FREE Websites

Design FREE Websites
With
FREE Internet Marketing Tools and Resources.

Free website design, free website templates, free design tools, free writing tools, free hosting, free domains, free content, free images, free clipart, free backgrounds, free audio and free video.

by

Christine Clayfield

Table of Contents

Acknowledgements

Thanks to my husband and children for supporting me in everything that I do. You are my life. Without you, I would not have a goal to work for and I would never have achieved what I have achieved so far.

Thank you to you, the reader, for putting your trust in me and buying my book.

I do not have a long list of people to thank because everything I've learned about the Internet and its money-making power, I've learned purely by hard work and making mistakes and, of course, learning from them.

> **If you never make mistakes, you'll never make anything.**
> *Richard Branson*

Foreword

Over the years, since I became a full time Internet Marketer, I have spoken to hundreds of people, all trying to make money online. Most of these people have one thing in common: they don't have any money to get started. I hear the same question over and over again: "How can I start to earn online if I haven't got any money at all?"

It is for these people that I have written this book. You can indeed create your own products or create a website without having to spend any money on tools, services, software or subscriptions.

Internet Marketing (IM) can be great fun and very rewarding but I fully understand that people don't have any money to spend. This book explains how anyone can start an online business using only free tools. In lots of cases, free tools are just as good as similar payable versions. In some cases, however, it is best to use payable options e.g. for hosting. Most free hosting companies will have limitations and the end result will be that your website might not load fast enough and visitors will leave your site, resulting, of course, in no sales. However, you will find some free resources in this book for your hosting and your domain names.

As I am a full time Internet Marketer and all my other books I have written so far are all about making money online, this book will refer a lot to being an Internet Marketer. It could also be that you bought this book because you just want to build a personal website or just one company site, without wanting to be an Internet Marketer. You will also find plenty of free resources you can use to build your site.

This book is ideal for people who just want to test to see what Internet Marketing is all about and to see if they like the whole concept without having to spend any money. Once you've decided you like it and you are going to treat Internet Marketing as a "proper" business, I do recommend you use the payable, professional, well known services; definitely for your hosting and to buy your domain names.

Is free stuff just as good as paid alternatives? In some cases, yes. You don't have to spend hundreds to purchase Adobe Photoshop as there are very good, free, alternative programs that will do the job for you. Most people who use Photoshop only ever use 1 to 5% of what the software can do anyway.

Another important thing to mention here is that most Internet marketers don't advise you to use the free tools because then they can't earn any money from sending you affiliate links to the payable tools. I am different. I am not your typical guru Internet marketer. I don't bombard my subscribers with crappy affiliate links. That's not how I earn my money. I earn money from my own created products. I am known as an honest Internet marketer and I want to keep it that way. So, if I can help people who haven't got any money at all, to get started online, I am happy to do so. Hence, this book.

The purpose of this book is to wipe out your concerns about the costs of setting up websites. Many people think it is very expensive, but it doesn't have to be. All you need is time! Whether you use free or payable tools, you WILL need time, as Internet Marketing and building websites is very time consuming before you can earn money. Of course, you could outsource a lot of the work, but that wouldn't be free, therefore I don't mention outsourcing costs in this book, as this book is about doing it all with minimal expense.

It will walk you through the process of developing your own website and will do it without any cost but your time. I am not showing you exactly how to build a website as there are plenty of books available for that. I am just giving you the tools. The tools you will be introduced to are all free and easy to use. If you can write a letter in Microsoft Office and post an image to your Facebook page, you can create a killer website.

The Internet is everywhere around us. It has become a critical part of many people's lives, while at the same time, to most people it is still a mystery. In the late 1990s the Internet changed from a restricted educational/ military network to one that just about anyone from anywhere in the world could access. Millions of people use services such as Facebook to communicate with friends and family. In seconds you can find information on just about any topic. Major companies have created elaborate websites offering company information to consumers. Companies both large and small have accepted the Internet as a valid sales channel. They often spend tens of thousands of dollars developing their websites. You may have been considering having your own website or blog, but it is confusing and you don't know where to start. Also, most people are concerned about the cost.

We all get emails telling us that we should have our own website. It may be for self expression or as a means to earn a steady income from online sales. Many companies will offer you a turnkey business with the promise of soon being rich just by purchasing their web package at x dollars. It can be anywhere from 100's to 1,000's.

The reality is that purchasing and/or building a website can be very expensive. Many web designers bring years of graphic artist skills to website development. Add in marketing experience and the tools that they use to convert their artistic ability and marketing experience into a website, and the cost can run into thousands of dollars. Computer programs are very expensive. The Adobe Creative Suites Master Program is the most common collection of software that web designers use. The cost of this collection is about $3,000 (£1,700) and can vary depending on what country you are in. If you just purchase the two main programs in the collection, Dreamweaver for website layouts and Photoshop for image creation, you will be paying about $2,200 (£1,300) for the most professional versions.

That is the downside of purchasing a website from a designer. However, there are other options. Most people have art work hanging on their walls at home that they enjoy, most likely you do. Also most likely, that art work is not done by Rembrandt or Claude Monet. Personally I have purchased paintings from street artist for just a few dollars that I enjoy looking at more than the Mona Lisa. The creative knowledge of a high priced designer may not be what you need. The world is full of geeks, and I mean that in a loving way. As a stereotype, geeks do not like wasting money on software and they always believe they can do things better than anyone else when it come to computers. This "Geekiness" is one thing that has led to something called Creative Commons. Anytime a creative product is produced, such as writing, photography or even computer programs, a copyright automatically exist.

Creative Common is a copyright license that allows anyone to use the copyright material with the only restriction being that they cannot charge for it. Computer programmers build on each other's work and, over time, free alternatives appear. I will talk more about Creative Common later.

Important To Mention

Free is nice, we all like free stuff but free from the Internet sometimes comes with spyware, ads or SPAM e-mails. Some people will download anything without thinking about it first. Be VERY careful if you download anything from any website you haven't used before. It is *your* responsibility to check out that what you are downloading is trustworthy.

There are thousands of websites pretending to give you a solution to your problem when you download things, whilst they don't tell you that you are also downloading a virus or spyware to your computer. It can take you days to get the spyware or virus off your computer!

On top of that, most of the time the free anti spyware programs don't get rid of the serious spyware and you'll have to spend money on professional spyware software. Make sure you search thoroughly for "xyz + review" or "xyz + scam", etc... before using new tools.

Use the listed sites at your own risk as the publishers of this book cannot be held responsible for any harm done to your computer, cost of repairs, compromised or hacked accounts, or loss of production as a result.

Many of the mentioned "free" sites include advertisements, some to pay sites, others to non-related products or services, or both. Please be careful when navigating them as you are unknowingly led to other websites. Before downloading material, make sure you're on the original URL. When downloading free software, be careful not to accept applications that you were not looking for in the first place, such as free games, weather channels, financial service sites, shopping, etc. Avoid advertisements related to sweepstakes, winnings or free gifts. These are all malware.

Most of all, beware of requests for updates for software that you have installed on your computer, especially numerous requests. Rather than updates, many of these applications are malware instead.

There are a few important things you need to know before we start digging into building a website with free tools.

- I am not a lawyer, the information in this book is for informative purposes only and does not constitute any legal advice. Please make sure, before you use any images or content from any website, to check for copyright rules. Websites can change their conditions.

- You might think:"Why recommend free websites and write a book about it whilst they sometimes come with Malware and Spyware?" The simple answer to that is: MOST of the free websites are perfectly OK to use but I do need to warn about the possibility of Malware and Spyware in this book. Websites that are perfectly OK today, might not be tomorrow. Just check them out before you use them is the most important message!

- Be prepared to receive a lot of unwanted email in your inbox and advertising on your site if you use some of the websites mentioned in this book.

- You can get your feet wet in building websites with free hosting and free domains but in order to be a *professional* Internet marketer, you will need two things that are not free: a domain name and a hosting account. All the other tools mentioned in this book are free but for some I do mention a payable option. A lot of the free tools also have payable options, not always mentioned in this book.

- This book requires a basic knowledge of Internet Marketing. Internet Marketing is really well explained in my book *"From Newbie To Millionaire."* If you can afford it, get yourself a copy. People call it The Internet Marketing Bible. Check out the reviews on Amazon: it's not me saying it is a really good book!

- Don't expect a step by step plan on how to build a website in this book as that is not what this book is about. The only purpose is to give you free tools that can help you to build a free website. I do understand that many people simply cannot afford the payable tools but the good news is: you can build a site and earn money with nothing but free tools.

- You will find that there is a particularly large section about images in this book, the reason being that many people ask me about this, therefore I conclude that this is not clear to many people.

- My mother tongue is not English, and for the first 30 years of my life I spoke only Flemish (I am from the Flemish part of Belgium, not the French part), until I met an

English gentleman, who is now my husband. For that reason, if you do find some grammatical errors in this book, I apologise. This book has been proofread, but perfect proofreaders are very hard to find. It is not my goal to write a "perfect English" book; instead, it is my goal to write an informative book that will help you.

 - Readers who have read one of my other my books: you will find that I repeat some of information in all my books, but not much. The reason for this is that some people will read one or two of my books whilst other people might read all my books. Information that I have written in my first book might also be useful content in my other books, therefore it would be silly to re-write it all and I copy and paste that content.

- You will not find a lot of information about social media or free social media tools in this book as I am not a big social media fan. It is great fun for social reasons but I don't believe in making money from social media. People don't hang around on Facebook to buy stuff but to have fun and socialise.

When someone opens up Amazon, they already have a buyer's frame of mind because there is nothing else you can do on Amazon but buy stuff! When someone visits Facebook, they don't have a buyers frame of mind as they go to Facebook to socialise, have fun, watch some funny videos, etc...

I hope you can see the difference and you can conclude that selling something when people are in a buyer's frame of mind will give you more chance to get sales.

- I live in the UK, so this book is written in English spelling, therefore you will see 'colour' instead of 'color', 'optimise' instead of 'optimize', 'socialise' instead of 'socialize', etc.

- It is impossible to explain all the things I talk about in this book in detail. Should something not be clear to you, I suggest you search for more information online or search on www.youtube.com or www.Udemy.com. Udemy has thousands of informative videos.

- At the time of printing this book, all websites were fully functional. If you come across a website that is no longer available, as the Internet changes constantly, sorry.

- I don't endorse any of the websites I mention in this book, nor can I tell you which one is "THE" best as it all depends on your products, your priorities, your taste, etc.

You need to look after your health! Believe me, I know!

Consider this a very important message from one Internet marketer to another. Believe me, I have learned the hard way. For years I sat working on my computer for hours and days in the wrong position, in the wrong chair, without any breaks. On some days, I would switch my computer on at 8 am and work on it until 1 am the next morning. My punishment for this: I have been diagnosed with cervical spondylosis (a non-curable condition) in my neck, with the disc space between C5, C6 and C7 most affected. Want proof? Here it is. As I always like to prove what I say, here are an X-ray and MRI scan of my neck. You can see on the first picture that the space between disc C5 and C6 is thinner than all the other spaces. The second picture shows a bulging disc putting pressure on the spinal cord and its nerve fibres. Permanent damage can be caused when a bulging disc in the neck is compressing a nerve for a long period of time.

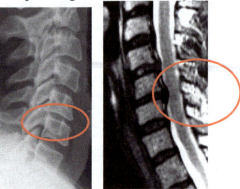

Now I cannot work on the computer as much as I would like to because when I do, my neck starts to hurt, my arm goes "dead" and I lose part of my grip and feelings in my arm. I have two choices: work a long time and give myself pain, or work less and have no pain. As health is more important than money, I obviously choose to work fewer hours. I can still work long hours on the computer but certainly not as long as I would like to, in order not to make my condition worse. I am not telling you this out of self-pity as I am very happy with what I have achieved. *I am telling you this so you don't make the same mistake.*

I am a professional, full-time Internet marketer and always will be; I love it. The fact that I cannot work as much as I would like to is not a major disaster for me, because a lot of my sites/products will provide me with income on autopilot for many years to come, and I do have staff members. *Please, please pay attention to the following. What I am about to say truly is very important for your health.*

I feel that it is my duty to tell everybody in an office environment about the dangers of working constantly on a computer. I would not want you to make the same mistakes as me. If somebody had told me seven years ago what I am going to tell you, I would not have a problem with my neck now. As an Internet marketer, you will be sitting in front of the computer for hours and hours and maybe even days.

Most people think that an office environment is a place with very low risk of injury. I thought the same until I had excruciating shoulder pain (cause by pinched nerves in my neck) when I woke up one day. The truth is a lot of musculoskeletal disorders are caused in office environments. These disorders are caused by repetitive strain to the body's tendons ,muscles, joints nerves and ligaments. Back, neck, shoulders, hands and arms are the most commonly affected by computer injuries (musculoskeletal disorders that are work related).

The two most important things that you need to know:

1. Make sure that you are sitting in the correct position at your computer. Search for "correct posture at a computer" and you will find a lot of information. Search for "ergonomic office chair" and change your office chair if you have to.

2. Make sure you take regular breaks. Staring at a computer screen with your head and neck always in the same position puts a lot of strain on your neck.

I use the software that I have developed, www.breakremindersoftware.com, and in my opinion this should be installed on each computer that is sold anywhere in the world. It is not available for Apple computers.

www.workpace.com is similar, more sophisticated software and available for Apple computers. The software monitors the time you work on the computer and it alerts you when you need to take a break. It shows you general exercises that you can do while sitting on your chair. You can set it to block your keyboard during breaks so you cannot work. My settings are as follows:

-   I have a break for 20 seconds every 10 minutes, and I've set the software so that my keyboard is blocked. Therefore, every 10 minutes I do some gentle neck exercises.

-   I have a 10-minute break every hour, and my software is set so my keyboard is blocked, which forces me to get up and do something else for 10 minutes.

If you can afford it, invest in www.breakremindersoftware.com. It is the best piece of

software available for an office environment. You have been warned: install it as a matter of urgency. If you cannot afford it, force yourself to take regular breaks. There are similar programs on the market. Simply search for "office timers" or "office break timers."
Since I installed break reminder software on my computer, I am happy to say I have no more pain at all, anywhere.

I'm sorry to be the one to tell you this, but iPads, laptops and mobile phones are a lot worse for your neck than a normal computer screen. This is because your face is always pointing downwards, so your neck has a lot more strain on it.
In addition, finger arthritis is predicted to be a major worldwide problem in years to come, as people use their phones and keyboards for too long. The finger movement involved in texting and moving a mouse causes repetitive strain injury, resulting in arthritis for a lot of people.

Correct posture at the computer: Bad posture at the computer:

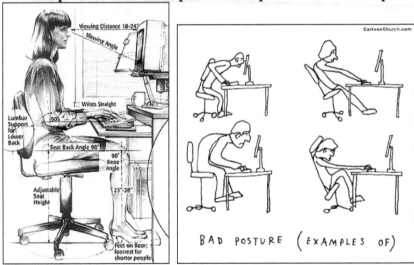

(Source: www.ergonomics-info.com)

Please do not ignore this message — it really is very important.
I cannot stress it enough.

18

My Other Products

My novel "No Fourth River". A Novel, based on a true story; my own personal story.

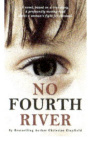

Buy the **eBook** here: www.ebooknofourthriver.com
Buy the paperback book on Amazon or other book websites.

My Bestselling Book "From Newbie To Millionaire"

Buy the **eBook** here: www.FromNewbieToMillionaire.com.
Buy the paperback book on Amazon or other book websites.

My Drop Shipping and eCommerce Book

"DropShipping and eCommerce. What You Need and Where to Get It"
Buy the **eBook** here: www.dropshippingandecommerce.com.
Buy the paperback book on Amazon or other book websites.

My Finding Niches Made Easy Book

"Finding Niches Made Easy"
Buy the eBook here: *www.findingnichesmadeeasy.com*

Buy the paperback book on Amazon or other book websites.

My Work From Home Ideas book

Buy the **eBook** here: http://www.makemoneyfromhomebook.com
Buy the paperback book on Amazon or other book websites.

My Self Publishing Success System Explained Step by Step in Video Tutorials

I publish a new book, on average, every 2 weeks. These books are all in different niches, and I outsource all aspects of the book, including writing and cover design, except for the publishing, which I do myself. I explain EVERYTHING I do, from finding a niche to publishing the book worldwide in watch-over-my-shoulder style video tutorials: www.WorldwideSelfPublishing.com.

My Break Reminder Software

I have to try to reduce the time I spend on my computer due to a neck injury (you will read about it later). I used to use www.workpace.com, which is software that forces you to take breaks while on your computer. I had my own simplified version developed, which you can buy here: www.BreakReminderSoftware.com.

My Repetitive Strain Injury Book

The real-life stories in the book will make you think and will, hopefully, make you take regular breaks on your computer/mobile phones, etc. The book is aimed at anyone who use our much-loved electronic gadgets too often, too long, without taking breaks. Nobody warns people about the permanent damage it can do to your body.

Buy the **hard copy boo**k: search for it on Amazon by author Lucy Rudford (pen name)

My Print Screen Software

When I was looking for a very simple print screen software application, without all the bells and whistles, I couldn't find it, therefore I had my own developed. I use it every single day and don't know how I could ever be without it.

You can buy it here: www.PrintingYourScreen.com.

Print a Kindle eBook

I don't like reading from a screen and searched A LOT for a reliable solution to print a Kindle book. You can grab your copy here free: www.HowToPrintAKindleBook.com. How to print a kindle book from your PC. If you are like me and you prefer reading books from paper, this is for you. Before I knew how to print a Kindle book, I never bought any Kindle books, now I do because I print them and read them.

Please note there is a one-time charge of $29.99 / £19.00 to buy the Kindle Converter that I recommend in order to convert your Kindle to a pdf format that you can print. However, you have 5 days to test the product free. This converter is not my product and I don't earn any money from it if you buy it but it is a product that actually works.

Works on PC, windows explorer. I have not tested it an Apple computer.

More Information About Me:

www.ChristineClayfield.com

For more information about how you can make money as an affiliate selling my products, please refer to the end of this book.

Chapter 1) What Skills Do You Need To Succeed?

Whether you will be building a website with free or payable tools, you are going to need some skills. This chapter is copied from one of my other books as I believe is vitally important that every Internet marketer is aware of this.

First of all, you need to know that running a website can be compared to running a normal business, and secondly you need to realise that you will need a blend of skills to be able to build a website that will make you money. Building a website is relatively easy but in order to build a website that will make you money, you do need a few extra skills.

1) Comparison To Running A "Normal" Business.

All you need is a computer and an Internet connection to make money online, right? Well, I am afraid it's not that simple. In my opinion, anybody with a tiny little bit of business acumen and common sense can make money on the Internet. A person with a lot of business attitude and business knowledge has a better chance of making it.

The buying attitudes, reasons and motives of customers buying on the web are very similar to the customers buying on the High Street. Many business principles can be applied to both marketing online and offline, so people who are aware of these business principles are just one step ahead of others. Having said that, you certainly do not need business knowledge to make it. It is just an advantage and not a necessity.

The traditional elements of marketing are the "four Ps". These also apply to Internet Marketing (IM) businesses. The point I want to get across here is that IM is comparable to doing business outside the Internet. An Internet business is like running a normal business; it will need your full-time attention to succeed.

Here are some business terms that are very well known in the marketing/business world outside the Internet and can also be applied to the Internet Marketing environment.

a) The 4 Ps are:

- **Product**. Your product is whatever you are selling, online or offline.
- **Price**. Your price needs to be realistic compared to comparable products on the market, in our case on the web.
- **Placement** is about your distribution channels. Where and when are your products going to be available? There is one big difference here between Internet Marketing and normal marketing because Internet products are available online 24/7.
- **Promotion** is the channels of communication you have with your customers and prospects.

If there is a problem somewhere with your sales, on the web or outside the web, you need to investigate each P to see which is causing the problem.

b) AIDA

A = Attention. Get your visitor's attention, in our case by building an attractive website.
I = Interest. Get your visitors interested in what is on your site.
D = Desire. Give your visitors the desire to click on the order button.
A = Action. Your visitor takes action and clicks on your order button.

c) 80/20 rule

The rule that 80% of your sales come from 20% of your customers applies very often in any business environment. This also applies in keyword research, as 80% of your sales will come from 20% of the keywords that you've used. It is therefore important to look after that 20% of your customers and to focus on the important 20% of your keywords.

d) Rule of 10

A sales representative can get 100 prospects gathered at an exhibition. Out of these 100 prospects, he might get ten more interesting leads, and out of those ten leads, one person will buy his product. If he is lucky, the sales rep could get between 2% and 5% of sales out of his 100 prospects. That is a principle that I have always applied in all my businesses. How does this work in Internet Marketing? If 100 people view your product online and one person buys your product, you have a conversion rate of 1%, which is acceptable in Internet Marketing. A realistic IM conversion rate is between 1% and 5%. A 10% conversion rate is very good and not very common.

e) Know your competitors

Knowing your competition is vital whatever business you are in. You will need to analyse your competitors' websites.

f) Supply and demand—pricing policy

If a manufacturer makes a product and there is strong demand and no competition, they will probably sell the product with a high profit margin. If other manufacturers start to produce similar products and bring them to market, the first manufacturer will probably have to reduce his price, as it is likely that the other manufacturers will have a lower selling price.

The same applies to your products: if you find a niche and there is no competition, you can sell your product for a high price. If twenty other people sell exactly the same product at a lower price, you might have to lower your price to stay competitive in the market.

g) Benefits, benefits, benefits

When selling any products, you HAVE to concentrate on what the benefits are for the customer when purchasing the product. If you are selling a product online, exactly the same applies: benefits, benefits, benefits. Don't say: "This is a good quality chair." Instead, say: "Your back pain could disappear forever with this chair." Focus on what it does for your customer!

h) Why do people buy "stuff"?

You should always keep in mind the reasons why people spend money, online or offline. Purchases are made for the following reasons in all walks of life, (not just online):
- To solve a problem they are having
- To fill a basic need
- For convenience
- To give them peace of mind
- To increase their image or ego/peer pressure/showing off
- For their entertainment
- To make them wealthier (this could mean either saving money or making money)
- To increase their knowledge
- To replace something they've lost or broken

- For value - people can't resist bargains

i) Put on other people's shoes

If you want to be in business, you need to put yourself in your customer's shoes. What would you like to see if you were a potential customer? Look at the world, your product, your product description, etc. as a potential customer. If you visit a website, what would you like to see? Develop the website in that way.

j) KPI indicators

KPI stands for Key Performance Indicators—also called Key Success Indicators. These are used a lot in businesses outside the web environment. As an Internet marketer, you also need to analyse as many aspects of your website as possible and try to improve it all the time. Just like the giant supermarkets know more about your spending habits than you do, you need to try to find out what the searching habits of your customers are. The purpose of a KPI is to measure a certain activity, analyse the data and learn or improve.

k) Your USP = Unique Selling Point

Last but not least: What is unique about your product or your website? How do you stand out from your competition? Why would people buy from you?

2) What Skills Do You Need You Succeed?

Are you dreaming of your own mansion, like many other people do? Are you hoping to retire early? Perhaps you just want to earn a nice income to be able to pay for all your expenses AND have some disposable income as well. Everyone these days wants to sell on the Internet! But the question is, can you do it? Can anybody build a website to earn money with?

As a web designer, you will have countless jobs to do: managing pictures, writing new content, putting new content on your website, calculating your product prices and profit margins, deciding how you are going to make money with your website, adjusting your style of writing to the audience you are targeting, etc…

My success in the IM world did not come overnight. I have read, I have analysed, I have tried, I have learned, and what I've learned, I've put into action. I have made lots of (expensive) mistakes.

You can forget about working only one hour a day to earn millions. That is living in a dream world. If you are prepared to spend a lot of time on the computer and if you are prepared to work hard and learn from your mistakes, you have a good chance of making it. However, you will have to learn a lot of skills in a short time, in a very competitive business.

To succeed on the Internet you need to have some knowledge in a variety of fields. There is no need to be an expert from the start in all the different fields, as you will learn as you go along. Once you know how to do it yourself and you have the money, you can always outsource things. I believe that, before you outsource something, you need to know how it is done yourself. Otherwise you won't be in a position to check the work that the outsourcer has done, to judge if he has done a good job. Any business owner will tell you that it is hard work running a company. The same applies for an IM business. If you are planning to do all the work yourself, without outsourcing any of it, you will need some skills from all the professions listed below. To succeed, you will need a mixture of these 25 skills:

- **Website builder.** You will need these skills as that is the aim of the game: build a website that will sell your products. In order to build good websites, you will also need lots of the skills listed below.

- **Graphic artist.** You will have to be creative in how you arrange the layout of your website. You must think about where to put images and text. You have to know what colours match and what colours clash when seen together. You have to know what typeface to use and what size the typeface should be.

- **Computer expert.** You don't really need to be an expert but you certainly need to have some computer knowledge. You will have to be able to work with different software programs (such as graphic layout programs and graphic design programs), as you will need to resize pictures or reduce their resolution. Knowledge of some basic HTML, a web coding language, is an advantage but not a necessity.

- **Marketing expert.** You need to have some marketing knowledge. It will be a huge advantage if you know what the 4 Ps, AIDA, Maslow's triangle and market segmentation are. When your website is designed, you need to know what your target market is, who your target customers are, and who your competition is. Not only do you need to know about it, but you also have to be able to analyse the information to your advantage.

- **Salesperson.** You need to know how to sell, what price to sell for, and who to sell to. One big advantage: you do not need to wear a smart suit, shiny shoes, red socks or a polka-dot tie ☺.

- **Accountant**. You need to work out your profits and you need to know how to calculate 65% profit on a product. You need to know how much profit is left after you've deducted your purchasing prices, your shipping costs, etc.

- **Mathematician**. You need to work out conversion rates and use spreadsheets to work out a total of your profits.

- **Writer.** You need to write content for your site and write product descriptions.

- **Photographer.** You need to work with photographs, so you will need some basic photo editing skills to know what resolution means, what pixels are, how to save a photograph as a JPEG, and so on.

- **Logo designer.** You will need to design a header for your site.

- **Psychologist.** You need to know about your customers' behaviour. Analyse in what style to write and to sell for your target customers. You need to realise that selling to teenagers and silver surfers is different, and you must adjust your style of writing accordingly.

- **Behaviour analyst.** You need to know where on your screen to put a "buy it now" button. You need to know which part of your screen your visitors look at first, according to studies.

- **Video expert.** You are likely to work with videos, so you need to know the best format to save a video for the quickest download. You need to know what MPEG and WAV mean.

- **Typist.** You need to be able to type more than five words per minute. If you are a very slow typist, you are losing valuable time.

- **Logical thinker**. You need to think about the logic of the page order on your site. Also, think about whether your text flows logically.

- **Businessperson.** You need the business instinct to spot money-making opportunities and exploit markets. You will need to make business decisions and foresee any changes needed, and be able to adapt to those changes.

- **Analyst.** You need to analyse information from several sources, put it all together and make decisions based on your analysis. Ask yourself: what market are you selling to? Who are you are selling to? What are they buying? Are they spending money?

- **Organiser.** You will, without a doubt, need some organisational skills. You need to organise the files on your computer into folders. You will need a system to instantly find a password when it's required. You will need to organise your orders, your incoming and outgoing payments, etc...

- **Risk taker.** You need to be able to make calculated risk decisions in case you are going to spend money on paid traffic methods.

- **Copywriter.** You need to be able to write in a style that makes people order from you. The ability to write interesting sales copy is very important.

- **Researcher.** You need to research your niche and be able to conclude what is important information for your potential customers.

- **Planner.** You need to be able to plan when you will design your site, when you will drive traffic to it, and when you will try paid traffic.

- **SEO expert**. The most important thing for your website is to rank highly in Google search results pages, therefore SEO (Search Engine Optimisation) knowledge is essential. I'll talk about SEO later.

- **Webmaster.** You will need to be able to publish your site to the search engines. You need to know what an IP address is and what hosting means.

- **Judge.** You need sound judgment and the ability to recognise a lie. There are lots of scam artists on the web who are often very convincing.

So there you have it! That is 25 skills that you will need to become a successful Internet marketer. And I am not joking. To become successful, you need a blend of these skills, abilities and talents. Most of all you need entrepreneurial flair and business instinct.

Maybe now you understand why most online businesses fail and why a lot of people give up. Even if you will be using ready-to-use templates and software, you will still need the majority of the skills above. Even if you decide to outsource everything, you still need to know all the basics about IM, as you will have to check and correct the work delivered to you by outsourcers.

But there is hope: you do not need all these skills from the start, but you will need most of them to become a successful Internet marketer. Fortunately, you can learn a lot of these skills by reading about them.

No one was born wise; it comes from making more good choices than bad ones and learning from the bad ones.

If you are reading this book because you want to become a full time Internet Marketer, in the beginning, you will probably just like me, feel like you're not getting anywhere. Be positive and stay focused and keep your spirits high. I want to say a few more words about **Judgment** (the 25th skill), as it is especially important. You need to STOP living in a dream world and STOP believing the overhyped sales letters. If you DO believe in them, you must STOP it. Right Now. Here are some rules to believe in, starting today.

- If it is too good to be true, it IS!
- Get rich quick schemes DO NOT EXIST and DO NOT WORK. EVER! I don't care who promises you what. If you do believe in these, sweet dreams!
- No one can guarantee you success, and if anyone does, run fast in the opposite direction!
- Pushing 1, 2, 3 buttons does not work either, EVER.
- Don't believe anyone will hold your hand all the way! YOU will have to do the work and figure out things for yourself OR wait four weeks to get a response to your support ticket.
- If you desperately need a lot of money immediately, don't start an online business—or any business, because building a business takes time. Doing business online involves work and determination.

Successful people are successful because they have put in the work!

On top of the blend of skills, you must also:
- Be prepared to work hard
- Be determined and persistent
- Have a strong desire to earn money
- Have the willpower to keep going when things go wrong
- Be willing to outsource once you have the funds
- Invest your profits in your next project
- Focus on one thing at a time. Don't start with ten websites. Start with one or two and make them a success. Only then duplicate them. Be like a stamp: focus on one thing until you get there.

Chapter 2) What Is Your Niche?

I am going to keep this chapter short. I explain everything about niches and how to find a new profitable niche really well in my book "Finding Niches made Easy."

You see the word niche being used a great deal on the Internet. Many product promoters make it sound like a mysterious secret weapon to become a millionaire in online sales. The word niche is primarily a marketing term used to identify a specific market within an overall market. As an example: a real estate company might limit themselves to private islands. Their niche is private islands. The more you can narrow down your niche, the more focused your market becomes. One advantage of niche marketing is that it is easier to make yourself be seen as the expert. On the Internet this can also be seen as the ability to get search engines to move you to the top of results list.

The first thing you will have to do before you start building a site is decide on your niche: what are you going to build a website about?

A niche is a small part of a topic or subject. A car market is a niche where all people are interested in cars. Mercedes is a sub-niche from the main niche (a niche within a niche), as it is a manufacturer of cars. You can keep digging deeper into a niche: a yellow Mercedes would be another sub-niche of the Mercedes niche. A yellow Mercedes with yellow leather seats (digging deeper again) would be a micro-niche in that sub-niche.

1) Your Website's Purpose

What do you expect from your website and what type of website do you want? These are basic questions you need to fully understand as you start on your journey.

If you are just looking for a personal website, then you are your own niche and most of the items about niche marketing are not critical. It is still possible to "monetise" your website. Monetising is a term that is used to express the concept of adding methods of earning an income from your website. It is not the proper meaning of the word but it is widely used. Some of these methods include selling advertising space and using affiliate links. The opposite end of the spectrum is the e-commerce site; these sites are designed to sell products e.g. online shops.

Here are some ideas to monetise a niche web site:

1. Opt-in box (so you will earn money from your list)

2. Adsense

3. Clickbank products

4. Recurring affiliate products

5. Other affiliate products

6. Sell a book

7. Amazon products with affiliate links

8. CPA offers

2) Niche Marketing

Once you have the basic concept of what you want to do, it is time to zero in on a niche that will be profitable and something you are comfortable with. Use a keyword tool to find out how many people are searching per month for certain keywords. I use Google's Keyword Planner for my initial research, which is also ideal for finding long tail keywords.

So here is your first free tool: Google Keyword Planner (KP).
What Google once called Keyword Tool has now been replaced by Keyword Planner. Before you can use Keyword Planner, you need to have a Google Adwords account (this is free). Important to mention: you DON'T need to spend any money with Adwords, you just need an account.
Obtaining a Google Adwords account is simple and can be done in five to ten minutes. Signing up is pretty self-explanatory.

KP tells you how many people per month are searching for your keyword. I am not going to show you here with screenshots how to sign in to your Google Adwords account, as Google changes that all the time. Sign up here:
www.adwords.google.com
www.adwords.google.co.uk

- On www.wordstream.com/keyword-niche-finder, you can search a limited number of keywords free of charge.

Enter the primary keyword that describes the type of products you intend to promote. It will return some related niches. Note some of the niches that you are interested in the most.

Next you should see how competitive those keywords are. Do a search on the keyword in Google's search engine and note what type of websites are listed and analyse them.

There are more sophisticated keyword tools available that you will need to look at for analysing your competitors and targeting keywords but KP is a great tool to start with.

3) Importance of Long Tail Keywords

This is covered in my book "Finding Niches Made Easy" but as it is important for success in Internet Marketing, I am copying it in this book.

Keywords are an important element in finding your niche. Without them, you wouldn't be able to research any subject. A *keyword* is whatever you type into the search box in a search engine. *Keyword research* is using a set of tools to discover what keywords people are searching for. If we know this, then we can build a site that targets people's searches.

Long tail keywords are keywords with multiple words in them, sometimes called golden keywords. These types of keywords are less searched for, less popular and less competitive, but when you target these keywords collectively, they can drive a lot of traffic to your site. These keywords are very specific to what you are selling. Long tail keywords are also cheaper per click if you use paid traffic.

If you were looking for information on how to cook a fish pie, what would you search for? Would you search for "fish pie"? No, you'd more likely search for exactly what you want — "how to cook a fish pie" — as we are all getting used to searching with long tail keywords to find exactly what we are looking for.
"How to cook a fish pie" is an example of a long tail keyword. Google shows the keywords that the searcher typed in bold. Subconsciously, people will click first on the websites that show their keyword in bold. Long tail keywords have a much better conversion rate than short keywords because you will get quality, targeted traffic. People type in exactly what they are going to buy and land on your site.

TOP TIP: Always try and rank for long tail keywords.

If you could buy the domain name www.howtocookafishpie.com, that would be your first step towards success. But you must follow all the other rules for success; a good domain name by itself is not enough to make it in the Internet world.

It is much better to rank for lots of low competition, long tail keywords than *not* to rank for highly competitive short keywords.

As you know, using a one-word keyword when looking for a specific type of product is unwieldy. For example, if you're looking for men's Nike running shoes and you type in the word "shoes", you will pull up a listing of every site about shoes. More likely, you would have to spend a great deal of time scanning the many listings in order to find the site you're looking for. Hence, to avoid generalized searches, you would have to use multi-word keyword phrases.

Long tail keywords, phrases containing three to five words, enable you to narrow your search down to only the sites that have the information you're looking for. They are used on a website to bring visitors to a certain web page or when the visitor is searching for something specific. Likewise, they are used by a web publisher in search engines to bring surfers to a web page within their site, rather than their home page.

If you are building a website about cheese, you would NOT target to be ranked for the word cheese. Instead, it is much better and easier to target for words like "Spanish artisanal cheeses" or "Dutch Gouda cheese" or "English extra mature cheese", etc.

An Example of Finding Long Tail Keywords

Once signed in to your Google Adwords account, go to "Tools" on the top of the page and select Keyword Planner from the drop down menu.

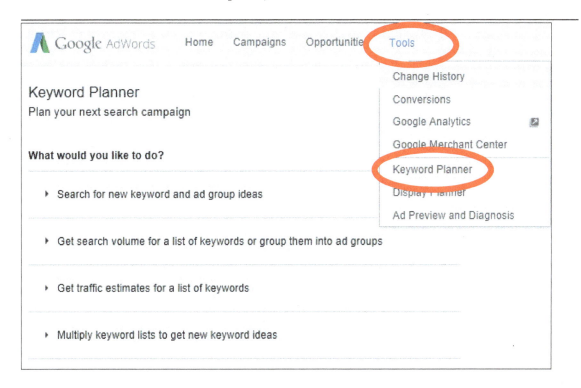

Click on "Search for new keyword and ad group ideas".

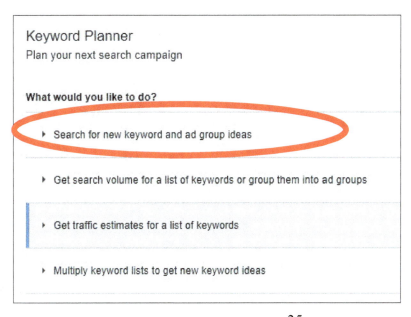

Type in your keyword and make sure to check the settings, e.g. Language, Locations, etc. I always set this to:

- All locations
- English
- Google: Here, you can also choose Google and search partners.
- You can fill in **negative keywords** if you wish, e.g. free. This will NOT display searches for someone who types in "free book", as clearly you don't want to target those people. You can also customise your search, but I always leave that as default. You could say, for instance, only give me keywords that have over 1000 searches per month.

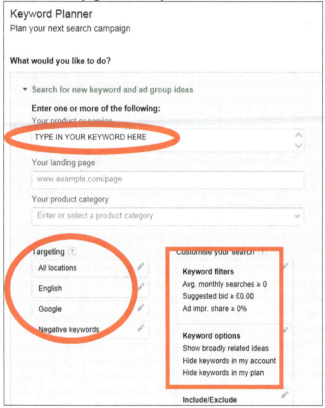

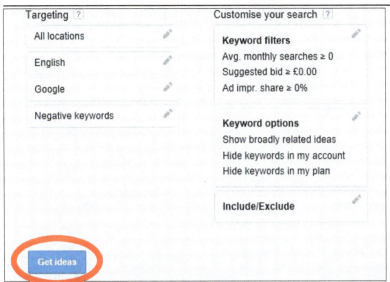

I have typed in "weight loss supplements" as keyword and clicked "Get ideas".

Next, you'll want to look at the average monthly searches that the keyword has. In our case, as shown on the above screenshot, there have been 223,450 **combined** searches for all the keywords (combined searches means the total of searches for different keywords added together).

Important to mention: the result of the monthly searches is based on exact searches.

When you type in [weight loss supplements] in the Google search box, you can see it shows 3,530.000 results. That is A LOT of results, so the competition for this keyword will be hard. We need to find another long tail keyword with less competition!

When you click on "Best Weight Loss", as shown below, you will get different keywords.

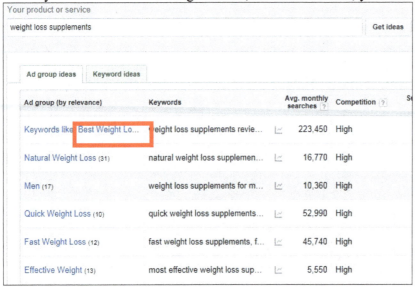

When you click on "Best Weight Loss", this screen will appear:

Ad group: **Keywords like: Best Weight Loss Supplement**		
Keyword (by relevance)	**Avg. monthly searches**	**Competition**
best weight loss supplements	9,000	High
weight loss tablets	6,600	High
weight loss supplements for women	3,600	High
supplements for weight loss	3,600	High
best supplements for weight loss	2,900	Medium
weight loss supplement	1,600	High
best weight loss supplement for women	1,600	High
best weight loss supplements for women	1,300	High
top weight loss supplements	1,000	High

Note that you can see the search results for long tail keywords. Have a look at the keyword "best weight loss supplements for women" and paste that into the search box in Google.

"best weight loss supplements for women"
Web   Images   Maps   Shopping   Videos   More ▾   Search tools
About 1,020,000 results (0.33 seconds)

You can see that the number of results is immediately a lot lower, at 1,020,000, so it will be an easier job to rank for that long tail keyword.
While the competition is still higher than you would like, it is better than the first keyword you tried.

If I were building a website around weight loss for women, I would have at least three different pages on my website, each focusing on the three long tail keywords shown on the next screenshot:

- weight loss tablets: 6,600 searches per month
- weight loss supplements for women: 3,600 searches per month
- best supplements for weight loss: 2,900 searches per month

Note that some of the searches are basically the same, e.g. single vs. plural or "for women" added. I would combine these small differences in searches and focus on all of them on one page of my website.

See how easy it is to find long tail keywords to target. Of course, once you have a bunch of keywords, you also need to study your competition, but I am not going to discuss that in this book.

4) Trends

Before you decide on a niche, you need to make sure that your niche is not a "dead" niche. There are two free tools that I use to check this.

- Google Trends www.google.com/trends, can be a help looking for customer demands. This tool shows search patterns. Enter the keyword or a group of related keywords and the tool will give you a graph showing the demand for those terms over a period of time. This will help you determine if demand for the keyword, and hence the product, is growing or declining. The trend page also shows what is hot that hour, showing what search results are most active. Some marketers look at the now trending information seeking keywords to tie into their products.

- In Keyword Tools you can look at the trend for one year but in Google Trends you can see the trend for many years.

I've typed in "labradoodle" in Keyword Planner and in Google Trends.

Keyword Tools example trend graph (maximum 1 year):

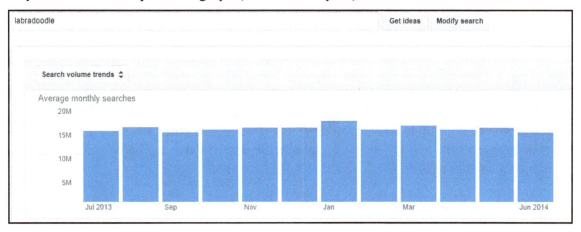

In Google Trends you can see the keyword for several years:

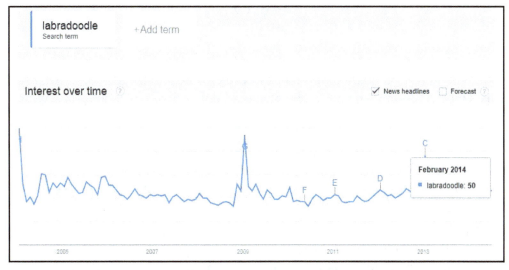

In Google Trends, you also get information about where the keyword was searched for the most. In the example below, that is Netherlands at the top, followed by United States, etc..

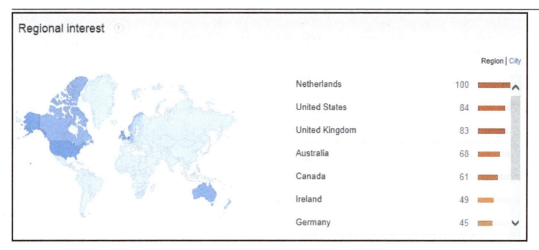

You can also learn things here about your geographical area e.g. you can see that Africa is not a darker colour on the map (dark colours on the map are the areas with searches) therefore you can conclude that it wouldn't be a good idea to build a website around the keyword Labradoodle and try and sell Labradoodle related items e.g books, collars, food bowls, etc... in Africa.

5) Keywords For SEO

I am sorry but I am going to refer here again to my book "*From Newbie To Millionaire*" in which I explain SEO really well. It wouldn't make any sense to just copy and paste it all here.

As the saying goes "Six of one, a Half dozen of the other" can easily fit looking for keywords to define your niche and looking for keywords for Search Engine Optimisation (SEO) reasons. Once you establish your niche, it should not be fixed, it should flow with customer demand.

6) Are People Talking About Your Niche?

A niche is not a good niche if people are never talking about it. If your competition is very high and the monthly searches are very high, usually you can conclude that people are talking about your niche.

I always like to double check though with Boardreader. (I've capitalised further instances of the word "Boardreader" on this page for consistency). Boardreader is a search engine for forums. It is a brilliant way to find what people are talking about, and so find new niches.

Type in any keyword, like [cat], and you will be presented with all sorts of forums on cats. It is also a very good site to find sub-niches. I use boardreader a lot.

Visit www.boardreader.com, where you can type in a keyword and you will see something like this:

I've typed in [drag racing] and Boardreader tells me 21,675 posts have appeared online in the last 3 months or 7,225 per month. That is a good result, showing clearly that people are talking about drag racing.

When I typed in [hot air balloon racing], only 27 posts showed up for the last 3 months. That is a not a lot and is a big NO for me, *unless* it does tick all the other boxes of the six step process. The reason why this step is not *that* important is that only a small percentage of people/customers hang around on forums/blogs and Boardreader does not pick up *all* forums.

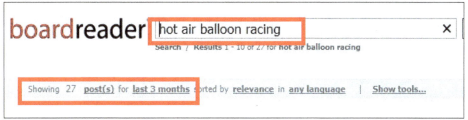

In Boardreader, you can also search for more advanced terms like: find videos, news, articles, forums, etc.

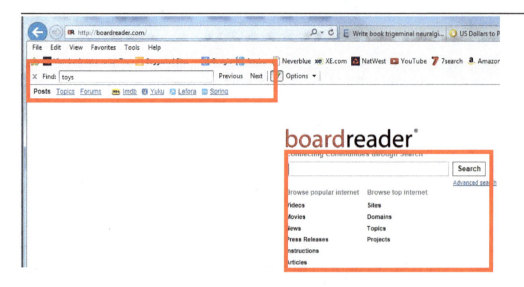

- Topsy www.topsy.com is similar but specifically for social media. Type in a keyword and Topsy will show you how many tweets there have been in the past five days or the past 30 days. You can search for links, tweets, photos, videos, influencers or everything.

Labrador had 11,098 tweets in the last five days so you can conclude that people are talking about labradors:

Chapter 3) Free Writing Tools

1) Writing Tools

Let's have a look at some free writing tools as, of course, you are going to have to write e.g. writing content. Microsoft Office sells complete packages costing from hundreds of dollars to a thousand dollars. Here are some free alternatives:

- Open office www.openoffice.org is free downloadable software that does everything that the Microsoft software does.

You can download it free and it contains a Word Processor, Calculation, Drawing Software, Maths, Charts, Templates, Screenshot Software, Slide Presentation Software.

- Libre office www.libreoffice.org is another good free alternative to Microsoft Office. You can download it free and it contains a Word Processor, Calculation, Drawing Software, Maths, Charts, Templates, Screenshot Software, Slide Presentation Software

Openoffice and Libreoffice are very similar but have some small differences in their software. You could even download both.

- NeoOffice www.neooffice.org is an alternative to Microsoft Office for the Mac.

- GoogleDocs. www.docs.google.com Google docs is easy and straightforward to use. This is a cloud based service. Although I am aware that millions of people use cloud services, personally, I don't like using cloud based programs to store my data as I don't like the idea of all my documents being in the cloud. I'd rather keep them personal, on my own computer.

- ThinkFree at www.thinkfree.com is another cloud based service.

- Noteplad++ www.notepad-plus-plus.org is a free open source text editor.

- Textwrangler is a very good text editor for the Mac www.barebones.com/products/textwrangler/

2) Create a PDF

In case you are thinking of producing an eBook: you can export your text document into a PDF document. Lots of writing tools have this feature as standard but here are some tools:

www.freepdfconvert.com	www.pdf995.com	www.cutepdf.com
www.doc2pdf.net	www.pdfforge.org	www.tinypdf.com

Chapter 4) Your Website

The web programmers and website designers have all sorts of buzz words and abbreviations to dazzle and buffoon you with. While each one of them has their value to accomplish a certain function, the truth of the matter is that 90% of the websites on the web do not need all the bells and whistles that are in the tool box of a web designer. Most of the websites that do have them really do not need them. Just like their expensive tools, there are inexpensive alternatives that will do the job just as well.

Everything on the Internet that you see in a browser is based on HTML. HTML, Hyper Text Markup Language, is how browsers communicate, it is a computer language. No matter how complicated a website gets, it has to be understood by the browsers, who speak only HTML. However, there are now many website tools available so you can build websites without knowing any HTML. The HTML language, when using these tools, goes on in the background but you don't actually see any of it.

HTML scares a lot of people because it consists of a lot of codes and looks like this:

```
<div id="container">
<div id="contentcontainer">
<div id="headertop"></div>
<div id="headerbottom"></div>
<div id="copycontent" style="width: 685; height: 13903">
<div style="TEXT-ALIGN: center">
    <p class="MsoNormal" align="center" style="line-height:150%">
    <span style="font-family: Arial"><br>
    <img border="0" src="images/headline2-650.gif" width="650" height="294"></span></p>
    <blockquote>
    <p class="MsoNormal" style="text-align: left">
    <span style="font-size:13pt;font-family:Arial;
color:black; font-weight:700"><br>
    </span><b><font face="Arial" size="3">I'll show you how to find a profitable
```

If you visit any website and right-click on any page and choose "View Source", you can see the HTML code. HTML is the small building blocks that make up a webpage. *Nothing* explained in this book requires any knowledge of HTML. Most website design packages do not require the website builder to know HTML, but it is handy to be able to work with HTML as you can then make changes to the site you would otherwise not be able to make. Wordpress, which I will talk about next, can be used without HTML knowledge but you can make extra changes if you DO know HTML.

The first thing you will need to do is decide what sort of website you want to build: personal site, business site, ecommerce site, blog, social network, forum, etc.. Here are some free website design tools.

1) Free Website Design Tools

a) WordPress

In recent years, a server side application has become very popular. That application is blogging. Blogging is basically a data base application. Blog programs originally were very boring until a developer created a shell program that became very popular: WordPress.

www.wordpress.com enhances the blogging program with the ability to wrap it in a web page style design. WordPress has grown since it was introduced and many users now use it to create a website.

Although Wordpress started as just a blog system, it can now be used as a full Content Management System (CMS). It is totally free. Millions of people are building websites with Wordpress. There are thousands of themes, plugins and widgets available, so your website can have its own unique look and feel.

Themes will change your layout and give you the website look that you desire. Plug-ins are small programs installed on your server that are activated by the web browser, and widgets provide information gathered from other sources. These items give additional functionality to the basic features. Using the WordPress website, you can be on your way to building a new website within minutes for free. For the majority of people looking to build their first website, WordPress has definite advantages. While WordPress technically still uses HTML, the website owner does not need to know anything about HTML to build and maintain their website.

To work with Wordpress all you need to do is install Wordpress on your domain name via your hosting company. It is totally free and done in a matter of minutes. Depending on which hosting company you are with, you need to follow different steps to install it. Just search for it or have a look at Youtube for some explanatory videos on how to install it.

Once installed, you can start putting content, page title, SEO, etc... on your site. You can download SEO plugins free so that SEO is done for you, all you need to do is fill in the keywords. Wordpress automatically fills in suggested keywords, based on the title and the content of the website.

When you create your content, you do it live online within the WordPress application. The basic WordPress is enhanced with different options.

Wordpress has made it really easy for anyone to build a website. Most people are a bit scared to set up a website. Just watch a few Wordpress Video Tutorials online and you will see how easily you can build websites.

I must admit, Wordpress did scare me a little bit when I first started online but now that I know it better, I keep wondering why it was so scary to start with.

Wordpress has so many plugins and widgets that you can achieve just about anything. Some plugins are free and others are payable. There are lots of good Wordpress themes that are totally free. Just search for "free Wordpress themes" and you will have plenty of choice.

There are three big downsides with Wordpress, in my opinion:

1) It is not very easy to use for special fonts e.g. if you want a font to appear as Font "Accord" in size 24, you might have to install a special plug-in to be able to do that.

2) Hackers! Wordpress is very popular amongst hackers. Make sure you protect your site!

3) Wordpress is not very user friendly for graphics. E.g. if you want to put a frame around a picture, it won't be possible to do that with a simple theme and you will have to either install a plug-in or know HTML language so you can put a frame around a picture with an HTML code.

Using Wordpress is not the same as using WYSIWYG (What You See Is What You Get) software applications e.g. Webplus from Serif is WYSIWYG software for designing a site. You draw a circle around text on your screen and the circle will appear on your website, once you've published the site. Simple things like this are not always easy to do with Wordpress.

The best thing: Wordpress is totally free to use. All you need is a domain name and a hosting account.

Download Wordpress: www.wordpress.org

Free Wordpress Themes:

www.wordpress.org/themes

www.wordpressthemesbase.com

www.freewpthemes.net

TOP TIP for Wordpress: Don't use "admin" as your user name to login to Wordpress as the hackers will look for the username "admin" to try and get into your Wordpress dashboard.

- Akismet www.akismet.com (payable) is ideal for blocking spam comments on your blog. I use it successfully on a lot of my Wordpress sites. On some sites, before I installed Akismet, I would receive up to 50 SPAM comments per day (I admit, my username was "Admin"). After installing it, the SPAM comments were zero!

- www.inboundnow.com is a free downloadable tool to improve your wordpress site, improve your marketing and measure your results.

b) Google Sites

Visit www.sites.google.com. You can create and share a group website and it is free. No HTML knowledge required, customisable look and feel. Easy to use and free hosting. They do have a limit on the storage and the number of pages you can have on your website. They also have a premier service for a very small monthly fee.

c) NVU

www.nvu.com is an open source web design application. You don't need knowledge of HTML and it an alternative to the payable Dreamweaver and Microsoft Expression Web.

Available for Windows, Apple and Linux.

d) MojoPortal

www.mojoportal.com

This is a free and open source content management system. It uses the Microsoft ASP.NET and it supports the best know databases: MySQL, MS SQL, etc...

e) Joomla

www.joomla.org is CMS (Content Management System) software and another free and open source solution for building websites.

f) CushyCMS

www.cushycms.com is very simple content management system. No installation is needed as it is hosted by them.

Other free sources are:

- www.pligg.com

- www.drupal.org (CMS software)

- www.silverstripe.org

- www.wix.com Create your own websites for free. Used by over 50 million people.

Remember most free sources also have payable options with more features.

- www.webs.com From only $3.75 (£2.25) per month. That's the price of a cup of coffee! As good as free!

2) Traditional HTML and FTP Programs

While WordPress is gaining in popularity, using HTML is still very popular. To create a website with HTML you will need an HTML editor. You design and edit the website off line and then upload your finished product to your url via an FTP (File Transfer Protocol) program e.g. Filezilla. which is called an FTP client. You can download Filezilla free from www.filezilla-project.org. It is totally free to use.

Search Youtube for how to use filezilla. A bit scary at first, but once you've used it a few times, it will become very easy.

Another FTP client is www.net2ftp.com . You don't need to download this software to your PC and it works on different browser.s

www.onebutton.org is a free FTP client that a lot of Mac users love.

While there are a ranges of different types of HTML editors, the most popular are called WYSIWYG editors. They work in a very similar way to a word processor program like MS Word. If you can type a letter and insert a photograph in Word you can use one of these editors. On the professional side Adobe Dreamweaver is the most popular, however, it is very expensive and it also has lots of features that you will probably never use. So let's look at some free sources.

- A program with almost all the features of Adobe Dreamweaver is the free Pagebreeze www.pagebreeze.com. You can download it free.

- Another free HTML editor is CoffeeCup: www.coffeecup.com

- Kompozer www.kompozer.net is also free and open source software. This is a WYSIWYG editor.

- Seamonkey www.seamonkey-project.org is another HTML editing tool

A payable option but not expensive is Microsoft Expression Web. Search for it on Amazon. I use this software for all my one-page-sales-wonders. I also use Webplus from Serif, not expensive either but easy to use.

Adobe Fireworks is also good, another payable option but not too expensive. I have never used this myself but I hear good things about it.

If you are not technical, Wordpress is the way to go for you as you don't need to upload your site to a server because Wordpress does this for you. However, you will still have to install Wordpress on your site but there are Youtube videos about this.

- On http://validator.w3.org you can check if any part of your website needs attention/improvements.

3) Themes and Templates

Themes and Templates are basically the same thing, predefined layouts for your website. WordPress calls them themes and HTML sites/editors call them templates. These layouts can range from very simple to very elaborate. A quick search on the Internet will reveal lots of different themes and templates to choose from.

- www.freecsstemplates.org has over 840 Creative Common website templates. We will explain Creative Commons in detail later when we talk about free content, but a brief explanation is: the Creative Common is free to use as you wish, the only restriction is that you cannot claim you developed it and you cannot sell it. WordPress themes are easy to find as well, in fact the wordpress.org website has over 2,000 free themes.

Whether you go with WordPress or an HTML option is like trying to decide what car you will buy. Much of it is a personal choice. Take a look at some of the available templates/ themes. See what you like best.

More free templates are available here:

www.freewebtemplates.com

www.templatesbox.com

www.e-webtemplates.com

www.templateworld.com

www.freetemplatesonline.com

Payable versions for all kinds of templates:

www.minisitegraphics.com

www.diywebsitegraphics.com

4) Important Things To Know About Building Your Site

Designing your website is not easy, but it is crucially important for your success. In the first seven seconds, customers will decide to leave your site or start browsing on it.

Your website has to:
- Convert well: this means that people have to buy from you, assuming you are selling something.
- Give customers enough trust to buy from you.
- Capture customer information for future promotions to these customers (build a list), even if the customers have not bought anything when they leave your site.
- Have most of the important information, e.g. who you are, what you do, what you sell, visible as soon as your customer visits your site.
- Give great customer service.
- Meet all the legislation in your country.
- Represent your brand well.
- Be appealing so customers will come back.
- Be easy to share with social media buttons.
- Have clear Buy buttons.
- Make it easy for the customer to check out when they have bought something (not seven pages to fill in).
- SELL your products.
- Display important information above the fold. 'Above the fold' is the first thing people see when the webpage opens. When a visitor scrolls down, they are then looking "below the fold". Important headlines should always be above the fold. I also recommend putting an opt-in box above the fold.

- **Important**: If you are in the EU, you must investigate whether your website complies with The EU Cookie Law which comes into place on 26th May 2012. Just search for "EU Cookie Law".
 www.cookielaw.org says: "Most websites must offer users opt-in consent tools to allow cookies that pass information about their browsing activities to 3rd parties".

Important things to know when designing a website

First of all, how NOT to design a website: make sure your site is never listed on this website: www.webpagesthatsuck.com

There are plenty of decisions to be made regarding the website layout and the visual appeal of the site. An attractive website is important, but don't let that take so much of your time that you forget to make sure your site is easy to navigate, as this is also of the utmost importance. Visitors will go elsewhere if they find your site too difficult to use. If your site is unprofessional looking or unattractive, they will leave your site and give their business to somebody else.

Here are the factors that will influence the credibility of your website; numbers below, represent the percentage of people saying that that particular factor is important.

Factor	Percentage of People
Design Look	46.00%
Information design/structure	28.50%
Information focus	25.10%
Company motive	15.50%
Information usefullness	14.80%
Information accuracy	14.30%
Name recognition/reputation	14.10%
Advertising on the site	13.80%
Information bias	11.60%
Writing tone	9.00%
Identy of site operator	8.80%
Site functionallity	8.60%
Customer service	6.40%
Past experience	4.60%
Information clarity	3.70%
Readability	3.60%
Performance on test	3.60%
Affiliations	3.40%

Source : Fogg / www.itu.dk

Perfecting the aesthetics of your website can be difficult and time-consuming. However, you can make things a little bit easier on yourself by checking out other comparable websites to see how they appeal to you as a web visitor. This can give you a lot of insight as to what you can do to your site to make it appeal to visitors.

Type in your keyword, in your niche, and analyse the websites that are on the first two pages of Google. Those websites are there for a reason. They probably have a low bounce rate, meaning visitors stay on the site for a while without clicking away, which consequently means that they are enjoying the site. A low bounce rate means money bouncing out of your pocket!

You will notice that you are drawn to websites that use simple and bold colours and graphics to create their visual appeal and impression of professionalism. During your search, you will also come across sites that make you want to turn your head away. When you find these, jot down what turns you away so that you can make sure that you don't do anything of the sort when it comes to designing your website.

We've spoken about the layout and appearance of your site, so now it's time to get to the nitty gritty and talk technical stuff. I know, it's the last thing you want to talk about, but I'll try to make it as easy as possible to understand. This is information that you need to know so that you can make sure your site is designed efficiently.
You want a website design that will appeal to your visitor, draw them in and encourage them to visit subsequent pages. You want a design that is efficient yet sleek and intoxicating, in a sense.

I am not going to go too deep into discussing web design, as that could take up an entire book all by itself. There are, however, a few important things that you should remember when designing your site. Here are my top design rules:

1. Navigation should be easy. Remember, you probably aren't a tech wizard, and neither are some of your customers. When designing your site, pretend that it is for a child—like an eight-year-old. If a potential visitor is on your website, browsing around, they want to be able to easily find what they are looking for. When they can't, they'll leave your site and find another one that's easier to use and understand to make their purchase. You'll be left in the dust without being given a second thought. Make sure all your information is easily accessible (homepage toolbar is always a good place to start).

Make sure your site has a search bar at the top of the page (I sometimes put my search bar on the left), not just on your homepage, but on every page of your website. Many customers like to type in what they want instead of scouring your site for it, so having this readily available for potential customers will result in more sales.
Of course, the above only applies if your site has lots of pages, not if your site only has 5 pages, as navigation will be very easy in that case.

2. Use graphics sparingly. Use graphics sparingly as not everyone has a broadband connection yet! Graphics (such as pictures and charts) take a long time to load. If you use heavy graphics that take a long time to load, you can lose one third of your potential customers because they will lose patience and move to another site. This is never easy: make the pictures too big and they load slowly, make them too small and they will not look nice on your website. Google the subject to find out more information; search for "what is best resolution for pictures on a website" or something similar. Most software programs now have the option "save for web" to save a picture, ideal for use on your website.

3. Avoid using moving images and streaming video. These can also seriously limit the speed at which your website loads. These slow loading times can cause visitors to leave your site before they've even read any of your content.
You can check the speed of your website with YSLOW from Yahoo! Yslow analyzes web pages and suggests ways to improve their performance. For more information go to http://developer.yahoo.com/yslow (not available for Windows Explorer)

A word about graphics and videos:
- Graphics and videos can make your site slow to load. You can find tools in this book to reduce the size of your images and your videos, without losing any quality.
- It is important that you pay attention to this as the loading time of your website is now also a factor that is important in Google's algorithm. This means if your site loads slowly, Google will take this into account and not rank your site highly (unless your site ticks all the other boxes to rank).

4. Simple is better. Simple is ALWAYS better! While you may want to get as much on your site as possible, even if it means cramming it all together, it makes the site look awful and often results in the customer never making it past the homepage.
If you don't want to convert visitors into sales, then by all means, cram as much as you can on your homepage. It's the best way to steer them away. But this isn't what you want.

You want to design a simple and attractive homepage. Your homepage should clearly state your business purpose while offering a short and sweet roadmap to your site. Even if you don't do the latter, make sure that your site is simple and to the point whilst being appealing to the eye.

5. Creativity gets a thumbs up – but don't go too far. Creativity is how you will stand out from the rest of your competition. However, you can go too far with it, which is the last thing you want. You want a website that is unique and visually appealing, but there are some things that you shouldn't aim for. For example, visitors are typically accustomed to having a tool bar at the top of the page, search bar in either the upper right-hand or left-hand corner, contact information at the bottom of the page, etc. When you get too creative with your web design layout, your website may become confusing, ultimately causing you to lose sales.

6. Nobody likes side scrolling. Keep your website suitable for 1366 x 768 screen dimensions, and you'll ensure that over 90% of people can see all of your content without annoying side-scroll bars. 1024 x 768 screen used to be the best dimensions, but in 2013 this changed to 1366 x 768. If you go any larger than that, there will be visitors who have to scroll left and right. You will be able to set your screen size in your web design software.

7. A word about colours. While it's true that having a clean and simple website is important, you need to consider other aesthetics of your site as well. Think of your target audience and consider the product(s) that you are selling, and then decide on the graphics, colours and fonts that you believe would appeal to them while creating an image for your products and your business as a whole.

Let's do an example to help you understand a little bit better. Your customers will likely get excited with some vividly bright and bold colours; however, if you are selling spa items, then you may want some soothing, pastel colours, as bold colours wouldn't fit well. If you are selling baby items, you'll also want to consider pastel colours or primary colours, as well as really cute baby graphics. Bold red would just look out of place for a baby website.

If you decide a site specifically targeting men, pink would not be a good colour. Use your common sense when you choose your colours.

While themes are great, don't go over the top with them. Try to limit your design to no more than three main colours, and make sure each one of them complements the others. Research shows that blue is one of the most popular colours to use for commercial websites. Why? Blue supposedly signifies freedom, professionalism, security and intelligence. However, if you are selling sweet stuff, you'll want to avoid blue, as it is known to suppress appetite. Other colours to note and what they stand for:

- Green represents relaxation and wealth.
- Red denotes strength, energy and passion—it's a good one for men.
- Purple indicates luxury and sophistication. Purple is also known as the colour of the independent woman!
- Black represents elegance and authority as well as drama.

Keep in mind that if you use trendy colours, you'll need to update your site should those colours go out of style. You also want to remember that colours mean different things in other countries, so if you are selling internationally, make certain that you are careful with the colours you use. The colour of serenity and purity for those in the United States represents death and sorrow in a number of Eastern countries. So, just be careful.

Don't use lots of colours on your site or non-matching colours. Below is a chart that interior designers use. The same rules for interior design apply for websites: it all has to be pleasing to the eye and have a cosy and comfortable feel. The rule from the wheel below is: opposite colours are complementary colours. Colours that are next to each other should never be seen together. Google "colour chart" and click on "Images" to see the colour wheel.

A set of colours that complement each other is called a colour scheme. These colours simply look good together.

Here are some tools that can help you choosing colours:
www.colorcombos.com
www.colourlovers.com

Here's another interesting tool, where you can see how colourblind people will see your website: http://colorfilter.wickline.org

8. A logo or banner is worth your money. Essentially your virtual thumbprint, your logo or banner defines your business and your website. Your logo provides information on who you are, in one memorable, yet simple, design. You can design a logo on your own if you wish to tackle it, as there are numerous tutorials online that will help you learn how to. r you can choose to have a professional graphic designer create a business logo for you, which will cost anywhere from $50 (£31) to $500 (£310), depending on where you find the graphic designer and how much experience the individual has. You can find people on www.fiverr.com who design a logo for a fiver! I know this is a book about free resources but hey, a fiver is as good as free!

A logo or banner is incredibly important, especially if you plan on expanding operations in the future. Your logo/banner needs to be attractive and recognisable, but at the same time, it needs to be readable and understandable. You don't want some crazy design script that someone isn't going to be able to decipher easily. Ultimately, your logo should be basic—your company name with some type of symbol or picture.

Your logo/banner can be used for more than just representing your company on your website; it can also be used on stationery, letterheads, brochures, etc. Keep in mind that the simpler a logo is, the cheaper printing will be, as a one-colour logo will be cheaper to print than a three-colour logo.

If you're not good at creating your own images and logos, then here are some places where you can get someone else to do them for you:
www.elance.com
www.fiverr.com yes for $5 (£3) someone will design a logo for you!
www.20dollarbanners.com Get any website banner done for just $20 (£12.50)
www.99designs.co.uk People compete to design your logo or website, driving the price down and getting you a serious bargain
www.agentsofvalue.com
www.freelancer.com
www.guru.com
www.ifreelance.com
www.microworkers.com
www.mturk.com
www.odeskresources.com
www.peopleperhour.com

9. Formatting. Ensure that your website is formatted so that it can be viewed on all the different, yet common web browsers. These include Internet Explorer, Google Chrome, Mozilla Firefox, Opera, Safari, etc. You can't expect a new visitor to download a brand-new browser to their computer just so they can view your website. They'll want a website that has already tailored to them and is properly formatted for viewing on their current browser.

Perhaps you didn't know that there are different Internet browsers? Years ago I didn't either, but not everybody uses the same one. Wikipedia defines Internet browser like this:

A web browser is a software application for retrieving, presenting, and traversing information resources on the World Wide Web. An information resource is identified by a Uniform Resource Identifier (URI) and may be a web page, image, video, or other piece of content.

If you do not want to download the browsers, ask a friend with a different browser to look at your site, but as a serious Internet marketer, you should download them all yourself. You will lose potential customers if your website does not view properly with Firefox or other browsers. Not all your visitors use Internet Explorer. You can easily switch between the different browsers, so you can use the one you prefer most of the time. But when you need to test your new site, you can look at it using the five main browsers.

www.browsershots.org gives a lot of information about different browsers.

10. Under construction. Never, and I mean, never, use the "Under Construction" term anywhere on your website. Don't even use it if it really is under construction. This represents to your customers that the website isn't finished, and who really wants to visit or buy from a site that is still under construction? Sites generally stay in the "Under Construction" mode for months, if not years, so it's unlikely that visitors will come back to your site often to check and see if that section of your site is up and running yet. Plus, some search engines, such as Yahoo, for example, will reject your site and will not list it in search results if a page has "Under Construction" on it. Don't publish your site to the world until the design is finished.

11. Background music. Should you have background music? Most people don't like it, although there are a select few out there who love it. The problem is that you could play metal music and cause visitors to leave your site because they don't like that type of music. The same is true with hip-hop, country or classical. Music genres are loved and hated, and it's impossible to know what each and every one of your customers is going to like, so it's better to steer clear of background music, which can often be more annoying than anything else.

Consider this: what if your customer is on the phone and browsing the web at the same time? They have their speakers on because they were listening to music a little while ago and forgot to turn them down when they got on the phone. They are surfing the web and come across your site, click on it and get blasted with roaring music. This unexpected sound is definitely unwelcome to the customer and will result in them closing your site. More than likely, they won't venture back to it. So, it's better to opt out of background music.

If you DO put music on your site, you MUST clearly display where the visitor can turn the music on or off.

Make sure that you use royalty-free music or risk a heavy fine (discussed later).

13. Pop-up boxes. Pop-up boxes are the boxes that appear on a website, usually rising from the bottom of the page or appearing in the middle of the page, where you are asked to fill in your email to receive further information or to receive something free.
These are a BIG no! Sure, they may gain some sales here and there, but honestly, they are more annoying than helpful in gaining sales. They seem desperate and are often obnoxious when it comes to content. All in all, it's just better not to use them. 15 years ago, they were different and great, now they are just annoying for most people.

If you DO use pop-up boxes, use them when a visitor leaves your site without buying anything. You could offer a discount voucher or a free gift. That way, your customer will be on your list. It is better to use a subtle opt-in box than one with lots of colours.

14. Use simple fonts. Always use simple fonts that are easy to read. Don't use some drastic font just because it looks good, as it may not be easily readable, which will cause customers to leave your site. If you use unusual fonts and your visitor does not have that font on their computer, they will not be able to read the text very well.
Sans serif fonts are easier to read on a computer screen, while serif fonts are easier to read in a physical book, therefore sans serif fonts are best for use on websites.
Millionaire = Serif font = more rounded letters and curls.
Millionaire = Sans Serif font = simple letters, no decorative letters.
The best fonts for the web are:
- Arial
- Calibri
- Verdana
- Tahoma

The above-mentioned fonts are simple, professional and easy to read. If your favourite font is easy to read and doesn't have some crazy cursive or obscure approach, then by all means, use it. Just make sure it is easy to read, professional and simple. By choosing a popular, plain and simple font, it will load faster for visitors and you are guaranteed that they'll see it properly as opposed to an obscure font that many people aren't even aware of, resulting in the inability to view the text on your website. Nothing is a bigger turn off for a customer than not being able to read a website. You've lost your sale immediately.

15. Your font size should be minimum 12pt. Remember that your visitors can be of all ages and older people often even find size 12 a bit too small to read. Some analysts say that font size 14pt is better. Try it and test it.

If you are targeting the older audience, I suggest you use size 14. Also worth mentioning here is that "the older" generation are used to reading newspapers, there simply wasn't anything else available to read in "the olden days". This means they are used to reading black text on white background: design your site the same way.

16. Flash ain't cash! Don't use Flash elements. Flash (Adobe Flash) is a multimedia platform for creating animation, video and activity on web pages. It is very often used for advertisements and games. Google can't read Flash (not yet anyway) and so won't know what your website is about. This will be a real problem when you start trying to get on page one of the search results. A person who does not have Adobe Flash Player installed will not be able to see your site. Although sometimes Flash can look great, flashing elements can put people off.
Don't build a website full of pop-ups, flashing images and moving graphics. Research has shown that people immediately leave sites like these and, on top of that, Google cannot see fancy stuff on your site, so it is better to use the space for content and targeted keywords.

17. KISS. Remember to KISS, which stands for: Keep It Simple, Stupid. Ugly and earning money is better than beautiful and earning nothing. The key to web design is simplicity, not sophistication and overload. Don't try to look like an Internet giant; instead, focus on what makes you money.

18. Low resolution videos. If you do use videos on your website, make sure that you use low resolution ones as otherwise they will take too long to load. You can use www.handbrake.fr or www.zamzar.com to convert videos.

19. Be clear. Your visitors must see in **the first few seconds** what the site is all about.

20. The 'above the fold' screen. The above the fold screen is what the visitor can see when they first open your site, without having to scroll up or down. When a visitor scrolls down, they are then looking "below the fold". The first screen visitors see is your website's prime selling space, and what you put on it can determine your success. Don't make it "overcrowded".

21. Put the opt-in box above the fold. Important headlines should always be above the fold. I also recommend putting an opt-in box above the fold if it is important for you to get people on your mailing list.

 22. Make sure a link is a link. Only underline text if it is a link. Don't underline to emphasise text, otherwise people might not click your money-making links. Make sure that a visitor can clearly see what is clickable and what isn't. The standard is to underline clickable links. You could change the colour of the links, too.

23. Leave enough white space on each page. Pages that look too busy are abandoned very quickly, and your chance of making money is gone.

24. Don't put thousands of words of text without any sub headers. Use sub headers and bullet points wherever possible. Visitors will not read every word on your site, but they will scan through it and read what interests them.

25. Text must be easy to read. No green text on a green and red floral background, please.

26. No white text on black background. Research has shown that a lot of people do not like white text on a dark-coloured background. Older people especially, and people with impaired vision find it hard to read. Stick to black text on a white background, as people are used to reading it. There is a reason why big sites, e.g. Amazon, Ebay, Google, Youtube, etc... just use a white background and mainly black text. Amazon and Ebay's websites have been unchanged for over a decade, and no one seems to mind. Why do they not change anything? Well, simply because it works well as it is. Why change something that works?

27. No welcome/intro/splash pages. I have never understood why somebody would want intro pages on their site. They say "enter". Yes, of course I want to enter your site, that's why I clicked on it. Duh!

28. Check your content for spelling mistakes. Get friends to proofread it, as you are unlikely to see your own mistakes.

29. Include lots of internal links. Have links to your other pages at the top, left and bottom of the page because Google likes this. Learn more about this in my book "*From Newbie To Millionaire*".

30. Make sure that ALL the pictures, music and videos that you use are royalty free.
There are institutions out there who only try to find websites that use non-royalty free products. You might get a letter in the post one day with a heavy fine if you do not abide by the royalty-free rules. The consequences could be huge and result in a lawsuit.
For that reason, you should always either buy stock photos or stock images, or make sure you use images that are under the Commercial Commons license (i.e. royalty free). Stock images are pictures on stock photo websites to be used or bought by other people. Sometimes you are required to provide a link to the source where you got the picture from, but read the terms and conditions of the site.

31. Photograph of yourself or not. A photograph of yourself on your site lets people know that you are a real person. If you don't like your own photograph, you can always create an avatar (payable options listed):
www.sitepal.com
www.cartoonyourworld.com
www.mywebface.com

32. Make your site trustworthy with security images if you are selling something on your site. You can have the best-looking site out there, but if you don't have that image of security that customers need to see in order to hand over their credit card to you, you will lose sales.
Third-party Security Icons are one of the easiest and quickest ways to build that image of security and let your customers know that your site is safe to shop at. Companies such as TRUSTe will review your website. They have security standards that they follow, and if your site meets those, they will give you permission for your site to hold their icon.

You must have a legitimate website with genuine, justifiable security measures.
Security sites, such as TRUSTe, say that when their icon is posted to a website, the site's sales increase anywhere from 7% to 12%. If this works out for your site, then it is well worth the money that you spend to retain their permission to display their icon.
33. Limit your ads, concentrate on direct content. The more advertisements and

irrelevant links that your site has, the more your potential customer will realise that your income is coming from affiliate links and ads rather than a quality product. Web users know what a online store or informative website looks like, and it isn't one covered in ads. Therefore, your content needs to be competent, direct and free of mistakes (namely spelling and grammar). Sloppy content indicates amateurism, and most customers don't want to deal with amateurs.

Conclusion: A website must look and feel good for the visitor. The visitor must immediately have a good impression when landing on your site.

Remember: You never have a second chance to make a first good impression!

Chapter 5) Domains, Hosting and Email Accounts

This set of topics can make or break your website's profitability. This will also be the only area that I recommend spending a little money on. However it is very small, compared to the professionalism it will bring.

1) Free Internet Access

www.freedialup.org offers free access in some states in the USA

www.free-Internet.name

www.all-free-isp.com

www.wififreespot.com

www.12free.co.uk

www.myfreeisp.co.uk

Keep in mind that free access usually means slow Internet speed and also intrusive advertising on your site.

2) Domain or Sub-domain?

Domain vs. sub-domain is a topic that people will line up and draw sides on. The Internet works on what is called Internet Protocol (IP) addresses. Each computer attached to the Internet has one. The server where your website is stored has one. However, numbers are hard to remember. A process called domain names was developed to make remembering locations easier. Domain names are made up of two components, the site name and the top level domain. The top level is at the end of the domain name, some top levels include: com, net, org, edu and mil. Each country except the United States has a country code. Your site name such as Amazon is combined with a top level such as.com, to create the domain name amazon.com. A period is used to separate elements of a domain name. The computer where the files for this domain are stored is reported to the Internet authority and a look up is created. Think of a look up as being similar to the phone book in your cell phone, you select the name and the phone dials the number.

A sub-domain is an address that belongs to a domain. As an example joes-store.amazon.com. Joes-store is a sub-domain of amazon.com. Generally companies that use sub-domains such as Amazon provide them for free. Most companies that offer free hosting also do so with sub-domains. When you start out that may seem like an outstanding option. However, you do not own the name and the domain owner has complete control over it.

Having your own domain is preferred and more professional and a must if you are going to become a professional Internet marketer.

3) Domain Names

You can get free domain names e.g. www.yourdomainnamehere.weebly.com from www.weebly.com.
A domain name like this just doesn't look professional but is perfect to use if you just want to test some stuff e.g. how does hosting and ftp work, etc...

www.yourdomainnamehere.wordpress.com is another option. Register with Wordpress at www.wordpress.org

To start with, to find out how Internet Marketing works, you can try a free domain. Keep in mind that very often it will be more difficult to rank in search engines with these domain names. Google knows that most of the time these domain names are not professional, therefore often have poor content and, consequently, Google thinks that they are not good value for visitors.

You can get a free domain name from:

- www.codotvu.com If you don't use your domain for 90 days from the date of registration, someone else can register the same domain so you will lose yours. You are not the owner of the domain.

- www.freenom.com You can get free domain names with these extensions:.cf,.ga,.ml,.tk. You are not the owner of the domain.

- www.uk.to You can get free domain names with these extensions: uk.to, us.to, fr.to, qc.to

If you really cannot afford a domain name e.g..com or.co uk, you can always buy a.info domain name as some of these only cost $2 (£1.50) per year for the first year. So, in most cases, getting your own domain name is by far the best option. Most hosting companies offer domain name registration. Host companies like

- Go Daddy www.godaddy.com

- 1and1 www.1and1.com

- Hostgator www.hostgator.com offer domain name registration. A year's registration of a domain name is about $15 (£9) for a domain with an.com top level. Many companies will offer a first year price at a much lower rate. Some companies will even provide the domain name for free if you purchase a hosting package from them.

The process of buying a domain name is very simple. You start with a search to see if the name you wish to use is available. It is best that your domain name is related to the niche that you wish to target. Visit a hosting company, click on [Buy Domains] and enter the domain name you are thinking of buying, hit [search] and it will let you know if it is available and with what top level extensions. Often the search will also show closely related names that are available as well.

Once you have selected the name you wish, it is just a matter of filling out a simple form and submitting it with your payment. Generally it takes about 24 hours to process and another 24 hours to set up the hosting if you've purchased that.

4) Hosting

Once you have decided on your domain name, which is the name of your site, such as www.yourdomainnamehere.com you need to make sure that somebody will host your website. This means somebody has got to store your website somewhere so people can access it. When you have built a website on your computer and it has been published to the web, people need to be able to see it. If 1000 people want to look at your site, they won't come to your home or office to do it, so you need to have a place where your site is "hosted" so that all 1000 people can look at it at the same time. This is what a hosting company does; they will give your site a space on their massive computer servers so people can view it. You pay the hosting company a fee to host, or store, your site.

When choosing a hosting company, you need to look at two factors: web disk space and bandwidth, both explained in the next few paragraphs. Another reason why you need a hosting company is because of the bandwidth (see explanation below) on your computer. If you host your website yourself and have an Internet connection speed of 1MB on your home computer, it will take several hours for a customer to download a movie. A hosting company might have a 250MB Internet connection speed, meaning your customers can download the movie much quicker.

Choose your hosting company carefully. You can spend a heck of a lot of time designing your site but if it is slow to load due to a poor hosting plan, visitors will move on to another site. I recommend strongly not using the free or very cheap web hosting companies.

- What is bandwidth and what is the difference between it and web disk space?
This often confuses IM newbies.

What is 'disk space'?

Disk space is also called data storage or hosting space. It is the amount of data that the hosting provider allows you to store. Images, audio files, visual files, multi-media files and graphics all take up a lot more space than simple text. If your site has 20 pages of mostly text, your total disk space needs will probably be under 1MB. If you have a site with lots of graphics and multimedia, you need a lot more disk space.

TOP TIP: To find out how much disk space you need for your website, simply put all your website files into one folder on your PC. Right click the folder and choose 'properties', which will show you the total space needed to store your website.

What is 'bandwidth'?

Bandwidth is the amount of traffic that your hosting company allows between your website on their server, and the visitors to your website. It is a measure of total data transferred in one month to and from your site. Each time a visitor looks at your site, it is downloaded from your hosting company to be viewed on the Internet. If you go over the amount of bandwidth with your hosting company, they could charge you an extra fee, visitors might not be able to see your site or it will be downloaded very slowly. Think about bandwidth as cars on motorways (highways in the US). If you are the only car on the motorway, you can drive quickly, but the more cars, the slower you're forced to go. You are also not able to overtake another car when you are stuck in a queue. With low bandwidth your visitors cannot download things quickly and will be stuck in a queue when wanting to download a file if two people want to download it at the same time.

How much bandwidth do you need?

For most small businesses or personal sites 2GB of bandwidth per month is usually enough. Most hosting companies will include this in their cheapest package. Traffic to your site is the number of 'bits' that are transferred on the Internet. One gigabyte (GB) is 1,024 megabytes. To store one character, one byte of storage is needed.
Imagine that you have 100 filing cabinets in your office.

Each of these filing cabinets has 1000 folders in it
In each folder there are 100 papers
On each paper are 100 characters
The total of all this is 1 GB (100x1000x100x100)

How much bandwidth you need depends on what type of website you are building. If people can download MP3 songs or movies from your website, and you are expecting a lot of visitors, you will need a very high bandwidth because each MP3 song is, on average, about 4MB. A movie can be up to 1000MB or 1GB. In this case, if you only have a bandwidth of 1GB, when two customers want to download a 1GB movie, they cannot do it at the same time. Remember, in my comparison with motorways and cars, you cannot overtake a car when in a traffic jam. The second one in the queue will probably receive an error message. This will result in your customer having a negative impression of your site, which of course you must avoid. If you are expecting ten thousand visitors to your site per day, you need to choose the correct bandwidth plan with your hosting company. Most hosting companies offer the facility to start with low bandwidth and upgrade it at an extra cost.

Companies offer a variety of bandwidth options in terms of your monthly gigabyte allocation. Working out how much bandwidth you need is not as simple as calculating how much disk space you need. But the following formula will give you some idea: Size (or disk space) of all your web pages including all graphics X numbers of visitors you expect each day X number of pages your visitors will view X 30 days per month = total monthly data transfer, or bandwidth.
The amount of emails that you send also counts in the bandwidth. If you often send hundreds of emails with very large files attached, it will count towards your bandwidth usage.
If your website gets lots of visits per month, through Google or from affiliates sending traffic to it, you need more bandwidth, not necessarily more space.
More and more hosting companies are starting to offer unlimited space and unlimited bandwidth.

Conclusion: disk space is the amount of storage space your website needs on the server of your hosting company. Bandwidth is the traffic that passes through your hosting company to your website.

Important to mention: Some hosting companies proclaim that their hosting includes unlimited traffic and unlimited storage. However, most of the time, there is a limit and most of the time the hosting means that your website will be placed on a shared server. If your site will take up too much space and too much time on the space allocated to you, your website will suffer, work slowly, etc.... or the hosting company will start charging you. You would have agreed with this when you ticked that you have read their terms and conditions when you signed up.

Should you use free hosting and are there different types of free hosting is a question that often comes to mind to those building their first website. There are a number of sites that provide free hosting, however, remember the old saying "there is no such thing as a free lunch."

The biggest trap you need to look out for are the free web hosts that place their advertisements on your web pages. Many companies place banners that are often in competition with your own efforts. Still, as you start out, there are some outstanding offers. If you are just getting your feet wet with Internet Marketing or building a wesbite, free hosting can be for you, just to find out if you like the whole "Internet Marketing thing". However, once you start to earn a little bit of money, it is highly recommended to change to a well know hosting company.

- Freehosting www.freehosting.com has an outstanding free hosting package. The "No Free Lunch" rule is that you have to register your domain with them, you get only one email address and 250 GB of bandwidth. 250GB is adequate for most websites.

- Byethost www.byethost.com has a free package that offers free sub-domains and 50Gb of bandwidth. They do not offer email or having your own domain.

- Weebly.com has a good reputation for free hosting www.weebly.com

- 50webs www.50webs.com also offers free entry-level hosting with 60 MB storage. You need to be able to create your own web pages and transfer them via FTP to your hosting account.

Batcave www.batcave.net offers free hosting with 1000MB of disk space and 5GB monthly traffic. They also have payable options that are very affordable.

- Bravenet www.bravenet.com is a very popular free web hosting site. They offer free hosting with their Site Builder software. They also offer an ad-free hosting for a very small monthly charge. The site has millions of members.

While there are some costs involved, paid hosting should definitely be considered. General hosting with unlimited bandwidth can be purchased for as low as $5 (£3) a month. The providers listed above with the domain name services, all have attractive hosting packages.

Using Hostgator as an example, their "baby" package includes unlimited bandwidth, unlimited storage and unlimited number of email accounts for about $8 (£5) a month or less. However, another attractive feature is that you can have an unlimited number of domains on your server. This means, as you expand your business, the one account can host them all. The program also allows you to have your own sub-domains. This will allow you to create different websites within one domain name.

I use GoDaddy www.godaddy.com, 1and1 www.1and1.com or www.hostgator.com for my hosting. Whatever company you use for your hosting, make sure that you go for one that offers unlimited bandwidth and unlimited space. If you don't, your website might load too slowly, or not load at all, resulting in visitors leaving your site immediately.

5) Free Email Accounts

There are many companies such as Google and Yahoo that will offer you a free email account. Consider this, who would you trust more to do business with: Sam@SamElectronicstore.com or Sam@yahoo.com ? Millions of people use Gmail and Yahoo email addresses and that's fine, free and easy. I have one too but hardly ever use it. In my opinion, from a **professional** point of view, it is better to use an email address that has your domain name in it.

When you get your own domain and a hosting service, you can create an email address that reflects your website, your business. If you are not willing to invest a few dollars a month for a professional email address, why would your customers trust you with their business? Having said that, a free email account e.g. joebutman1@gmail.com is perfect if you are trying out Internet Marketing. Once you want to go more professional, you really need an email account that goes with your website e.g. yourname@yourdomainname.com

If you have a website www.MakeEasyTables.com, it is generally accepted as more professional if you have an email e.g. info@MakingEasyTables.com compared to richard145@gmail.com

So, to start with, if you can't afford a domain name with an email account, get yourself a free Gmail address: https://mail.google.com/ or visit www.yahoo.com for a free Yahoo email.

Conclusion re free access, free domain and free hosting: you can use these free services to start with but in order to build a PROFESSIONAL website that will make you money, you really do need hosting with a monthly charge as this hosting is more professional and therefore faster. With www.1and1.com your email addresses are free, with some other hosting companies they are payable.

Chapter 6) Search Engine Optimisation

Building your website is useless if no one sees it. While many people believe it is, the Internet is not the field of dreams. "Build it and they will come" does not apply to the Internet. Before we get to the meat of building your site for free, there is one more very important concept that you should understand, Search engine Optimization (SEO).

One of the biggest methods of getting visitors to your site is by the search engines. Search Engine Marketing (SEM) is the means by which you get visitors to your site by way of the different search engines such as Google, Bing and Yahoo. SEM can have both paid and free components. The search engines rank pages using secret methods, called algorithms. They take numerous items into consideration and the end result is where you are listed for each keyword on your site. The better you rank compared to someone else, the higher you are in the rankings. This ranking is called an organic result. If you develop your website and publish it without some basic knowledge of SEO, is very likely your site will not be mentioned in the search results The basic concepts of SEO and how to prepare for it when you design and write your pages is, therefore, critical before you start.

1) Basic Training for SEO

No pushups or long runs required but some basic training in SEO is a requirement to get ahead with Internet Marketing. One of the best, if not the best, SEO training programs can be found for free on the Udemy website www.udemy.com.

- Udemy is a online training site. The whiteboard SEO course www.udemy.com/whiteboard-seo is presented by MOZ which is a leading SEO company. seomoz.org.

- MOZ also has a online guide: www.moz.com/beginners-guide-to-seo that is very good and it is free.

- Another course worthy of looking into, also on Udemy, is the SEO content writing course www.udemy.com/seo-for-content-creators

- The website seo-hacker www.seo-hacker.org has a nine lesson introductory program. - Hobo Internet Marketing in the UK has an outstanding 75 page book that is offered for free www.hobo-web.co.uk/seo-eBook

- The Kindle book section of the Amazon websites www.amazon.com and www.amazon.co.uk has a great source of free books in the Kindle format. There are free reader programs for computers, tablets, iPads and even cell phones so you do not need a Kindle device to read the books. Amazon has a program that encourages and rewards authors to offer their books for free for a few days. So check in for a few days and see what is on sale for $0.00. You can get books free that might be priced at $20 (£12) one week later.

- The "bible" of SEO is by Google itself and can be found at www.google.com/webmasters/docs/search-engine-optimization-starter-guide.pdf

If the above url no longer works, just search for "google search engine optimization starter guide 2014" and you will find where you can download it.

- SEO is really well explained in my book *From Newbie To Millionaire*". I build websites successfully on the principles based in this book.

Ranking in Google is over complicated by many people. A simple site with the elements listed below will get you a long way:

- regular visitors

- good SEO

- targeting long tail keywords

- good content

- most of the 'must have' elements, as already discussed

- some videos

- low bounce rate. A high bounce rate means that visitors opening your site close it again after a few seconds. Google will conclude from this that there is nothing interesting on your site for visitors to see, therefore your site will be ranked lower. Slow pages are annoying for people, the slower your pages load, the less Google likes your site. Google WILL rank your pages lower if your site loads slow.

- Never ever use anything automated e.g. articles, automated content, automated website building, automated backlinks, etc.. You WILL be punished by your site not showing in the search engines.

- Adsense on your site. Many people say this doesn't work but here's my opinion on it: if Google never showed websites with Adsense in the first rankings, Google's income from Adsense would stop. Of course, Google being a commercial institution, they will not stop showing sites that have Adsense on, otherwise they would lose that income.

A great SEO plugin for Wordpress is Yoast. wwwyoast.com (payable).

2) Duplicate Copy Penalty

Duplicate copy means that the text on your website is exactly the same as on someone else's website. With duplicate copy all over your site you don't have a lot of chance to rank in Google, even if you have applied good SEO on your site. This is because Google, or any other search engine, doesn't like duplicate content. The most common obstacle that sites have to getting a top ranking is duplicate content.

The search engines do not want to present to their clients a list of identical or very similar pages. Most users of search engines seldom go past the first, or at the most, the second page of results. If you are not there, for your targeted keyword, you won't get many visitors.

Many affiliate programs will provide you content for your web pages. However, they are providing the same content to hundreds, maybe even thousands of other websites. As a result, search engines will not give much consideration to sites that use the affiliate provided content.

One practice that many people use to try and create duplicate content, is to spin an article. In a spun article, certain keywords or phrases are replaced with similar words to create new articles. As an example, an article about inexpensive hotels might spin the article replacing the word hotel with accommodation, resort, lodge, or room. It might also replace the word inexpensive with cheap, budget or value. The result could be a dozen or more "different" variations.

Years ago, you could fool the search engines into seeing your spun articles as different. That is not true now. It is always best to use original content, to write your own content.

3) Plagiarism and Copyright Violations

In the search engines the concept of duplicate content often overlaps plagiarism and copyright law violations. We will discuss these issues in detail later. As a general concept the search engines only look for duplicate copy and use that to determine your rankings, they do not concern themselves with who really owns the material. An exception to this viewpoint is if a copyright owner notifies the search engine of a violation. As a copyright holder, if I see my content in a search engine listing, I can inform the search engine that they may not publish my information in their listing. As a result the page where the information is located could be banned by the search engine.

- The website www.plagiarism.org has a very good primer on plagiarism and how to avoid it.

- Copyscape www.copyscape.com is the Internet standard for checking for duplicate copy and plagiarism. Their free version is limited, however it will meet the basic requirements of checking for duplicate content.

You can become a premium member for $25 (£15). This will give you 500 documents you can scan during one year. Copyscape says that for best results, you can search for a document with no more than 2,000 words. I ignore that and I search a whole book e.g. 30,000 words and it will still find all the duplicated results. Copyscape Premium is the most advanced plagiarism search on the web. You can visit www.copyscape.com/premium.php for more information on the premium version.

I use Copyscape each time I outsource the writing of my niche books. When the outsourcer gives the book to me, finished, I paste the content of the whole book in Copyscape. That way I will find out if the outsourcer has copied and pasted content from the web in my book.

In the example below, you can see that on one occasion, Copyscape told me that the content of my book was exactly the same as content found on the web. In this instance, I made the change in my book myself as it is quicker than sending it back to the outsourcers and waiting for them to send it back to me, with the changes made.

However, if the result in Copyscape is, for example, four results found of duplicated content, I send it back to the outsourcer, with a screenshot of the results so it can be changed to original content.

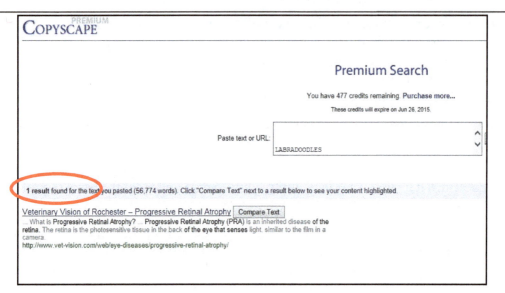

Once your document has been scanned by Copyscape and has Zero results of duplicate content, you can visit www.copyscape.com/banners.php?o=f , where you can see banners that you can put on your site or in your eBook. Here is one example:

Note: When you upload a Kindle book with lots of duplicated content, Kindle will reject your book and send you an email asking you to confirm that you own the copyright to the material you have uploaded. If you say yes, when you don't really own the copyright, your Kindle account can be banned.

- Grammarly www.grammarly.com is a website that will check your content for misspelling and grammar errors and will also check for plagiarism at the same time. Its free version will give you an overall rating. You have seven days to try it for free but you will have to sign up with the paid plan when you sign up. Don't forget to cancel your payable monthly subscription before the seven days end.

- The website Small SEO toolbox www.smallseotools.com is a 'must have' for site builders.

4) Keywords: The SEO Cornerstone

When you review the basic SEO material, one of the major topics is geared towards keywords. We discussed long tail keywords when we discussed niche marketing earlier. There are a couple of points that should be reinforced. Each page of your website is ranked for the words on your page. A page should be optimised for just a few words and should also include long tail keywords. With Keyword Planner, as already discussed, you can find long tail keywords www.adwords.google.com/ko/KeywordPlanner/home

- www.soovle.com I love this site. Type in your keyword in Soovle and you will be given a lot of suggestions for other keywords in different search engines and websites: Wikipedia, Google, Amazon, Answers.com, Youtube, Bing, Yahoo. Do a screenshot of the suggestions and analyse each keyword for potential. That's what I do.
If you click on a keyword, it takes you to the relevant website.

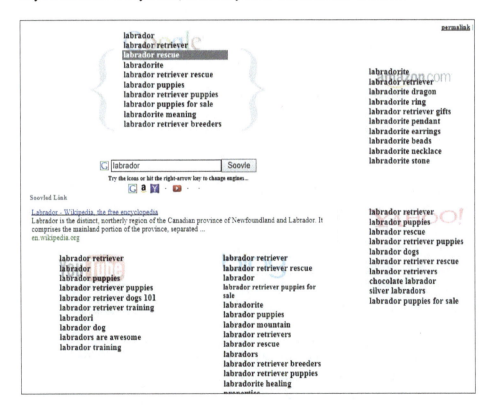

- Wordstream Keyword Niche Tool www.wordstream.com/keyword-niche-finder

- Keyword discovery www.keyworddiscovery.com/search.html

- Bing search tool www.bing.com/toolbox/keywords

- Word Pot www.wordpot.com

While you are designing your pages it is important to keep your target in mind: getting the right visitors to your site. Using the keyword tools will help keep you focused.

5) SEO Tools and Webmaster Tools

There are thousands of different free tools that you can use to check and develop your SEO and web optimisation practices. There are two, however, that are critical for you to know how well you are doing. Both of the tools are from Google, are free and they do both work together.

- Google Analytics www.google.com/analytics

- Google Webmaster Tools www.google.com/webmasters/tools

About the Google Analytics Tool:

Google Analytics is a website statistics program that you can use for free. It is not visible to the visitor to your site. It tells you all sorts of detailed information about your site including:

- Number of daily/weekly/monthly visitors
- Your site's page views
- Bounce Rate
- From which search engines your visitors came
- What country your visitors are from
- Which browser people use
- Traffic sources
- How long people stay on your site
- How visitors found your site
- Which keywords were used to land on your site

It's crucial to have this in place so you can see exactly how well your site's doing. You only have to sign up once and you can put Google Analytics on all your sites. The way it works: Google gives you a code and you put that code on your website.
 Sign up and have a look at their tutorials www.Google.com/analytics – it is completely free.

The following pages show you an example of Google Analytics from one of my sites. As you can see from the first graph, the site did not get ANY traffic before September but it did after I improved my SEO.

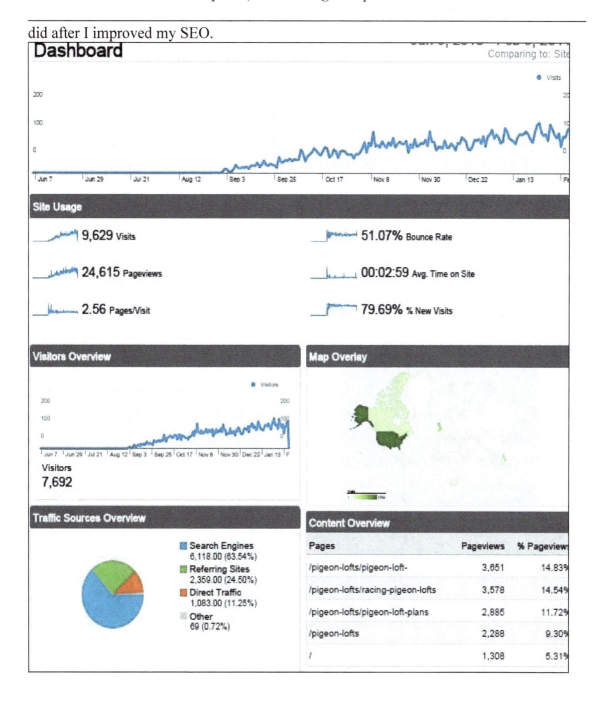

Visitors Overview

Comparing to: Sit

● Visitors

7,692 people visited this site

9,629 Visits

7,692 Absolute Unique Visitors

24,615 Pageviews

2.56 Average Pageviews

00:02:59 Time on Site

51.07% Bounce Rate

79.69% New Visits

Technical Profile

Browser	Visits	% visits	Connection Speed	Visits	% visi
Internet Explorer	5,256	54.59%	Unknown	3,473	36.07
Firefox	2,322	24.11%	DSL	2,996	31.11
Chrome	1,114	11.57%	Cable	2,366	24.57
Safari	657	6.82%	T1	561	5.83
Opera	102	1.06%	Dialup	187	1.94

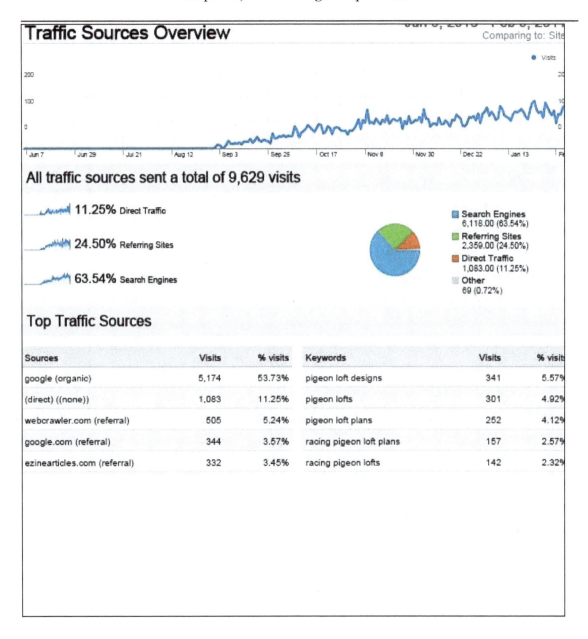

Traffic Sources Overview

Comparing to: Site

All traffic sources sent a total of 9,629 visits

11.25% Direct Traffic

24.50% Referring Sites

63.54% Search Engines

■ Search Engines
6,118.00 (63.54%)
■ Referring Sites
2,359.00 (24.50%)
■ Direct Traffic
1,083.00 (11.25%)
▨ Other
69 (0.72%)

Top Traffic Sources

Sources	Visits	% visits	Keywords	Visits	% visits
google (organic)	5,174	53.73%	pigeon loft designs	341	5.57%
(direct) ((none))	1,083	11.25%	pigeon lofts	301	4.92%
webcrawler.com (referral)	505	5.24%	pigeon loft plans	252	4.12%
google.com (referral)	344	3.57%	racing pigeon loft plans	157	2.57%
ezinearticles.com (referral)	332	3.45%	racing pigeon lofts	142	2.32%

81

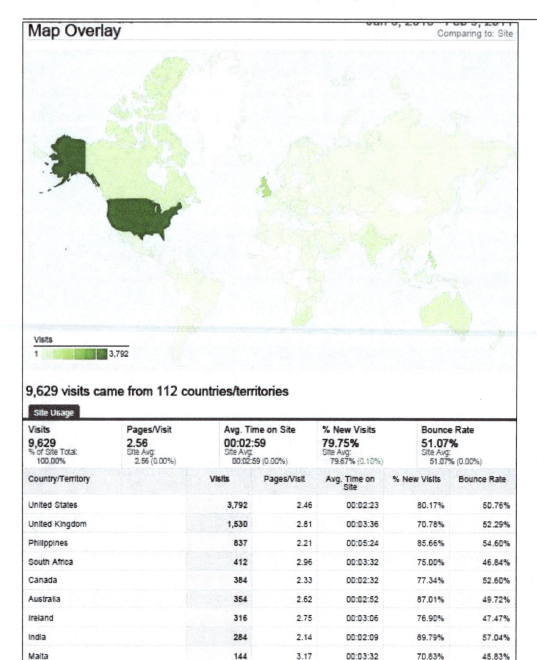

Map Overlay

Comparing to: Site

Visits
1 ▮▮▮ 3,792

9,629 visits came from 112 countries/territories

Site Usage

Visits	Pages/Visit	Avg. Time on Site	% New Visits	Bounce Rate
9,629	**2.56**	**00:02:59**	**79.75%**	**51.07%**
% of Site Total: 100.00%	Site Avg: 2.56 (0.00%)	Site Avg: 00:02:59 (0.00%)	Site Avg: 79.67% (0.10%)	Site Avg: 51.07% (0.00%)

Country/Territory	Visits	Pages/Visit	Avg. Time on Site	% New Visits	Bounce Rate
United States	3,792	2.46	00:02:23	80.17%	50.76%
United Kingdom	1,530	2.81	00:03:36	70.78%	52.29%
Philippines	837	2.21	00:05:24	85.66%	54.60%
South Africa	412	2.96	00:03:32	75.00%	46.84%
Canada	384	2.33	00:02:32	77.34%	52.60%
Australia	354	2.62	00:02:52	87.01%	49.72%
Ireland	316	2.75	00:03:06	76.90%	47.47%
India	284	2.14	00:02:09	89.79%	57.04%
Malta	144	3.17	00:03:32	70.83%	45.83%

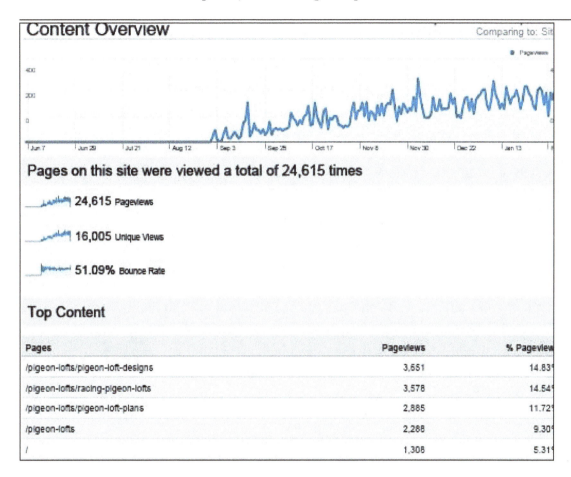

About The Webmaster Tool:

The webmaster tool will tell you how you are doing in the search engines. It will let you know how many times your web pages appeared in searches and how many of those searches resulted in someone visiting your website. The tool will allow you to see how many of your pages are indexed in the Google search engines, how many links are pointing to your pages and what your average position is for keywords that brought visitors to your site. Google will also let you know if there are any broken links or other problems with your site. Overall it is an outstanding tool to see how effective your SEO is and where you could improve.

- Bing has a similar tool www.bing.com/toolbox/webmaster. After you start your analytic account, you will register your website. Each website that you register is given a site ID code. The analytic page will give you instructions on where and how to insert a script on each one of your web pages.

- Wordpress has a tool for this www.wordpress.org/plugins/google-analytics-for-wordpress Once the code is installed, you will be able to see statistics on how visitors act on your website. You will not be able to follow single visitors but you will see traffic flow. Things such as 50% of web visitors only visited the main page, while 30% went to widget "A" page and 10% to widget "B" page. It will show you in percentages and total numbers what the entry point was of your website and where visitors were before they visited your site. You can get a geographical breakdown of where your customers are. One interesting piece of information is the real time data. The real time data will show you which pages currently have people looking at them and how long they have been on your page and on the website. It will also tell you how many are first time visitors and how many are repeat visitors.

- Visit www.footprintlive.com and you can see which search term your visitor has used to find your site. You can also observe visitors real-time. By analysing how your visitors/customers interact with your site, you can also find ways to improve your SEO or other aspects of your site.

- There are some other good analytics tools available:
www.accesswatch.com - free
www.extremetracking.com - free
www.statcounter.com - free
 www.webtrends.com - high end to pay solution

6) Search Engines Don't Buy Products, People Do

One overriding rule about search engine marketing and search engine optimization: your buyer is a person, not the robot from the search engine. The text you have on your website must make sense to a person. Too often developers get so carried away with the concept of keywords that they end up writing nonsense. Search engines are getting smarter and they are applying grammar rules to pages. Always write to your target audience and write in a way that reads well but is not overstuffed with keywords.

Chapter 7) Legal Content

When we talk about legal content, we automatically talk about DMCA and OCILLA so it is important that you understand these terms.

To put it in one simple sentence: DCMA is a law that protects against copyright infringement and OCILLA is the same, but specifically for online service providers.

Infringement means that you are using something that is legally not yours or that you do not have the right to use e.g. content, photographs, videos, etc...

I quote from Wikipedia:

*- DMCA = The **Digital Millennium Copyright Act** is a United States copyright law that implements two 1996 treaties of the World Intellectual Property Organisation (WIPO). It criminalizes production and dissemination of technology, devices, or services intended to circumvent measures (commonly known as digital rights management or DRM) that control access to copyrighted works. It also criminalizes the act of circumventing an access control, whether or not there is actual infringement of copyright itself. In addition, the DMCA heightens the penalties for copyright infringement on the Internet.[1][2] Passed on October 12, 1998, by a unanimous vote in the United States Senate and signed into law by President Bill Clinton on October 28, 1998, the DMCA amended Title 17 of the United States Code to extend the reach of copyright, while limiting the liability of the providers of online services for copyright infringement by their users.*

The DMCA's principal innovation in the field of copyright is the exemption from direct and indirect liability of Internet service providers and other intermediaries. This exemption was adopted by the European Union in the Electronic Commerce Directive 2000. The Copyright Directive 2001 implemented the 1996 WIPO Copyright Treaty in the EU.

*- OCILLA The **Online Copyright Infringement Liability Limitation Act (OCILLA)** is United States federal law that creates a conditional safe harbor for online service providers (OSP) (a group which includes Internet service providers (ISP)) and other Internet intermediaries by shielding them for their own acts of direct copyright infringement (when they make unauthorized copies) as well as shielding them from potential secondary liability for the infringing acts of others. OCILLA was passed as a*

part of the 1998 Digital Millennium Copyright Act (DMCA) and is sometimes referred to as the "Safe Harbor" provision or as "DMCA 512" because it added Section 512 to Title 17 of the United States Code. By exempting Internet intermediaries from copyright infringement liability provided they follow certain rules, OCILLA attempts to strike a balance between the competing interests of copyright owners and digital users.

You can read the full explanation about DMCA here:
http://en.wikipedia.org/wiki/Online_Copyright_Infringement_Liability_Limitation_Act

You can read the full explanation about OCILLA here:
http://en.wikipedia.org/wiki/Digital_Millennium_Copyright_Act

- On a lot of websites, usually at the bottom, you will see a link that says "DCMA". Use that link to report any infringements of copyright that you can see on the site e.g. if a website is using your content or your image, you can report it to that website via that link.

- "DMCA Takedown" means that something has been removed because of copyright infringement e.g. a writer contacts the DMCA office to report a website that has his content illegally on that website. The DMCA office will then demand the website owner removes the content.

In case you are the owner of a photograph and you can see it is illegally used on a website, here is an example email you can send the webmaster:

****

Subject Title of email:

Your company is currently in violation of US software copyright protection laws

Content of email:

Your company is currently in violation of US software copyright protection laws in relation to an illegal upload and link to a photograph that is my property.

I am *"your name here"*, owner of copyrighted work *"url of image here"* or name of *photograph here.*

My photograph is downloadable for free on your site. The use of the material in the manner complained of is not authorized by me, the copyright owner, its agents, or the law.

Please remove my photograph immediately from your site. Providing this product for free download is against all copyright rules. I have never given written permission for you to make it available for immediate download, therefore it is against the law.

Infringed material that needs to be removed from your site immediately is here: **p***ut the url of the photograph here.*

Your immediate reaction is required to remove intellectual property from your site.

If this software isn't removed within five days from receipt of this notice I/we will be forced to commence legal proceedings and related costs for copyright infringement and loss of earnings for the above product.

In the U.S., software and intellectual property rights are protected under the U.S. Copyright Protection Act as amended in 1964, 1980 and 1990, the No Electronic Theft Act of 1997, the Digital Millennium Copyright Act of 1998, the Software Rental Amendment Act of 1990.

The information in this notification is accurate and I am authorized, as the owner of the photograph, to put in the claim.

Name: *Your Name Here*
email: *Your Email Address Here*

Regards

Your Name Here

****

OK, that's that said about DMCA and OCILLA. Information in this chapter is presented as an overview of the topic and should not be considered legal advice. Please refer to knowledgeable persons in your own country for legal advice if necessary. I am not a lawyer and cannot be held responsible for any legal consequences, of any sort.

Another item to keep in the back of your mind is that while in some countries certain content may be acceptable, in others the same item can bring criminal charges. A recent case in Thailand: a group of individuals were arrested and found guilty of the crime of insulting the King. They had liked and shared an article that contained some insulting comments about the King.

CONTENT IS KING. FACT. Content is definitely what can make or break your chances of ranking highly more than anything else (besides SEO) and it is what makes you different from your competitors. It also makes other websites in your niche want to link to your site. The links that other websites give you is a sign for Google that your site is worthy of ranking for your market. More links means more traffic from other sites and traffic from other sites means Google will rank you higher. Content and SEO are the two most important things you have to do well to be successful.

1) Being on the Internet Does Not Mean it is Free to Use

Many people believe that anything they see on the Internet they can use. This is not true. You have a few different problems that can happen if you indiscriminately use material you find online. As mentioned before, using duplicate content will get you penalized by the search engines. This can happen even if you have permission from the owner of the information. The other, more important issues are those that deal with copyright violations and plagiarism. Some people are under the misunderstanding that the © symbol must be shown for a copyright to be protected or that an item must be submitted to the copyright office in order to have a copyright. Neither of those statements is true.

In the United States the requirement for the © symbol and registration was removed in 1989. See Cornell College website www.copyright.cornell.edu/resources/publicdomain.cfm for a full breakdown of US copyright periods.

UK law encourages it but does not require it. www.ipo.gov.uk/types/copy.htm . A copyright is created at the time of creation of a work. This includes items such as writing, photography, art work, and music. Any item of a creative nature is protected. So if you write a book, you are automatically the copyright owner or if you take a photograph, you are automatically the copyright owner of that photograph.

Generally the creator of the work is the copyright holder, however that is not always true. If the work is created by an employee then the employer owns the copyright. When a creative work is made as a derivative of a copyrighted work then the original owner owns the copyright.

If you write an outstanding novel showing Harry Potter going to college, J K Rowling would have a number of choices:

- She might offer you permission to make a derivative from her copyrighted works (doubtful)

- She might bring a lawsuit against you for damages (more likely)

- She might thank you because she would own the copyright and all rights to the book you wrote.

Taking a picture or a screenshot of a copyrighted item can also be considered a derivative. Want to take a photograph of a sexy bikini girl or a muscle man laying across a Porsche? If the photograph clearly shows that the car is a Porsche, such as being able to identify the Porsche badge, you need permission from Porsche.

Most companies will allow you to use their name e.g. in the above example, Porsche will get free advertising. Amazon is copyright protected but thousands of Internet Marketers use the Amazon logo on their site to promote them with an affiliate link. Amazon doesn't mind as it is free advertising for them.

The Olympic Games© copyright does not allow you to use their name in a domain name and will take you to court, if need be, resulting in heavy fines for you.

The bottom line is: always investigate whether you are allowed to use a company's logo that is copyright protected.

2) Creative Commons

To use the work of another creator you must obtain their permission.

A non-profit group Creative Commons www.creativecommons.org has created a website where copyright owners can select a free license agreement that allows other to use their work.

The Creative Commons (CC) site has a directory of websites where all contributors agree to the Creative Common licenses. There are six different agreements available. The most common is use with attribution (this means referring to the source of the image, video, text, etc...).

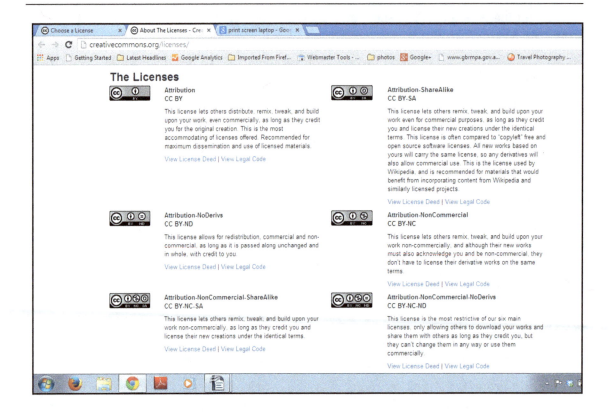

The image above is from the webpage www.creativeommons.org/licenses *and shows the variation of CC licenses. Note that each one of them requires that the copyrighted material is attributed.*

This allows you to use the item whether it is something written or a photograph, in its original form for non commercial purposes, provided that you give a credit to the copyright holder. The CC definition of Non-commercial purpose is: "CC's NonCommercial (NC) licenses do not allow uses that are mainly intended for or directed toward commercial gain or monetary compensation."

A photograph or article used as a part of a website or an eBook generally fit the definition of NC. This concept of Creative Commons has been instrumental in the development of many of the free computer programs on the market that mimic expensive programs. Open office is an example. CC FAQ has further information on what is commercial use at www.wiki.creativecommons.org/FAQ

Each product in Creative Commons has an icon or some text explaining that the material is available under a Creative Commons License. If you click on the icon, you will see the full details of the license. Make sure to check out the type of license so you know what you are allowed or not allowed to do with your article, image, etc..

TOP TIP: You can search for your keyword and add "cc license" to your search to find material on the web that you can use e.g. "labrador +cc" or "labrador + Creative Commons"

Important to mention: A Creative Common License does not give you legal protection (some paid images sites do) against legal disputes: for instance, if there is a person in a photo who did not give permission to be in the photo, that person can protest and file a legal dispute. Another example: you are using a picture with a woman holding a Coca Cola bottle. Coca Cola could file a legal dispute saying you are using their trade mark.

When you use a Creative Common image, YOU are responsible.

3) Public Domain Information

You will also see and hear about items that are in the public domain. Works in public domain are works whose copyrights have expired, are inapplicable or have been forfeited. Items in the public domain can be used by anyone; generally you don't even have to have to attribute. With public domain works, you have unrestricted access to the work and you have unlimited creativity! An image in the public domain has no legal owner.

Items can become public domain in different manners. The most common is expired copyrights. While terms differ by country and even when it was created, a common copyright length is 70 years after the author's death. If the author is unknown or when they died is unknown, the length is set at 120 years. An item created before 1989 without a copyright notice is in the public domain. A copyright holder can also declare their work as public domain.

In the United States, the US government cannot be a copyright holder. Any material created by an employee or contractor of the U.S. Government is in the public domain. For example, Ansel Adams is a landscape photographer from the 1930s. Reprints of his photographs cost hundreds if not thousands of dollars. His estate only allows limited use of the photographs in books and magazines. However he created a number of images for the National Park Service of the US Government. www.archives.gov/research/ansel-adams Those images are public domain and are free to use.

I will not give a definition here about copyright free and public domain because the rules and regulations are different in each country. Check your country for all legalities. Just Google "public domain" or " when is a product copyright free", etc… In general, royalty free and public domain means that you can use content and change it without permission from the author or the creator. Anything which legally has no owner is public domain, so it belongs to the public and they may use it any way they choose. If something is under Copyright Protection, you cannot use it without the author's permission.

Public domain used with a business attitude, or an "I-want-to-make-money" attitude, can earn you money. With public domain work, you can even remove the author's name, edit the book and sell it as your own. Once you have modified a public domain product, it becomes your property.

In the USA there are some general rules for a work to be considered public domain:
- If the work was published in the United States before 1923. This applies only to unpublished works.

- All work created after 1 March 1989 is Copyright Protected for 70 years from the date the author dies. This applies to published works.

- All work made for hire after 1 March 1989 is Copyright Protected for 95 years from publication or 120 years from the date it was created.

There are more factors that determine whether something is Public domain or not in the USA. Investigate if the book or article you want to use is indeed Public domain.

Did you know that there is work available as Public domain by William Shakespeare, Mark Twain, Jane Austin, Hans Christian Andersen, Charles Dickens, Agatha Christie, Albert Einstein, Charles Darwin and more?

Is there money to be made with public domain content? Sure there is!

- Walt Disney started his billion dollar empire with a public domain source: The fairy tales of the Grimm Brothers.
- Did you know that almost all the movies played on TCM (Turner Classic Movies), the cable network company were public domain when they started? The creator had a business idea, using public domain work to get rich. As it has become a very popular TV channel, he now earns lots of money from advertising.

How can you find public domain work ?

- Visit www.books.Google.com where you can find books on many different subjects. In the advanced search you can select books that were published before

1923. For books that are out of copyright, you can read and download the entire book.

Click Advanced Search:

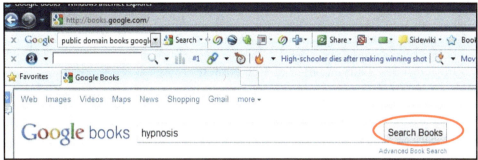

In the publication date, set the last date as January 1923 and hit the 'Search' button. This will show you all the books that were published before 1923, which are public domain books.

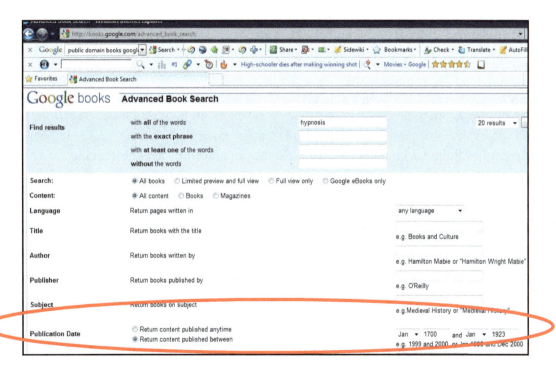

To find Public domain works:

- www.archive.org for material that is available to the public

- www.gutenberg.org for royalty free books

- www.authorama.com has a large list of public domain books

- www.bartleby.com has a large choice of free content

- www.bibliomania.com

- www.literature.org

- www.publicdomainreview.org

- www.digital.library.upenn.edu/books/cce

- www.web.law.duke.edu/cspd

- www.librivox.org for free domain audio books

To find public domain work in your niche, Google:
" your keyword + public domain work"
" list of public domain books + your keyword"
" public domain websites"

There are plenty of Public domain books, articles, music, and films available in the following niches:
- Children books
- Mind reading
- Natural remedies
- Home cures
- Handwriting analysis
- Television series and radio programs
- Business books
- Books on hobbies
- Books on collecting
- Masterpieces of literature e.g. Shakespeare, Dickens, Poe
- Thousands of non-fiction books
- Family books about education, children, relationships

- Historical books
You will be amazed what is available as public domain material.

4) Fair Use

In some cases you can quote copyrighted material under the free use clause. This however allows only limited usage and the laws do differ from country to country.

5) Royalty Free is Not Free

Royalty free can apply to any copyrighted work but it is generally used for images and music. Many people see the word free and think they can use it without any payment. A item that is royalty free can be used without a per use fee, however you still have to pay an initial payment. Royalty free means that, when you have paid a license fee to obtain an image, you can use the image many times without paying an extra fee but you do need to pay for the initial license. You can use the image in almost any application, as often as you like and for as long as you like but of course, you have to make sure you comply with the terms of the license that you bought. You could purchase the right to use a song as an example. Often that will allow you to play it a certain number of times and after that you have to pay a royalty each time you use it. A Royalty Free arrangement allows you unlimited use within the scope of the license. You can only use it within the scope that you purchased it for and you may not transfer your rights to others.

There are also rights-managed images for which the use of these images is restricted e.g. you can only use them for certain industries or a certain geographical location. This will be specified in the license agreement.

6) What is Copyright Infringement?

Copyright Infringement can be explained in a complex manner but to summarise it in one simple sentence: Copyright Infringement is doing something that you are not allowed to do, according to the rules. The item can be a book, an image, music, etc..

Infringement is a violation of the rights of the rights holder or the creator of the original work. Infringement for an image can be any of these:

- Making changes to the image without permission

- Using the image in another way, not permitted within the license

- Using an image without permission of the rights holder

Copyright infringement is to be taken very seriously as it may result in lawsuits and very high legal fees.

7) Personal Rights

Closely related to copyright law are Personal Right laws. While most people are not aware of the laws, and the issues of Personal Rights are not raised as often, it is still a concern at times. You may use a photograph of a person without their permission if the photograph is newsworthy and timely. Also, the photograph must have been taken in a place where the subject could not reasonably expect privacy. Paparazzi have used this as the base of their taking photographs of celebrities. Newsworthy can also be extended to editorial use if it can be shown that the image relates to the time reference in the article. It does not, however relate to commercial use. To use an image of a person that is used as a product or to illustrate that the individual endorses a product, requires the permission of the individual. Such permission is referred to as a model release. The website of the American Society of Media Photographers www.asmp.org has an excellent overview on model and property releases.

8) Personal and Commercial Use

When you are looking for images, you will most certainly come across the term "personal use" and "commercial use" e.g. you can use the picture that you are downloading only for personal use but not for commercial use. What does this mean?

Personal use means you can use the picture but not for commercial gain e.g. you can use it in a newsletter or an invitation to a party.

Commercial use means that you can use the picture for commercial purposes e.g. advertising, a company brochure, a company website or a catalogue.

9) Must-have Elements on Your Website

- You can download free (and payable) legal policies for your website from Website Law - www.seqlegal.com

- Whilst talking about legal policies: visit www.legalzoom.com and www.legalzoom.co.uk for information on all aspects of setting up and running a business (payable).

Here are the most important things your website must have to look and feel professional, and to increase your chances of ranking for search engines. These are all free so I recommend that you put most of these on your site.

Note: you don't HAVE to put these on your site by law (except for the cookies information). These are just my recommendations to put on your site to make it look and feel professional.

a) Disclaimer

Compulsory if you're running a site that has anything to do with health, earning money or contains information and products that could be potentially harmful.

b) Privacy policy

It's a good idea to have a privacy policy anyway, but if you're planning on installing AdSense, then this is something you have to do. Add the Easy Privacy Policy plugin to your Wordpress page and this will be set up automatically for you.

c) Contact form

To install the Contact Form Plugin, visit
http://wordpress.org/extend/plugins/contact-form-7.
The minimum that should be on your contact form is your name and email address. It is better to also give your address and even phone number to create more credibility.

d) Terms of use

This is a contract that the user automatically agrees to by using your site. Make sure that all legalities not covered in the Disclaimer and Privacy Policy are included here.

e) Sitemap

A sitemap is a must-have if you want Google to accurately find all the elements on your site. If you use Wordpress, http://wordpress.org/extend/plugins/xml-sitemap-feed the sitemap will be done for you. If you are not using Wordpress, search for " HTML sitemap" in the help section of whatever web design software you use.

f) Copyright policy

At the bottom of every page you should have: "Copyright 2014, All Rights Reserved". This helps protect your intellectual property from people who may wish to steal your content.

g) Guarantee or refund policy

If you are selling something, make sure that you always put a money-back-guarantee on your website or a refund policy. The visitor will be more likely to buy when there is a money-back guarantee.

h) Testimonials (if applicable)

If you're selling a product or services, it is crucial to have testimonials visible.

Testimonials add proof to your site and will help persuade your visitors to spend money on what you're offering.

Video testimonials are very effective.

If you put testimonials on your site, always put the full name and, if possible, the website of the person giving the testimonial. If possible, add a picture.

Video testimonials are the best. Audio testimonials convert better than written testimonials.

Here are two websites where you can create or buy audio testimonials.

- Audio Generator - www.audiogenerator.com
- Article Video Robot - www.articlevideorobot.com

Unfortunately testimonials are not always real (you can buy testimonials from www.fiverr.com. People get paid to do them. I am sorry if I have shocked you by saying this, but it is true. If you are going to be in the IM business you need to know. I suggest that you never use made up and fake testimonials.

i) 'About Us' page

If possible you should put a photograph of a person on the 'about us' page. People want to know who they are buying from. If you say something about yourself and put a photograph on your page, you become a real person, which helps improve your credibility. After all, you don't buy just from "anybody" on the web, so compel your visitors to buy from you. Increase your chances by increasing your trustworthiness with an 'about us' page.

Putting a signature on your site also improves your credibility. You can create a signature at www.mylivesignature.com It is free.

j) Home page

If the home page fails to say what the site is all about, or what users can find on the site, people will leave the site more quickly.

k) Google Analytics

Google Analytics (already discussed) is a website statistics program that you can use for free. It is not visible to the visitors to your site.

l) Cookies

Don't forget to put information about cookies on your website www.cookielaw.org

Chapter 8) Content is King

Up until this point in the book, I have been discussing the basic concepts and how to incorporate them into your website for free. I am now going to suggest some ways and places you can obtain content for your websites. The previous chapters had a great deal on information and concepts, from this point forward it will be more suggestions of where to find things for your sites. Before you actually start implementing the suggestions, it will help to be focused on what you want to do. You should already know and maybe even established, if you are using WordPress or HTML, your own domain or sub-domain, free hosting or paid, starting from scratch or using a provided design or a template/theme. When you are first getting started you might want to add some SEO tool bars to your browser.

Virtual Real Estate has a tool bar that will help you find content. It can be found at www.vretoolbar.com .

Special Note: About three years ago, Google started to change the way it ranks web pages. Overnight websites that held the positions of number one or two for keywords, found themselves unlisted or at least hundreds of pages down. You may come across references to Google Panda , Google Penguin and Google Hummingbird, these are the code name for the three programs that have changed how websites are ranked.

Building websites, I believe, is overcomplicated by many people. I am *not* the "The SEO Expert of The Year" by all means. So, if I can build websites that rank on page one, so can you! I apply the rules as explained in my Newbie book when building a website. To give you one example, to show content is important: my website about micro pigs, www.micropigshed.com.

Three years ago, when I built the website, there wasn't much competition in Google. There is more competition now, but the site still ranks on the first page of Google, even after the Panda, Penguin and Hummingbird updates. I have NEVER updated the site, not even with fresh content. The only aim of that website is to sell my micro pig book in all three versions: Kindle book, eBook and a hard copy book. I have also put some Adsense on this site to create extra income.

This site ranks on the first page of Google for the following targeted keywords:

- Looking after a micro pig
- Micro pigs care
- Micro pig care
- Micro pig
- Micro pigs
- Keeping micro pigs
- Micro pig diet
- How to keep micro pigs
- How to keep micro pigs as pets
- Micro pig food
- Micro pig food UK
- How big is a micro pig
- Micro pigs book

Well, I hope the website is still ranking well when you are reading this book. It was when I finished writing this book you are reading now (August 2014).

My racing pigeon sales letter is another example: www.howtoracepigeons.co.uk. It is on the first page of Google for [how to race pigeons] and has been for many years. This website is a "one-page-sales-wonder" or a sales page and Google usually does not like sales letters so they don't rank very well.

Lesson to remember (from my own two sites mentioned above): it is not THAT difficult to rank a website, all you need is:

- regular visitors

- good SEO

- targeting long tail keywords

- good content

- most of the 'must have elements', as already discussed

- some videos

- low bounce rate. A high bounce rate means that visitors opening your site close it again after a few seconds. Google will conclude from this that there is nothing interesting on your site for visitors to see therefore your site will be ranked lower.

- Never ever use anything automated e.g. articles, automated content, automated website building, automate backlinks, etc.. You WILL be punished by your site not showing in the search engines.

- Adsense on your site. Many people say this doesn't work but here's my opinion on it: if Google never shows websites with Adsense on the first rankings, Google's income from Adsense would stop. Of course, Google being a commercial institution, they will not stop showing sites that have Adsense on otherwise they would lose that income.

By the way, I am fully aware that I have already mentioned this under the SEO section, but I am repeating it here to stress the importance of how simple it CAN be to rank a website on the first pages.

My micro pig site is also a good example of the fact that a site hasn't got to be stunningly beautiful as that site is very simple, nothing beautiful about it at all.

OK, back to the content, as that is what this chapter is all about. It is time for you to visualise how you want your web page to look. How much text is needed, how many photographs, will you being using videos, are all basic requirements you should think about. They say a photo is worth a thousand words. While photos and videos are important, the primary focus of the site should be the written word. Let's look at some sources.

All the methods discussed in this chapter are totally free so why not use them all!

1) Creating Content Without Having to Write Anything

Here are some ideas for creating content for your site without having to actually write anything.

- Turn some of your most valuable blog content into an eBook/book.

- Use public domain works

- Host a webinar and record it to send to your list

- Turn some of your most valuable blog content into a newsletter

- Use an old slide presentation and put is as content on your site, as a pdf

- Make an info graphic and put it on your site

- Do a Skype interview and use it as content

- Use internal and external links on your site

- Put links to videos on your site

- If you have a video, why not get it transcribed and use the content for an article?

- Turn some of your content into an MP3, all you need is a microphone

- Make a phone call and record the conversation. You can do this with www.freeconferencecall.com. Use the content to put on your website.

2) Guest Blogging

Generally Guest Blogging does not jump to the top of the list of getting content. However, I have some suggestions for getting content that is easier to understand if you understand Guest Blogging. Guest Blogging is a tactic where the guest blogger writes content and looks for a place to post it with links back to their own site. Many people make submissions to article sites for the same purpose.

- Kissmetrics has an interesting guide for writers that want to guest blog www.blog.kissmetrics.com/guide-to-guest-blogging/ giving the benefits they can achieve and hints on how to be successful.

- The website Myblogguest www.myblogguest.com is a platform to bring together blog owners looking for content and writers looking to get published. If you and a writer match on themes, then you can get unique content and the writer can get a back link and the exposure he was looking for. Try to find a few writers that will do a few posts a month. Spread out the content. Ideal to get free unique content and also to get free traffic to your site.

They also have a premium payable option: you submit your articles, visit their websites and you can check the PR rank of the website and accept their offer. This way, you can get back links to your site from PR3/PR4 websites.

- Blog Synergy www.blogsynergy.com is another site with the same service. However, you need to be established to use their service.

- BloggerLinkUp www.bloggerlinkup.com allows you to sign up for a free account and fill in a form requesting people to post on your blog. Within a few days of your request, you will get several people wanting to post on your blog.

- You can Facebook Guestpost Portal and you will get a notification when people have posted about a certain niche.

3) Article Sites

There are hundreds, maybe even thousands, of article sites out there that allow you to use their content on your website, providing you abide by the terms and conditions of the article.

> Important: taking content from article websites very often means that you won't have unique content as other people might have exactly the same article on their site. Google doesn't like duplicate content. Therefore if you are looking to rank in Google, it is always best to write the article yourself or outsource it.

- DMOZ, an open site directory has a list of free article websites www.dmoz.org/Business/Publishing_and_Printing/Publishing/Services/Free_Content/

- www.vretoolbar.com/articles/directories.php lists the Top 50 article directories by traffic and page rank. Some of the sites listed allow automatic feeds. The automatic feeds only require you to place a line of code on your site and will update your site with fresh content.

- Article city www.articlecity.com/rss.shtml has a good feed system and it also has a WordPress plug in that does all the coding to add headlines and new articles to your website.

- Amazines www.amazines.com is another leading article site that allows you to publish its content.

- Articlebase www.articlesbase.com allows you to embed articles in your website in a number of different ways, such as HTML and RSS features. To re-publish the articles, check out the rules, as often you need to leave the link in the articles intact.

- Ehow www.ehow.com will allow you to share articles. However, you are not allowed to use them on your site. So check the terms of use carefully. Ehow is a good place, though, to get ideas for future articles. Over the last few years Google has been changing the ways it rank sites, and article sites have been hard hit with duplicate content penalties. The number of sites allowing you to post articles on your page has dropped because of this. Also most SEO experts now are advising against using free content like articles as your primary source. Still it is a good way to get started.

Many of the authors who post articles on these article directories are doing so to create links. If you find an author who writes in a style you like on a related topic to your website, approach them by email and offer them the opportunity to write an article for your website that links back to the author. This is similar to the guest blogging we opened this chapter with. Getting your content in this manner, instead of directly from the articles already online, is a win-win situation. You get fresh original content and the author gets the links and recognition that he is looking for.

- Scoop.it www.scoop.it a great search engine to find content. Type in your keywords and you'll discover lots of articles in your niche.

- ContentGems www.contentgems.com find and share great content.

4) RSS News Feeds

News feeds that have been tailored towards your niche are still a good way to get free content. Google and other search engines will index and rank news content rapidly. RSS News Feeds are very popular but I have several sites that are doing well without an RSS feed. RSS stands for Really Simple Syndication and is a way for users to check on your recently updated content without having to visit your site. Users have content posted automatically to their site, or keep themselves updated on your latest posts.

If you're having trouble understanding exactly how this works then take a look at this example below. I have an RSS feed set up for the latest headlines on the BBC website. If I want to see the latest news stories I just click the button marked "Latest Headlines" and it shows me the latest news:

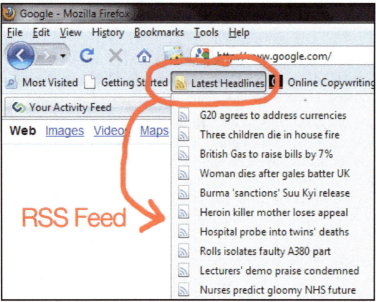

Here are some RSS resources:

www.bloglines.com
www.feedvalidator.org
www.rssfeeds.com
www.rssreader.com

To get an RSS feed on your website (with weebly.com), follow these steps:
- search for keyword + blog or keyword + rss
- look for the orange feed button that looks like this:

 or

- Click on the button which will take you to the RSS feed
- Copy that URL and paste it on your RSS feed in weebly.com. The URL to paste will usually be something like: www.rocketnews.com/feed . Now your website will always have fresh content.

Many international news companies have their own feed that you can add to your site or you can use a consolidator that gets information from different sources such as fresh content www.freshcontent.net and Feedzilla www.feedzilla.com

5) Private Label Rights

Private Label Rights (PLR) is a marketing concept for intellectual property where the copyright holder transfers broad license for the use of the property. Generally these are articles or groups of articles in an ebook. While agreements differ, generally the purchaser is allowed, even encouraged, to make minor changes and can even claim authorship. I personally never use PLR articles as I am a believer in new, original content but I am covering it in this book as many people use PLR.

Often PLR allow resale writes. Resale rights means that there is no control on the number of copies that have been purchased and are being used. A few years ago, when Amazon cracked down on duplicate content in its Kindle offerings, it deleted over 150 versions of the same beauty tip book by different authors. Most of them even had the original cover with just the author's name changed. The value of PLR articles and ebooks are very low. They should not be used as content on your website as they will be seen as duplicate content.

You will NOT rank high with nothing but duplicate content on your site and Amazon will not rank your eBook high either.

While some PLR sales sources preach that they make great giveaways to customers visiting your website, in reality they often reflect negatively on the quality of service you provide. Having said that, people who are buying eBooks that don't know a lot about Internet Marketing, don't even know what PLR is so they don't think that they are receiving a PLR eBook, for example, someone buying an eBook on how to train a dog, will be happy to receive the eBook free (if you want to build a list, you can give the eBook away for free) providing there is interesting content in the eBook.

The most important things I have to mention about PLR are:

- make sure it is a product with GREAT content, not an eBook that is 10 pages long and therefore can't really be categorised as a book, but more as a long article.

- PLR can be brilliant to give away for free after a visitor has opted-in. However, the same applies here: check that the eBook has great content. If you give a "crappy little eBook" free to your new potential customer, they are not going to be impressed, therefore they are unlikely to buy anything else from you. If you impress them with what you give away, you have a lot more chance that they will buy from you through your email marketing.

- If you do use PLR articles, I always recommend re-writing them so they become unique content.

- You can buy several PLR eBooks in the same niche, put them all together and give that away as an eBook free. I stress again, most of the time, the content will not be very valuable content though. There are, of course, exceptions to the rule.

- Don't publish a book (one that you are selling rather than giving away), with PLR articles put together. You will receive negative reviews from readers saying: " Nothing new in this book, it is all stuff you can find on the web easily". I know this as I have published a book that had a negative review because the outsourcer copied a lot of text from PLR articles. He admitted so after I pointed out that the book had a negative review. Lesson learned and I am not using that outsourcer again. I also did forget to check that book with www.copyscape.com

Here are some PLR sites:

www.specialreportclub.com very affordable pricing

www.cloneforsuccess.com = PLR with squeeze page
www.contentgoldmine.com
www.gutenberg.org
www.allprivatelabelcontent.com
www.plrpro.com

www.resellrightspack.com
www.sitecontentideas.com
www.easyplr.com
www.super-resell.com
www.theplrstore.com

6) Copyright is The Law

I've mentioned this before, so just a reminder: always be respectful of a creator's copyright. If in doubt as to whether it can be used, err on the side of caution and do not use it.

Article sites generally state how the content can be used, some require you to show it as a RSS feed, others allow you to cut and paste. Read the FAQ of the site and see the requirements. Most websites require that a link be maintained. Fail to follow the guidelines exactly and you can make the license invalid, resulting in your use being a copyright violation. This applies also to images and videos.

7) Places to Find Free Written Content

There are many places on line to find free content but remember that any free content you find can be found by everyone else who is looking for free content. Duplicate content will undo all the hard work that you have done.

- www.INeedAGreatStory.com: Royalty-free stories, videos and infographics. You buy credits to allow you buy material.

- www.curationsoft.com This software finds content you can share on your website. They have a free version which is pretty good. You will get more advanced tools with the payable version.

8) Places to Find Ideas For Content

- www.alltop.com This site gives you top blogs in any niche. Great to visit to find some ideas to write about.

- www.quora.com A Question and Answer site.

Question and Answer sites are always great to visit as you can find out what problems people have in your niche, which is always great content.

In my book Finding Niches Made Easy, I've listed a lot more websites to visit to find ideas for content.

9) Google Maps

If applicable to your site, for instance, if you have a website about physiotherapy in London, and you want to attract visitors, you MUST put a Google Map on your site to increase your ranking chances. You simply need to get the code from Google Maps www.maps.google.com or www.maps.google.co.uk and paste it onto your site.

In Serif WebPlus X4, web design program, there is a tab "insert Google map" and all you need to do is put in your postcode (zip code).

10) Images

Google, or any other search engine, cannot recognise pictures on your website (not yet anyway), but if you give each picture a keyword, Google will recognise the keyword. Each page should have at least one image on it, and that image's filename should be in the format: your keyword.jpg /.png/.gif (suffix depends on file format).
When you insert the image onto your site you also need to set the "alt tag" as your keyword. This is easy to do in Wordpress, as shown below:

If you are not using Wordpress then you should put the alt tag in manually. The code for this is:
[img src="http://www.yourdomain.com/images/your-keyword.png" alt="your keyword" /]

If you're using a website design program, then try right-clicking the image and clicking [properties]. There will be a section marked "alternate text" or "alt text". This is where you enter your alt tag keyword.

You must give every picture on your website a name because Google counts it as a keyword.

Do the test on your website, or on other websites. When you see a picture on the page and you move your mouse over the picture, you will see the picture name either on the screen or at the bottom left corner of your browser window. This is the Image Alt Tag. If no name appears when you hover over the picture, it means that no Image Alt Tag was used or, in other words, the picture was not named with a keyword in the title.

Google's picture search won't find your picture of a Ferrari 658 if you put it on the web with a reference " DCMB999002". It might show it if you give your picture a name like "My Ferrari 658".

When adding images. make sure their filenames are the same as the keyword you're optimising your page for.
e.g. You've created a page on a keyword you've researched and want to rank in Google for. Let's say this keyword is "fly fishing". Your image should be named *flyfishing.jpg* and the alt text for the image should be *fly fishing*. If this is hard to understand, then let me give an example of how the HTML for the image should look:
[img src="http://www.yourdomain.com/images/flyfishing.jpg" alt="fly fishing" /]

All professional software for building websites will have an in-built feature to give your image an alt-tag, or in other words, a keyword.

If you give your image a keyword, it also means that it will be listed under Google Images. A lot of people will look under 'Images' in Google. By including a lot of images on your site and giving these images a name, you will increase traffic to your site. You must give the images a name that is relevant to the page they are on. Always make sure you include Alt and Title in your image tags.

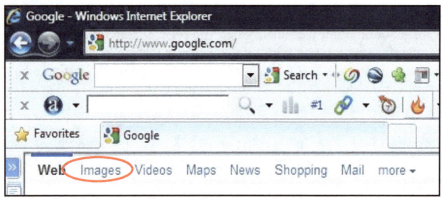

Further in this book, I discuss where to get free images. Getting the image is free and putting an alt-tag or keyword on the image is free too, so make sure you use this tool.

11) Videos

Videos are a great way of creating content and keeping visitors on your site, while offering real SEO benefits and getting you more traffic. YouTube videos frequently appear in the first page of Google for highly competitive keywords so you know that it's worth doing.

Most consumers today expect video sales pages, video testimonials and so on. I must admit that I don't use enough video myself but hey, things are going well for me without videos.

You don't have to create the videos yourself. If you find a video that you really like (eg. on YouTube) and want to promote it, you can email the creator asking to buy it or get permission to use it on your site. The owner of the video will often sell it to you. Sometimes the owner will simply give it to you. Then you just add your URL to it and upload it to your various video site accounts! To give an example: you are in the chicken niche and someone has a video about the chickens in his garden on Youtube. That's the type of video I am talking about. The owner has just put it on Youtube for fun so if he can make money with it, he will likely do so.

Keep your videos short e.g. not 50 minutes. You must either mention your website or include your website in the video.

There is a lot more information on how to create for videos free later in this book.

12) Audio

Never put audio on a page if customers can't turn it off easily. This is especially important with music - if they don't share your taste it may put them off.

There are two ways of using audio content well on your site:
- Give your visitors the chance to download audio that they can listen to it in their own time - every time they listen to it they'll be reminded of your site and, not only will it keep them coming back, it could be shared, bringing more users to your site.

- Have auto-playing audio that directs the visitor to the different areas of your site, gives them a clear call-to-action or testimonials from other users.

I'm sure you can think of more creative ideas. If you can fully utilise sound and video content then you'll find your content is better received.

www.sourceforge.net – a free download that lets you create audio recordings on a PC.
www.applian.com – lets you record the music that is playing on your PC.

For royalty-free music clips:
www.publicdomain4u.com
www.royaltyfreemusic.com
www.shockwave-sound.com
www.slicktracks.com

More on audio in a later chapter.

13) SEO is Free

Good content means good SEO. SEO is totally free and with good SEO you will have more chance that your site will rank well in the search engines. Always apply relevant SEO to your content.

14) Other Free Tools to use for Content

Content doesn't necessarily have to be text. There are lots of other things you can put on your website. You can provide useful tools or things that are just plain interesting. I will discuss a few.

Note: expect a lot of unwanted email in your inbox and advertising on your site if you use any of the following tools.

a) Visitor counter

- If you are not keen on analytics but you just want to find out how many people have visited your site, you can put a free visitor counter on your website. All you need to do is grab an HTML code from any of the websites below and place that on your site. Some counters come with advertising and others don't. You want to place this somewhere where your visitor doesn't see it but the information is there for you to see.

TOP TIP: Start your counter from 2000 (or something) instead of 1. A visitor counter with only three visitors is not good for customers to see. Here are some websites where you can get page counters or trackers:

www.stats4all.com
www.extremetracking.com
www.bravenet.com

b) Weather forecast tool

You can add free maps and weather forecasts to your website.

The Weather channel www.weather.com allows you set up a profile and create a weather feed based on your specifications. You can control the location, the size and what information is included.

www.worldweatheronline.com Definitely No Spyware or ads with this one, I use this myself.
www.qwikcast.com
www.accuweather.com
www.weatherzone.com
www.myweather2.com

c)Free chat room

Word of caution: sometimes people may become abusive in your chat room. That is a big downside of this tool. It can drive visitors away from your site rather than keeping them on your site.

You can download free chat rooms from www.bravenet.com

d) Online polls

Putting a poll on your site is interacting with your customers, which is always a good thing. Customers can guess what the answer is and they can view the correct answer instantly.

You can get a free online poll from www.bravenet.com

e) Surveys

www.surveymonkey.com is a great survey site. They have a free version that includes 10 questions per survey and 100 responses. Good enough to start with.

f) Horoscopes

These websites all offer horoscopes for your site:
www.eastrolog.com
www.adze.com
www.astrology.com

g) Jokes

www.comicexchange.com delivers free comic strips to your site every day. www.jokesgalore.com is another great site. The website Free Sticky www.freesticky.com has links to sites with cartoons, jokes and converters that can be added to your site.

h) Games

www.flashgamesforyourwebsite.com
www.gamesforwebsites.com
www.miniclip.com

i) Quotations

www.greatquoteslibrary.com
www.brainyquote.com

www.quotationspage.com

- ReciteThis www.recitethis.com lets you create a quote and turn it into a graphic design that you can use as content or post on social media sites.

- QuotesCover www.quotescover.com is similar to ReciteThis. You can turn simple text into stunning pictures.

- Quozio www.quozio.com is another tool similar to ReciteThis. You type in a sentence and a design will be created for you.

j) Greeting cards

Why not offer a greeting card on your site? Your visitors will be able to send an online greeting card from your site to their friends. Many card recipients will visit your site. Visit these sites:
www.regards.com
www.bravenet.com

k) Financial tools

In case you are in the financial niche, here are a few interesting websites where you can find things to put on your site.
www.investing.com
www.moneychimp.com
www.mortgageloan.com
www.thefinancials.com

l) Other tools and gadgets you can use for content

- www.wisdomcommons.org Poems, essays under Creative Commons.

- www.intratext.com Over 12 million texts, including some B.C. A lot of them under Creative Commons.

- The grand daddy of gadgets is Google. The Google gadgets listing

www.google.com/ig/directory?synd=open has over 350,000 gadgets that can be used to add information to your website.

Search for "Google Gadgets For Your Webpage" if the above url doesn't work, and you will find hundreds of games listed to add to your web page.

You can browse by category or search by keywords. The gadgets are free and most of them are automatically updated at a prescribed time.

- Now here's a great tool: http://newspaper.jaguarpaw.co.uk. This will create your own newspaper that you can use as content and save as a pdf file. Be aware, though, that the content will be duplicated content.

- Wordle www.wordle.net Use this to create word clouds that you can use as graphics on your website.

- Recordit www.recordit.co (There is no "m" missing here after .co). You can record videos and make animated GIFS to use as content.

- Evernote www.evernote.com Another great free tool. You can record audio and change it into text and use it as content. You can also write blogs in Evernote.

- Slideshare www.slideshare.net You can embed presentations on your site and use them as content.

- Pinstamatic www.pinstamatic.com Create great Pinterest boards in a few minutes

- Pinwords www.pinwords.com Create a picture from a quote to add to your Pinterest account.

m) Creating headlines

- TweakYourBiz www.tweakyourbiz.com is a free tool to generate titles for blogs and articles. This is a great tool.

- Portent www.portent.com Here you can get ideas for headlines.

- Title-Builder www.title-builder.com lets you find the best keywords for your headlines and titles

- ContentRow www.contentrow.com Click on [Tools] and choose Link Bait Title Generator, then go get some great ideas

- Instant Sales Letters www.instantsalesletters.com is a payable option to create headlines and sales copy where you just fill in the blanks.

Chapter 9) Graphic Design Tools

When you are designing your web pages, it is important to have a good balance on your page. You want to ensure you have images that break up the text and support it. While all the copyright laws that apply to the written word also apply to photographs, currently there is no duplicate content penalty for images. When you are designing your web pages, images are added in a very similar fashion as that used for a Word document. You find the image you want and insert it into the page at the location you want. Most word processors like Word and Open Office have limited image editors built in. WordPress and HTML editors also have some graphic ability, however, it is much better to use a graphics program. As mentioned earlier, Photoshop is the industry leader when it comes to creating quality images. It also often comes with a large price tag. Images that are going to be used on a website that is being sourced from an online location, seldom need the power tools found in Photoshop.

1) A Word About Colours.

While it's true that having a clean and simple website is important, you need to consider other aesthetics of your site as well. Think of your target audience and consider the product(s) that you are selling, and then decide the graphics, colours and fonts that you believe will appeal to them, while creating an image for your products and your business as a whole. I have already mentioned the colour wheel in this book: make sure you use colours that complement each other.
You can visit www.html-color-codes.info to get the correct HTML code for the colour you want to use. Please refer to the section in this book where I talk about the colour wheel for more info about using colours.

2) Zero Cost Alternatives to Photoshop

The most widely used alternative to Photoshop is a program called GNU Image Manipulation Program or GIMP for short. It is an open source program developed with a Creative Commons license. That means that it is free.

- The official site for GIMP is www.gimp.org However, since it is open sourced, you can find it on other sites as well. The program has a built in help system and a full user manual is also available for download. Some users may find themselves overwhelmed with the variety of tasks that can be accomplished. Just start with the basics and go from there. The most common task that you will have to perform on your images is resizing and cropping. Both of these tasks are easy to do.

- A slightly different interface, one very similar to Photoshop, is available from the website www.gimpshop.com

- The second most popular alternative is Paint.net, available from the website www.getpaint.net This program does not have all the features of GIMP, however it does have all the features you are most likely to use. It is a good tool for those who have no experience with graphics.

- BeFunky www.befunky.com Totally free and no need to register. They call it the world's best photo editor. It is really good.

- Pixlr at www.pixlr.com has levels for beginners, intermediate and advance users. It is a browser-based editor.

- Splash up at www.splashup.com is designed for beginners. It has an easy to use interface and will have what you need to help create your website.

- Canva www.canva.com Create free designs without possessing any design skills. They also have lots of templates for social media use. Search for a photo or graphic and then use Canva to create a new design.

- Timeline Slicer www.timelineslicer.com is a cool tool to design images for your Facebook Profile or Page.

- Another great online graphics creator is Sumopaint. Download it free from www.sumoware.com. They also have a paid version but I am sure you can create some great things with the free version.

- Photovisi www.photovisi.com No need to create an account. This is a photo collage tool that is easy to use.

- TinyPNG www.tinypng.com Shrink PNG files. High resolution images can slow down your website. You can convert them to a smaller size with Tiny PNG.

If you do have Photoshop, here are some free tools:

www.brusheezy.com/patterns

www.brusheezy.com/textures

www.getbrushes.com

www.freephotoshop.org/styles

3) Using Imaging Software

The purpose of using imaging software is to adapt the image to your needs. The most common things you will do with images is cropping, resizing, changing file size and making thumbnails. Thumbnails are useful to link to full size images. You could use the full size image on your page and use the web design software to have the image fit the location. However, doing so would require the full file to load. A smaller thumbnail would load faster and the full file would only load if someone clicked on the thumbnail to see the full image. Imaging software can also do other tasks but altering an image, replacing elements or adding to them could be considered creating a derivative, which would require an authorisation.

Making a thumbnail could not be easier than with www.MakeAThumbnail.com. You can import a graphic and choose to make a thumbnail of that image and save it as a Jpeg. Tip: the size 150 x 150 is the closest size to an Amazon Book Thumbnail.

4) Banner Creation

Banners are a very important element on a website. They are one of the items that help create your brand and provide continuity across your website. While creating your own banner using an image tool is very easy, many designers prefer to use a banner tool. There are many good online tools, however, some of the "free" ones will have a watermark shown, unless you purchase their paid version.

- With www.3dtextmaker.com you can create your own 3D banner, totally free. Nothing to download.

- Banner Fans at www.bannerfans.com/ is a nice program that will help you create a banner in just minutes.

- BannerBreak at www.bannerbreak.com is another great website

- Fotor Banner Maker at http://banner.fotor.com is also a very good free program. Both of these programs has a set of common preset sizes and allows you to create your own size.

- Html5 maker at www.html5maker.com will help you make animated banners using flash. This site can also be used to make slide shows and presentations.

5) Logo Creation

- Want to design a simple logo? Have a look at www.TheLogoCreator.com. Makes logos and graphics that look like a Photoshop design but are actually created with this free software. Suitable for both PC and Mac and super easy to use.

6) Favicon

A favicon is that small image that shows in the address bar before the site's URL, and as the icon when a page is bookmarked. It is a small image 16x16. Most browser will accept any image as a Favicon, however, Internet Explorer still requires it to be in the.ico format. An example of a Favicon (the small monkey face on the left of the domain name):

To have a favicon show, you need a line of code in the page's header saying what the favicon file name is and its location. You also need the file. There are many free generators on the web such as:

- www.favicongenerator.com

- www.favicon.cc

7) Book Cover Creation

- On www.myecovermaker.com you can design book covers free. There is a payable option for unlimited designs.

- www.diybookcovers.com You can get great ideas here for book covers.

- www.bookcoverpro.com is a good payable option

- www.PicMonkey.com lets you convert a graphic into different sizes, etc... I use this tool to convert my high resolution book covers to Kindle covers.

8) Slide Creation

If you would like to build slide presentations but can't afford Powerpoint, here is a good alternative: Prezi. Visit www.prezi.com and you will be able to create great presentations, with or without video. Prezi has an impressive art board to create all sorts of interesting effects.

9) Reverse Image Search

Photographers and graphic artists have the rights of ownership to the images they create in the same way as a composer or author. They have a number of tools available to them to identify unauthorised use of their property. Here are 2 tools:

- Google Advance Image Search www.images.google.com/advanced_search?hl=en&fg=1

- TinEye program www.tineye.com If you are using an image of a product, you might want to search for it to see how many other websites are using the same or similar images. TinEye is a reverse image search engine. With TinEye, you can find out where an image came from, if there are modified versions of the image on the web, how the image is being use, etc..

10) Infographics

An Infograph is a graphic representation of a topic, sometimes also called Pictographics. It is often used to express complicated data. A layout of the London subway system is an example of an infograph. A number of companies provide software to create infographs; many use templates to get you started.

- http://ui-cloud.com/free-vector-infographic-design-elements Find free vector infographic design stuff here.

- http://all-free-download.com/free-vector/free-infographics.html

- www.piktochart.com: use their free templates to add your own data and create an infographic that way.

- www.freepik.com/free-photos-vectors/infographic

- www.easel.ly Create your own infographics.

- Infogr.am www.infogr.am To create interactive infographics. Over 2,500,000 infographics have been created with this online tool.

Chapter 10) Images

Very important to mention: While some image sites are perfectly safe, others may be compromised or infected with spyware, malware, or adware. A site that is currently safe to use may not be days, weeks, months, or even years from now. When writing this book, I have omitted many of the malicious sites.

To begin this chapter, let me tell you a story about images and copyright. The story is titled: "Man Versus Monkey". Well, actually, it is not a story, it happened in real life and it was in the news today, 7th of August 2014. A British photographer, David Slater, who was taking pictures of monkeys in Indonesia wanted to take some close-ups of monkeys, more specifically of the Crested Black Macaque Monkey. After a few attempts at taking not very satisfactory monkey photographs, one of the monkeys got hold of his camera and took some "selfies" (for the older generation reading this book, this means taking pictures of himself by holding the camera in front of him). Mr. Slater's camera was stolen and somebody put the pictures on Wikipedia. David, the photographer has demanded Wikipedia remove the pictures as he is the copyright owner because he took the pictures. The US organisation behind Wikepedia says that Mr. Slater is not the copyright owner but the monkey is, because the monkey took the picture! The pictures are now considered public domain because a monkey, (or any other animal), cannot hold copyright. Mr. Slater was planning to earn a lot of money from the pictures and claims he has suffered a large financial loss. This is one of the pictures:

Source: www.wikipedia.org

I have already mentioned this at the beginning of this book but to stress the importance, I am repeating it here:

Use the listed sites at your own risk as the publishers of this book cannot be held responsible for any harm done to your computer, the cost of repairs, compromised or hacked accounts, or loss of production as a result.

Many of the mentioned "free" sites include advertisements, some for pay sites, others for non-related products or services, or both. Please be careful when navigating them as you are unknowingly led to other websites. Before downloading material, make sure you're on the original URL. When downloading free software, be careful not to accept applications that you were not looking for in the first place, such as free games, weather channels, financial service sites, shopping, etc. Avoid advertisements related to sweepstakes, winnings or free gifts. These are all malware.

Most of all, beware of requests for updates, especially numerous requests. Rather than updates, many of these applications are malware instead.

A few words about "scam" updates:

If your current video editor, HD, MP3/4, or audio player should be updated, you will be prompted accordingly. Make sure that their name and/or logo (such as Adobe Flash Player, etc) is on their update prompt. Well-known software brands have an option to check for updates. Use this option when in doubt. Do not install any application that you're not familiar with.

If pop-up ads repeatedly appear and make the website hard to navigate, it is best to avoid this site altogether. If problems persist, consult your computer technician.

This section explains the potential perils in pirating pictures and how stolen images can be found. It also serves as a comprehensive guide to understanding licenses and copyrights of online images. Although you may have heard of many of these sites already, there are some in this book that are not so common.

On some image sites you can purchase individual photos outright, but on others, you pretty much have to be a member of their club or organisation and thus, pay a monthly fee. If you happen to have a great chunk of money to throw around, you can be choosey and buy the best quality photos that are most appropriate for your projects. However, if you're living on a tight budget, venturing onto sites that sell photos and video material can seem like a huge gamble. After all, you need all the money you earn to meet monthly expenses. You don't dare spend a dime on images if you feel you don't need to.

However, there are totally free image and video sites out there and it's just a matter of finding them. While some are really good, others have a rather limited selection. To test how good each site is, input a search term that isn't too commonplace. Therefore, in my example, I chose the term "Bedlington Terrier" instead of "dogs" or "terriers" since this breed is not so common or well-known.

Take note that the sites listed in this book may undergo changes. Therefore, if you visit a site's home page, it may have an appearance that is somewhat or totally different than the one pictured in this book. How a site is navigated may change if its owner needs to make it more efficient.

Likewise, I refrain from disclosing prices for most sites as they may be subject to change without notice.

If you are absolutely set on receiving free images, I strongly advise that you read all the print on the websites you visit very carefully including their *terms and conditions*. Many of the so-called "free sites" do offer free pictures, but were mainly created to promote payable sites.

Remember: You are responsible for adhering to all copyright restrictions and licensing conditions. Using images without the proper, correct license, attribution or without the author's permission is against the law!

- First of all, I am going to talk about the Wordpress plugin PhotoDropper, which you can get here: www.photodropper.com/wordpress-plugin. This is a fantastic tool. PhotoDropper is a WordPress Plugin and it is designed to easily find pictures for your site.

With access to over 62,538,143+ for free (via Creative Commons license) you'll be able to impress your readers and search engines like Google.

PhotoDropper lets you add great photos to your website with just 4 simple clicks. You no longer need to visit 12 different photo sites to find the right image and license. PhotoDropper does all the searching for you… it even handles the attribution and licensing.

You can spend more time creating great content that your readers and search engines will love. Adding photos to your WordPress blog has never been easier.

> **Important:** Everything in this chapter about images applies if you are using royalty free pictures that you did not buy. If you buy royalty free images from stock photo websites, you can, most of the time, use those without having to refer to the creator of the pictures. That's why you paid for them, to be able to use the pictures. You do still have to check the terms and conditions for each picture e.g. if you can use the bought pictures in commercial projects.

1) The Dangers of Stealing Online Photos

Just because it is on the Internet does not mean you can use it and the term royalty free does not mean it is free to use. Images that you find via a search in Google are almost always copyrighted, so you can't just use them on your blog or website.

Visitor's eyes are often drawn to the images on your website so it's important to place an image, a visual that illustrates your point. Important: always check, whichever website you use to obtain images, that you credit the image, if required to do so.

Downloading copyrighted photos from the Internet without authorisation from their photographers or original publishers is risky and can lead to adverse consequences if these pictures are found in your creations. This is especially true if you use stolen images for commercial purposes. There are software tools, as already mentioned, such as TinEye and Google "Search by Image" that can find duplications of images.

If you're a beginner hoping to make an income online, and you're living on a tight budget, you definitely don't want to shell out big bucks for pictures. However, you still need images for whatever you're doing, whether it is a blog or a website or maybe even a video. Even if you own a camera, you may not have access to things you need pictures of. Let's say you want to write a blog about Labradors, but you don't know anybody who has a labrador so you can take a picture of the dog. Hence, you definitely want to find images online that you can use.

Ever since you were in school, you were assigned to write reports requiring some degree of research. Your teachers told you that plagiarism is wrong and a violation of copyright.

The thought of stealing photos can be quite enticing, especially if you must be frugal, but most of all, if you hate the painstaking and time-consuming process of hunting down images. More often than not, asking a source for permission to use images might take hours, days, or weeks before you get an answer. Then there are those fears that the originator will say "no" or ask you to pay them a fee. That means…on goes the search.

Like most creators, you want to complete your project and get it up and running TODAY! If you're one of those people, you need some images NOW! Hence, you may be more than willing to just steal the images and take the risks that come with it. In this great big world of exponential online growth, some may assume that their odds of getting caught are extremely slim, like a million to one. Some who have websites or blogs online may have the attitude, "It'll never happen to me!" Well, think again, as it happened to me.

Seven years ago, when I was new to Internet Marketing, I inserted an owl picture on a website about owls. I did an interview with an owl owner and he gave me the picture. Not knowing what royalty free pictures were at the time, I didn't think there was anything wrong. Three months later, I received a letter from a stock photo website demanding $12,000 (£7,000) because of infringement of the DMCA (Digital Millennium Copyright Act).The letter said I would receive a 10% discount if I paid the fine within 30 days. That was a shock! Where on earth would I get that sort of money? I wrote them a letter saying I had removed the picture and that I was given the picture and was not aware that I wasn't allowed to put it on my website. They replied, it is YOUR website, so YOU have to pay the fine. Countless letters were written between me and them. In the last letter to them I told them that I didn't have any money and that I would be able to pay them $5 (£3) per month. I haven't heard any more from them since. I guess they realised if it was going to take me 2,400 months (200 years) to pay off the fine, they'd better move on to another "case" and send somebody else a letter. Lesson learned!

Most important lessons for you to remember:
1) Don't steal photos - EVER.
2) Don't accept photos from other people. YOU are responsible if the photo is on YOUR website.
3) ALWAYS check the terms and conditions when you use a royalty free photo (free or payable)

You may wonder how the photographer is ever going to find out you stole their work. Will they check? Do they know how to check? Maybe they're so consumed in their everyday affairs or they have such a massive amount of content that they won't even notice or investigate? Possibly, they might not even care if one individual stole a few pictures from their site. All this depends on their character and how successful they are (how much traffic they bring to their site), online. They're not too likely to find out unless your project is for a commercial purpose and becomes a smash success, earning you a fortune.

Also, it depends on who you steal your images from. If you copy pictures from a small site which generates little traffic and was created by fewer than ten individuals, you might not have any problems. However, if you steal images from a large corporation that has its logos, brands, or trademarks (say Guess, Levi, Victoria's Secret, Google, eBay, Amazon, etc) quite frankly, you're playing with fire. Mostly, anyone who's invested a lot of time and money into obtaining their images will want to guard them with their lives. After all, why should you get for free what took them a lot of effort and money to acquire for their own use?

So, the consequences you face all depend on the individual or party you get (or steal) your pictures from. Some may check for image theft every so often while others never do. Many people are not aware of the image search applications out there. Yes, some might not care if you copy an image from them, while others can be downright pricks about it. If you use a picture for your own personal use or for an assignment, it usually is no big deal - but still illegal, so you should never do it. On the other hand, if you develop an application or website that becomes extremely hot, the author is likely to discover you and will seek out royalties or maybe damages, especially if their work of art is unique and took a lot of work to produce.

Copyright laws were made, not to enable an originator to disallow someone from copying or reusing their work, but rather to encourage the reproduction of it. Article I, Section 8, clause 8, of the United States Constitution states the reason for establishing copyright laws is:

To promote the Progress of Science and useful Arts, by securing for limited times to Authors and Inventors the exclusive Right to their respective Writings and Discoveries.

For example, if you need photos of German Shepherds, all you need to do is enter "German Shepherds" into your favorite search engine and voila! Thousands of websites containing them will appear. With so many sites to choose from, you're bound to find numerous pictures of these dogs. As you navigate through a few sites, you find lots of high-quality pictures of this breed in different settings or sitting and standing in various positions.

So, you've decided which pictures you would like to have. How do you go about getting them? Sure, you can make screen shots of them and edit or crop them in Microsoft Paint or a photo editor and suddenly you have free images, but is that right? Absolutely not!

People who steal photos typically say to themselves things like, "Who's going to know I stole that picture?", "So many other people do it so why can't I?", "Why pay for pictures if you don't have to?", "How are the site owners going to know I stole their images?", or "The odds that they're going to check are slim to none."

Some may think that once the original publishers post photos, they give little or no thought to them afterwards. Even though publishers don't check their photos regularly, there may come about signs that indicate someone has pirated them. Likewise, the authors of online content may choose to randomly check their visual material to make sure no one else has used it. Some may not care, but others definitely do. Although stealing a few images may seem petty, that isn't always true.

Most likely, these companies or publishers paid good money to obtain their photos. Either they hired a professional photographer or a graphics designer to produce their images and maybe purchased an expensive photo editing program to touch them up. Possibly, they've invested in a high tech camera and the equipment to go with it. Some have travelled long distances to get their photos. If none of the above apply, it is likely they've obtained a membership to one or more paid photo sites like www.Dreamstime.com, www.Shuttershock.com, etc.. for which they pay a high monthly fee. Even buying individual photos can be expensive, especially if you buy them frequently.

Just for a moment, put yourself in the shoes of the site owner. What if someone stole one or more pictures you'd paid a lot to obtain? How would that make you feel? What if your images apparently made them successful?

Let's look at this from another perspective. Imagine, that you'd spent over $900 (£530) to buy and download a sophisticated software program (like Adobe Photoshop). Six months later, as you repair your computer from a crash, you reinstall this program only to find out that your registration number is invalid. Why? Simply because someone else has used it to register their copy.

How would that make you feel? Needless to say, you'd be extremely angry. Stealing someone else's photos has the same effect on the original publisher.

2) How Stolen Photos Are Found

Are you still convinced that if you steal a photo or two, the original publisher will never be able to find you? Think again!

Copyright owners can identify unlicensed images with new technology. Images can be "coded" or "fingerprinted" so they can be tracked, even if changes have been made to the images or only part of the images have been used.

Just like there are tools to find duplicated text on the web, such as www.Copyscape.com, there are tools that scour the Internet to locate duplicated pictures. Two of the most popular programs are *TinEye* and *Google Image Search*.

a) Tineye

www.tineye.com The TinEye application enables you to find images on the web that are exactly like or similar to yours. It is not 100% accurate, but it is effective. With it, you can upload at least one picture file, or the URL of an image assuming it's already online and viewable by the public. Once the file or URL has been uploaded, you will receive a list of results stating all the locations where the image resides.

It's so easy to use, and best of all it's free. Simply go to TinEye's site and start using it. See below:

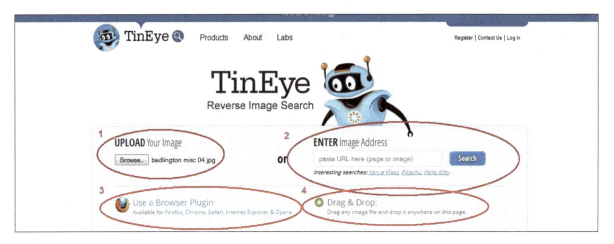

All you need to do is upload an image (1) by clicking the [*Browse*] button and searching for it on your hard drive or go to the webpage where it's posted on (2) by pasting the URL into the box and clicking [*Search*]. Within seconds, you'll receive a list of results of where the image was found (that is, if it was found).

With each result listing, TinEye provides two links: one to the page that the stolen image is on and the other to the original picture on the server. No matter how many times the image has been stolen and/or modified, TinEye lists all these images as a single match. To ensure TinEye works with your favorite browser, you may need to download a plug-in for it. Below the *Upload An Image* area, there is the *Use A Browser Plug-In* (3). There's another convenient option which enables you to drag a picture anywhere onto this page, called *Drag & Drop* (4). What can be easier?

b) Google "Search by Image"

For an introduction to this tool, visit the *Google Inside Search* page or go to the following link: www.google.com/insidesearch/features/images/searchbyimage.html. In fact, this tool is so self-intuitive, you can start using it in seconds. Below is the initial screen:

Click on the camera icon (circled) to enable your search capabilities as shown below:

Paste in the URL (1), upload an image from your hard drive (2) or search for one in Google's massive catalog (3). Easy as pie!

Google "Search by Image" not only helps you find pirated photos, but also gives similarities and suggestions to further your search (see below):

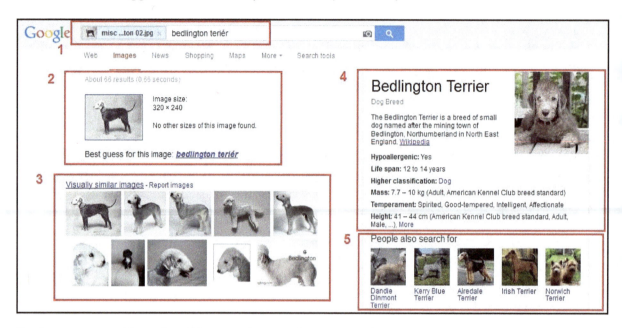

To demonstrate this tool, I did a search on a picture stored on my hard drive which I named, "misc bedlington 02" by uploading that image (1). Next, I got a listing for how many results and the size of the photo (2). Although the image was rather small, it came up with 66 results, but stated there was no exact image of 320 x 240 pixels as mine was. Following that was a listing from Google's catalog of exact, similar, or subject-related pictures (3). To the right was a description of the Bedlington terrier (4) as an informative supplement. Finally, was the *People also search for:* section (5) which basically shows other popular topics people hunt down that are like this topic.

Unlike TinEye, Google lists each stolen image separately, thus coming up with more matches than TinEye. Unfortunately, Google can turn up a lot of incorrect results.

3) Obtaining Permission to Use Images

This chapter describes the Fair Use Practice and its regulations governing how images may or may not be used. It explains commercial use versus non-commercial use. Also, if you wish to obtain a photographer's authorisation to use their pictures, it explains ways of doing so.

OK, let's say you are working on an online project, or perhaps your website, and you find a really nifty picture that you would like to use. By now, you know you just can't copy it and place it into your own creation. Who knows, the originator of the work will find you, assuming that he or she happens to investigate whether their images are being used elsewhere. Even though this visual work of art is copyrighted, that doesn't automatically bar you from using it, especially if it's for a non-commercial purpose of your own. If you really love this image and cannot recreate it yourself, you can always seek the author's permission to use it.

One term you should be familiar with is *royalty-free*. If an image or graphic is marked as royalty-free, that means that its creator or photographer cannot collect royalties from you under any circumstance. Hence, finding and using royalty-free images is best since you need not worry about paying out a percentage of your profits to photographers if your creation generates large sales. Another term you must be familiar with is *Creative Commons licensing*.

a) Creative Commons License

Some of these images under Creative Commons License are produced by amateur photographers while others are done by professionals. Professionals often release a few images under a Creative Commons with the required attribute linking back to their professional website.

In order to share and download digital content legally, you must understand the *Creative Commons license* (CC) concept. Creative Commons enables you to share your work or use pieces of content posted by others. Whenever content such as a photo, video, music track, or document is posted on the web, it is automatically protected by copyright. With CC, authors of such pieces can say who is able to reuse, remix, or share their works. CC provides free licenses and tools allowing artists, musicians, photographers, and writers to copyright their own works. Hence, these authors allow people to reuse and distribute their works providing the users give the authors credit.

To explain how CC licensing works, imagine that Barbara (Barb for short) is a photographer who posts images online and Carol would like to use Barb's images for her website. If Barbara allows photo sharing through CC, Carol can use her image. However, whenever Carol publishes one of Barb's images, Carol must give credit to Barb by stating her name or a link that takes visitors to Barb's site.

CC licenses are identified in three classifications:

1. **Commons Deed** – Expressed in icons and summarized in plainly understood language, this license is said to be *human readable*.
2. **Legal Code** – Legal terms of the work as stated as *lawyer readable*.
3. **Digital Code** – A licensing recognition method that is *machine readable* to aid search engines and other applications in identifying the terms of use of the licensed work.

Before reusing someone else's work, you should be familiar with the different types of CC licenses as symbolized with the icons listed below. *Source: www.creativecommons.org*

So each time you use a free royalty free image, you need to check which icon the image has so you know what you are, and are not, allowed to do with the image.

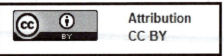

Attribution - This license lets others distribute, remix and tweak build upon your work, even for commercial use, but they must credit you for the original creation. This is the most accommodating of licenses offered. Recommended for maximum dissemination and use of licensed materials.

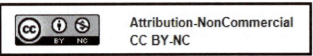

Attribution-Non-Commercial - This license lets others distribute, remix and tweak build upon your work. Their new works must also acknowledge you and be for non-commercial use, they don't have to license their derivative works on the same terms.

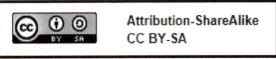

Attribution-ShareAlike - This license lets others remix, tweak build upon and distribute, your work, even for commercial purposes. But they must credit you and license their new creations under the identical terms. This license is often compared to "copyleft" free and open source software licenses. All new works based on yours will carry the same license, so any derivatives will also allow commercial use. This is the license used by Wikipedia, and is recommended for materials that would benefit from incorporating content from

Wikipedia and similarly licensed projects.

 Attribution-NonCommercial-ShareAlike
CC BY-NC-SA

Attribution-Non-Commercial-ShareAlike - This license lets others remix, tweak, distribute, and build upon your work, non-commercially but they must credit you and license their new creations under the identical terms.

 Attribution-NoDerivs
CC BY-ND

Attribution-No Derivatives - This license allows for redistribution, commercial and non-commercial, as long as it is passed along unchanged and in whole, with credit to you.

 Attribution-NonCommercial-NoDerivs
CC BY-NC-ND

Attribution-Non-Commercial-No Derivatives - This license is the most restrictive of our six main licenses, only allowing others to download your works and share them with others as long as they credit you, but they can't change them in any way or use them commercially.

It is very important that you understand Creative Commons licensing and how it works, even if you only use one free or low-cost photo site. Once you do, you can use photos without the worry of an owner coming after you.

b) Fair Use Practice

The terms *fair use* and *free use* are not the same thing. Fair use is defined as the legal exception to the exclusive rights an owner has for his or her own copyrighted work. The *Fair Use Doctrine* "is to allow **for *limited and reasonable uses* as long as the use does not interfere with owners' rights or impede their right to do with the work as they wish."**

Section 107 of the Copyright Act states:

- *the fair use of a copyrighted work, including such use by reproduction in copies or phonorecords or by any other means specified by that section, for purposes such as criticism, comment, news reporting, teaching (including multiple copies for classroom use), scholarship, or research, is not an infringement of copyright.*

- *In determining whether the use made of a work in any particular case is a fair use the factors to be considered shall include—the purpose and character of the use, including whether such use is of a commercial nature or is for nonprofit educational purposes.*

- *the nature of the copyrighted work; the amount and substantiality of the portion used in relation to the copyrighted work as a whole; **and** the effect of the use upon the potential market for or value of the copyrighted work.*

The above description was taken from 17 USC Section 107.

One fair use common use of photos is for product reviews. Whatever it is you want to review, say a book, skin cream, a cell phone, etc, if you don't happen to have an image you can use, you may copy one from the manufacturer's site. This is because a photo cannot be substituted for the product itself and reusing the product maker's picture will not affect them significantly.

Another fair use of images allows copyrighted works to be used without the owner's consent if they are being used to benefit the general public. If you're blogging about George Washington, of course you'll want to use a picture of him in your article or if you're writing an article about a car show, you'll need a picture of the car you're referring to.

c) Why Do You Want to Use an Image?

Before you go and copy an image (which is illegal), it is best to ask yourself five basic questions to determine if you really want to use a royalty free image:

1. **Do you comprehend what fair use is about?** Even if you take a picture and refer a link back to the owner, that is not sufficient. This is the same as plagiarism. Fair use means that you can use someone else's photo and there is no action they can take against you. If the purpose of using their images falls under the fair use classification, you need not even attribute the source, although doing so may be beneficial for you.
2. **What do you need the image for?** If the image is for news reporting, criticism, feedback, teaching (meaning providing a copy for each of your students), or research, then using this image is acceptable. On the other hand, if you intend to make a blog more appealing, you'll need to seek permission or buy a stock photo.
3. **Do you plan on modifying the image?** Just changing the proportions of the image or reversing it in Microsoft Paint is not considered sufficient transformation.

Altering the lighting effects can help as well. Once the picture becomes altered enough to where it no longer resembles the original, using it will likely be acceptable.

4. **How much of the image do you plan to use?** Using it for a thumbnail rather than posting the image on your site while linking it back to the original location may be fine. Cropping the picture or using only a small portion of it (less than 50%) may be sufficient transformation. For example, if you use an existing cat picture, but only showing its eyes, this is fair use.

5. **Are you willing to risk losing your site?** You must realize that if you steal a picture and post it on your site, if caught, your site can be taken down. This may result in a cease and desist bill from the *Digital Millennium Copyright Act* (DMCA) or you might simply get sued. The DMCA empowers the original owner to protect their work in the digital space. Choosing to publish this picture without permission may result in copyright infringement.

Commercial Use versus Non-commercial Use

Publishers are often willing to share their images with others providing that these images won't be reproduced with the intent of making money.

However, there are some sites that would like to use other peoples' pictures for commercial purposes. For example, an ecommerce site would like to have pictures of their products or game developers may want particular panoramic pictures as backgrounds in their games.

Obtaining permission to use pictures to build an application or website with the intention of making money is best approached professionally. This begins with a written contract between you and the owner of the art piece(s) you would like to use. It must state the agreed terms as to how the picture will be used and signed by both you and the originator.

Putting this in writing ensures that if anything should change, good or bad, the owner won't attempt to sue you later on. For example, if you are writing a game and it becomes a big seller, the original author of the image may decide that he wants a small percentage of your profits (royalty). You may decide to pay the owner a high flat fee with no future rights or pay a small fee with an agreed percentage earned on future sales. All details must be explicitly expressed in the contract.

My niche books are all written by outsourcers. Some outsourcers have their name as the author on the book, together with the pen name I use. So the authors at the bottom of the book are printed as: "Martin Summers and Dave Hoverton." Dave Hoverton, the writer of the book does NOT get any royalties from the book. He has no rights at all regarding the book he wrote. It is just an "ego-thing" for him so he can show his friends that he wrote a book. In these situations, the writer signs a simple agreement like the one shown below. If you are planning to write a Number One Bestseller, I suggest that you contact a lawyer for a "proper" contract. This one is the one that I use for my niche books:

****

Ghostwriting agreement

This Agreement ("Agreement") is entered into on XXXXX (Date and Year Here) between XXXXX (Your Publishing Name Here), also described as the '**Author**'; and XXXXX (Ghostwriter's Name Here), also described as '**Ghostwriter**'. Ghostwriter is also known on www.elance.com as XXXXX (Username on Elance Here). Both parties do hereby agree to all the terms described and given below.

1. Ghostwriter will write several books for the Author, as long as he still wishes to write books and as long the Author still gives him new books to write.

2. The name of the Ghostwriter XXXXX (Ghostwriter's Name Here) will appear as the Author in the book and on the front cover and spine of the book.

3. Ghostwriter is not entitled to any royalty or commission on the sales of the Book.

4. Ghostwriter has no say or decision power in the pricing of the book or where and in which book formats it is sold.

5. All rights, title and interest of the book shall be the sole and exclusive property of Author.

6. The above applies to all books published by XXXXX(Your Publishing Name Here) that will have Author XXXXX (Ghostwriter's name here) printed in the book.

7. Ghostwriter agrees not to publish any books with the same content in as the books he will write for the author. Gostwriter cannot use the content of the book in any other format e.g. blogs, articles, etc..

Ghostwriter hereby transfers and assigns to Author all rights for this book. The undersigned agree to the terms of this Agreement.

Ghostwriter

Signature

....

Name

....

Publisher

Signature

....

Name

....

****

How to Contact an Author

Getting permission to use other publishers' works is not as hard or as expensive as you may think. I will discuss totally free resources later.

How do you go about using someone else's published images without infringing on their copyrights? Using a publisher's copyrighted pictures is much the same as using copyrighted music or quoting blocks of text found in another person's article. Before you can use these things, you need to get authorisation first. Copyright infringement is not something to be taken lightly.

You can contact the website owner ask them for permission to use their picture and how much it will cost. To ensure that you're protected, you must get some type of written documentation evidencing that it's alright to use their material. As you seek permission, you'll want to give them the following information:

1. What you intend to copy and the link to each of the images or video material
2. What purpose you plan to use the images for

3. If this is for commercial or non-commercial use
4. Whether you will be publishing this work and in what ways (a website, eBook, printed book, etc) and the link where this material will be used
5. How long you plan to use their work (one time or indefinitely)
6. How the author of the material will benefit, including a keyword-rich link back to the author's site

Yes, obtaining authorisation does take some time, but if you plan to use it for purposes outside of the definition of fair use, going that extra mile will be well worth it. Hence, you must not be in a hurry to complete your website, video, eBook, etc and just start desperately grabbing pictures for the sake of it. It's better just to wait a few extra days, or weeks if necessary and lose potential traffic or sales as the completion of your work has been delayed, than to release it right away and get sued for it later. Even if you have to pay a nominal fee, it will be well worth it in the long run.

Also, getting permission can lead to a great relationship with authors in your same niche. Once an author sees that you are seeking their authorisation to use their works, to them, this is a sign that you're honest and someone they can trust. Not only can you build a good working relationship with them, but they just might also refer you to other sources that will enhance your future productions.
On the other hand, they can, and do, say "no." Whatever you do, don't let this discourage you. With the great number of stock photo libraries and videos on the web, you're sure to find another author with similar images.

Below is an example of an email requesting consent to use copyrighted material:

Hello Nathan,
I am writing an eBook about different Terrier breeds of dogs called "What to Know About Terriers." On your site I saw a picture of a Border Terrier being groomed at [link where picture is located] and thought this would be most appropriate to use as a grooming demo in my book. However, I would like your permission to use it first.
Once completed, I plan to sell this eBook online on an ongoing basis. At this time, I don't know how many copies of this book will sell, but those who read the chapter about grooming Terriers will see a rich-text keyword back link to your site. Once published, my eBook will be published on my website [www.nameofmywebsite.com].
Also, I love your site and will recommend it to others who own Terrier dogs.
Thank you,
Your Name Here

Best of all, you can sleep better at night knowing that you're not likely to run into legal problems with your production later.

For 99% of my niche books, I always buy the pictures from stock photo websites. However, for some niches, there are not many pictures available. In that case, I email a few websites asking permission to use their pictures e.g. if I am publishing a book about a fish, I will visit websites about fish and contact those websites. I tell the website owners that, in return, I will mention their websites in my book. Most website owners are happy with this and give me permission to use their pictures. Remember that the person who gives you permission has to be the copyright owner of the picture!

Three things are important here:
- make sure the webmaster confirms that he owns the rights for the picture, that he took the picture himself
- make sure you get a written permission by email
- keep that email as proof should someone question that particular image

4) Free Icons and Buttons

- www.iconfinder.com is a great site. You can find lots of free icons here.

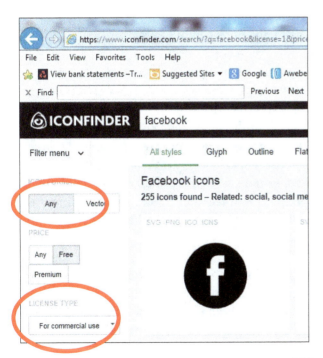

Click on "Free" and select "For commercial use" from the drop down menu and you will be presented with all sorts of icons you can download.

- Find Icons www.findicons.com

- Buttonland www.buttonland.com Lots of free buttons to download here.

- All Free Download www.all-free-download.com

5) Totally Free Image Sites

Important to mention: The quality and resolution of free images is often lower than paid images. If you are looking for images to put on a website, the free images are usually fine. However, if you are looking for images to print in a physical book, you will need images that are minimum 300dpi. If you use lower resolution images, your printer will likely warn you that the images might not look good once printed. There are a few free websites that do have large images but not many.

Here are several sites that offer free pictures with screen shots and instructions on how to download images for some sites.

For those of you who are just plain old frugal and absolutely hate paying for images if you don't have to, you will want to become acquainted with some of the totally free image sites. If you have a lot of time on your hands (which few people these days do) but not a lot of money, investigating free picture sites may well be worth your time. Also, if it's general type images you need (say skyscrapers), you may do well on these sites.
On the other hand, if you need pictures of famous buildings in New York City, either you must do a great deal of searching or just buy these images outright. I recommend the latter. Why do some photographers offer images for free? This is simply an act to promote themselves. That means, if you use their photos, you must mention their name beside the photo when inserting it into your creation. Some of them require a back link, so someone who views your piece of work can click this link and go directly to the page where the image is displayed (or their website).

If acquiring free images has always been extremely important to you, chances are, you've entered phrases like "free photos online", "where to find free photos", "how to get free pictures", and other similar phrases into your favorite search engine, only to be sent on a wild goose chase. Seems there are so many sites out there that offer free images, but there's one major catch for most sites: they are free only if you agree to comply with their free trial period (usually seven days).

However, there are *really* free image sites, but most of them are merely out there to promote paid image sites. If you're not careful on how you navigate them, you will more likely wind up on a pay site and end up backtracking to where you started from.
No need to go round and round trying to find free photos online. I've done the research for you.

Most of these image sites make money either from Adsense or from affiliate links to other stock photo sites, where you can buy pictures.
Note that when you save pictures from many of these sites, they will either put them in Windows Photo Gallery or in your Downloads folder unless you specify another directory.

Here are some websites where you can find free images. Remember:
- Always check the terms and conditions before you download an image
- Always check the CC License

a) Flickr

www.flickr.com has a very impressive range of Creative Commons pictures. There are over 100 million pictures on this site! Some free to use, others are payable. Type in your keyword and choose from the drop down menu under the License heading. I have searched for Bedlington Terrier and ticked [Creative Commons] Only"

Flickr is a superb online photo management posting and sharing application for which a community of fans contribute great personal photos and videos. Also members support one another's contributions by leaving comments and inserting tags. Flickr aims to make their photos available to interested members and to provide an online medium where members can upload, show, and store photos and videos. Here, uploading and downloading of pictures to and from the Internet via portable devices, users' home computers, or any software program that manages pictures, is easy. Users are free to transfer visual matter to and from the Flickr website, in RSS feeds, via email, and by posting to a variety of blogs.

All you need is a Yahoo account and you're set to go. If you don't have a Yahoo email account, well, sorry, but you can't use Flickr. I know, not good eh?

Once signed in, you will see the following menu choices: *You, Following, Community,*

Explore, and *Upload*.

The *You* menu simply enables you to store and access your photos and videos with its many options, such as storing pictures in your personal photo album.

Finding Pictures on Flickr

Communities options are great if you are a member of a group that shares photos online or if you want to create a group of your own.

The *Explore* menu gives you access to Flickr's great features for finding the photos or videos for your use or entertainment, such as:

1. **Recent Photos** – Simply what its name says, a page of pictures that were uploaded within the last week. Once you reach the bottom, you can look at images uploaded yesterday and any other day for which there is a button.
2. **The Commons** – In this section you'll find a great variety of photos from the world's public photography archives along with the list of industries who've contributed their own libraries. See below. To get a list of contributors, click the link [*Participating Industries*] (1), choose one on the right by its avatar (2), or put in your own search keywords to find a pictures from the archives that interest you (3).

3. **Getty Collection** – Whether you're looking to buy or sell and need to post images, this channel will enable you to do just that. Please see channel for additional details.
4. **Galleries** – These are simply collections of photos which fall under a particular theme that members contribute and viewers comment on. They are mostly hobbyist or subject related, such as the gallery of polar bears. If you're not looking for a particular type of picture, but are interested in what other members share, this category will appease you.
5. **App Garden** – This is a place where members write their own online apps and share them with the Flickr community.
6. **Camera Finder** – If you're looking to buy a camera or a portable device with one, this page gives lots of great suggestions for models and features.
7. **The Weekly Flickr** – Here, the latest and most popular photo sets and videos are displayed for viewers' entertainment.
8. **FlickrBlog** – Members who are writers are free to post blogs here. This is one great way a writer can be further exposed on the web.

Also, they offer some great extras that are hard to find anywhere else such as 1 terabyte of free storage space online. Those with tablets, cell phones, or other portable devices can take pictures on the go and upload them to *Flickr* for future use. Likewise, these images can be passed onto followers and friends. Also, images are available in high resolution ensuring superb quality, always as good as or better than the original photos.

Understanding Flickr Licenses

Before you download photos from Flickr, you need to observe the licensing information and know about Flickr's different licenses. There are four types whose symbols are shown below:

If you post photos and videos on Flickr and want to control how they're used by members, you must understand the four basic Creative Commons license types (see symbols for each in the figure above). I have already covered this but I am repeating it here to stress the importance:

- **No Derivative Works** – Users are free to use your photos providing they don't create *derivatives* of them. Derivatives are modifications made to an image such as resizing it, sharpening the contrast or brightness, reversing the image, using only part of the image as in cropping, inserting your image inside another picture, or any other changes.
- **Non-Commercial** – You allow others to display and distribute your licensed photos or videos as long as the users give you sufficient credit. Users may also produce derivatives of your works.
- **Attribution** – If you do use the photo, credit the photographer by referencing his or her name next to or on the same page as the picture is shown. Also, insert a link referring back to the author's website or online location of the photo.
- **Share Alike** – You allow others to distribute derivative works only under the exact same type of license your works are licensed under.

Searching and Downloading

One you are familiar with the licenses and copyright terms, you are free to download pictures or videos providing you abide by the rules. In order to find something quickly on Flickr, you will want to try their enhanced and *Advance Search* techniques as shown in the illustration that follows. The search bar area (1) is handy, especially if know where the photo you want is and you have a large *Photostream* of photos or are associated with groups that have a huge quantity of images.

If you don't know anyone with the pictures you have in mind, you can choose *Search Everyone's Uploads*, enabling you to find your desired video within Flickr's entire library. However, if you choose this option, you may be scanning through a large quantity of images brought up in your search results and will have to look at each one individually to make sure it has the attributes you desire (such as copyright data). To find only a specific type of photo, it is best to do an *Advanced Search* instead. Start by assigning parameters in *Search for* (2), *Search in* (3), and *SafeSearch* (4) as shown in the figure below:

There is more to *Advanced Search* as shown below:

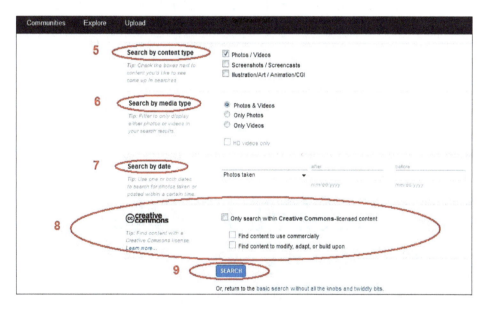

Search for (2) enables you to search by: *Any of these words, all of these words, the exact phrase*, with the full text or by inserting tags.

Search in (3) gives you access to the basic search libraries available in the search box plus *Getty Images Collection, the Commons,* and *US Government Works*.

SafeSearch (4) allows you to control the amount of safety in your searches by selecting *SafeSearch on*, *SafeSearch moderate*, or *SafeSearch off*.

Search by content type (5) gives you a selection of what to search for with its three checkboxes: *Photos /Videos*, *Screenshots/Screencasts*, and *Illustration/Art/Animation CGI*.

Search by media type (6) offers you a choice between *Photos & Videos*, *Only Photos*, or *Only Videos*. If you're looking for videos in HD, check the appropriate box. This box will be grayed out if *Only Videos* is not selected.

Search by date (7) lets you decide on a date range when a photo was actually taken or when it was posted. This is great if the photos you are looking for pertain to a specific event.

Creative Commons (8) enables you to find visual material for which commercial use and/or derivative works is allowed or if you want to *Search within Creative Contents license content.*

For further details on searches, please visit this page: www.flickr.com/search/advanced/?q When you type in a keyword in the search box, you are presented with this screen, where you can choose which license you want to see pictures for.

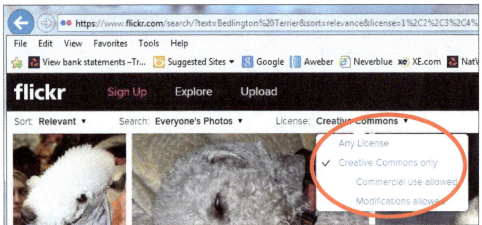

Now click on a picture you like and it will enlarge the picture and give you more information:
- You can Fave it (the star)
- You can Share it (the arrow)

- You can download it (the arrow pointing down)

Before you download it, you must check out the rights you have with this picture by clicking on "Some rights reserved".

When you've clicked on "Some rights reserved", it will give you the information on what you are allowed to do with this picture. In the example above, I was presented with this:

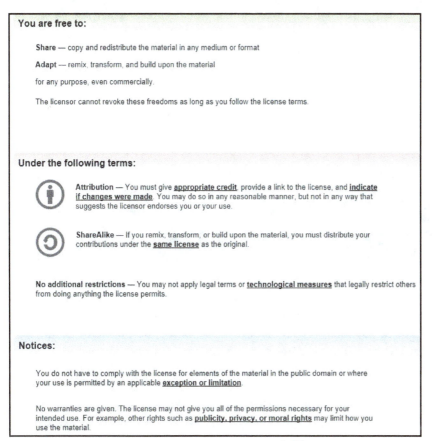

Read the information and make sure you apply it correctly to your picture.

b) FreeMediagoo

www.freemediagoo.com FreeMediaGoo.com was created for developers by developers. It provides a way for developers to gather free media that can be used in print, film, TV, Internet or any other type of media both for commercial and personal use. The site also has free textures, backgrounds, flash and audio. The content they provide is royalty free. **No need for annoying links and no limits to the amount of free media you can use!**

c) 4FreePhotos

As long as you don't mind hunting and pecking this site for free pictures and the images you're after need not be too specific, you might enjoy using *4FreePhotos* www.4freephotos.com

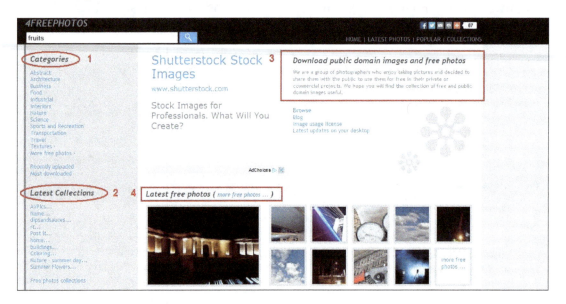

As seen in the illustration, look under the *Category* section (1) to see all of the categories of pictures available. For the most recent collections of images, see the *Latest Collections* (2) section. The area marked as (3) just gives a brief description of the public domain images and free photos on this site. To see what photos have been newly uploaded, see the *Latest free photos* section (4).

Most important of all, read their *Terms and Conditions* section before using their photos. These images are not warranted and 4FreePhotos takes no liability for damages caused by the misuse of them. They also have versions in other languages, but there may be slight inaccuracies in listings in these areas. The bottom line here is: Use these photos at your own risk.

Finally, if you choose to use their photos, they would appreciate it if you would insert a link in your website linking back to theirs.

d) Gratisography

www.gratisography.com A great collection of free images - high resolution - for personal or commercial use. They add new images every week.

e) Bigfoto.com

No joking! Here are some quality photos that can be downloaded and used absolutely free, even if you want them for commercial purposes. Best of all, there are no watermarks or terms and conditions to comply with. In fact, you need not even register. So, if you love to travel to different cities around the globe or are creating a piece of online work that requires the use of pictures from a particular city or country, you can find them here. Also, if you need images associated with a specific theme, there are such images as well.

The following screenshot shows what you'd expect to see when going to their site www.bigfoto.com:

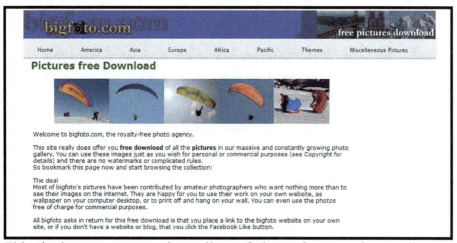

This site has an ever-growing gallery of photos from continents all around the world in categories including: *America, Asia, Africa, Europe, the Pacific, Themes* and

Miscellaneous Pictures.

The Themes dropdown menu contains the following categories of pictures: *Human, Nature, Background, Aviation, Close Up, Fountains, Sculptures, Fireworks, Amusement Park, Christmas, Architecture, Food, Railway, and Ships*. Pictures with subcategories on *Bigfoto.com* are not arranged in any particular order. Thus, you must scan for the ones you want. The *Background* category specialises in wallpapers or patterns which are ready to use.

Also, there are the *Download and Play* functions on each page of pictures. However, you must download iLivid software to enable the videos or pictures to download faster. Personally, I would not recommend downloading programs that I never heard of. Unfortunately, if you want download or play their videos, there is no way around this.

Bigfoto.com allows you to advertise your business on its site. Simply submit a.gif or.jpeg picture that is not animated and for a fee, this picture will provide a link to your website. You are also free to share any of them on your favorite social media sites such as Facebook, Twitter, Google+, Digg, etc.

f) Cepolina

Cepolina www.cepolina.com offers an online library of free images in subjects such as plants, animals, foods, architecture, and scenes from countries around the world. At the time writing this book, there were 20,000 pictures to choose from within 1,400 categories. Any image can be saved in up to six different formats and as large as 16,000 by 1,200 pixels.

There are eight sections of photos to choose from: *nature, geography, transport, food, art, objects, technology,* and *people*. Under each section is a description of each category, mostly in white lettering with some words in green. The green printed words are clickable keywords as they further refine your search and bring up pictures as if these words were entered in the search box. Cepolina's home page (lower section) contains a section with 18 different languages to choose from.

Suppose we enter "telephones" in the search box or click it under the objects photos section. A page with pictures of different types of telephones would appear as shown below. Now let's say we wanted to download the vintage telephone image as shown below.

As you can see, this image is enlarged and is ready to download. If this is not the image you want, you can click on the [*PREV/NEXT*] icon on the right (1) or input a new search word in the search box (2). If you want to see it larger, you can click one of the three magnifying glasses on the right (3). Next, right click the image and a menu will appear as shown in the next image. Click [*Save Image As*] on the menu, choose the directory on your hard drive that you want to save it under, give it a name or accept its default name, and click [*save*].

Registration is not required nor is there a place to register on Cepolina at this time. Although, this library is rather small compared to others, there are some great pictures here.

g) Freedigitalphotos.net

Free Digital Photos website www.freedigitalphotos.net has a very good range of photographs and vectors if you need some clip art. For web use the photos are free with an attribute. Lager images are available for a fee.

If you're OK with using small photos, *freedigitalphotos* may be beneficial to you. There are at least 10,000 pictures readily available for download and each is typically less than 500 x 500 pixels in size. Once you find one you'd like to download, all they ask is you publish a credit to the photographer who contributed the image.

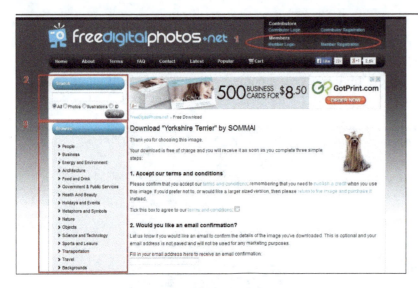

Referring to the screenshot above, simply sign in or register (1) then search by word or media in the search section (2) or browse by category (3). Although registration isn't required, doing so offers additional benefits such as adding pictures to light boxes, sending photos to friends, and viewing your order history with *freedigitalphotos.net*.

Standard License vs. Extended License

freedigitalphotos.net automatically grants you what they term a *standard license* (at no cost to you) once you have agreed to their terms and conditions and have downloaded your first picture. With a standard license you can use these free images for:

- Websites (including ecommerce)
- Avatars or pictures on social media sites as Facebook or Twitter
- Printed media in the form of advertising, booklets, flyers, magazines, newsletters, newspapers, or promotional matter
- Blu-ray, DVD, or CD covers
- Printed books or eBooks
- Films or videos such as those published on Vimeo or YouTube
- School or college projects
- Television broadcasts
- Wallpapers

However, you will need to purchase an *extended license* to use their pictures for:
- Images that the selling of a product is totally dependent on
- Learning type aides such as flash cards, online learning programs, or professionally published software for mass distribution
- Product packaging or labelling
- Any matter where the image(s) taken is a significant selling point of that product or service.

Again, their free images are small, but their terms and conditions are comprehensive. If you desire a larger picture, you may purchase one on the spot. There are no contracts or monthly plans to commit to or restrictions on the number of images you can download daily or monthly - you simply pay as you go.

Downloading images is an easy four-step process:
1. Find an image you would like to use (use the *Search* or *Browse* functions).
2. Click the [*download*] link (3) to the right or the green [*Start Download*] button in the figure below.
3. Complete the three requirements on the following page: 1) Agree to the terms and conditions, 2) Request an email confirmation if wanted, and 3) Fill out the security question to prevent automatic downloads of their material in the next figure.

Also shown above, are the sizes of the photos (1) and their dimensions in pixels (2) followed by the price. These pictures are low priced and for a medium, large, and high-resolution are $5 (£3), $7 (£4.20), and $10 (£6) respectively. You may even choose the currency you wish to purchase pictures with.

Before downloading, note the photographer's online user name (5) and be sure to check the box as marked in (1). The security code to be entered in (3) is accompanied in the short advertisement video. Just enter it in the box below. Finally, download the picture by clicking the [*Download*] button (4).

Still, there are other ways to find that image you're looking for. See below:

Scrolling down their entire home page, you will find sections of featured photos. Some are the latest submitted photos and illustrations while others pertain to special interests or even time of the year. Others are found under *Featured Contributors* (1) or in a photo slideshow (2). Take some time and look them over.

Best of all, these images can be used for commercial or non-commercial purposes providing you abide by the terms of the standard or extended license. If free versions are downloaded, be sure to give credit to the photographer or illustrator next to the photo used in your publication.

h) Getty Images

www.gettyimages.co.uk is an easy to use site.

www.gettyimages.co.uk/embed has over 50 million images that you can embed on your website.

Type in a keyword and tick "Royalty Free" to see all the Royalty Free Pictures.

i) Freepixels

www.freepixels.com As the name says, *Freepixels* is a site where you can get pictures for free. Let it be known that the main purpose of this site is to refer its visitors to sites such as www.Shutterstock.com, www.depositphotos.com, www.123rf.com , Google affiliated sites, and more. Though some may be free, others are pay sites. You can find some pictures here, but you must search for them carefully.

If you wish to avoid pay sites, ignore the selections in the green section at the top. The large picture shown above is a slideshow of many of the images that are on FreePixels.

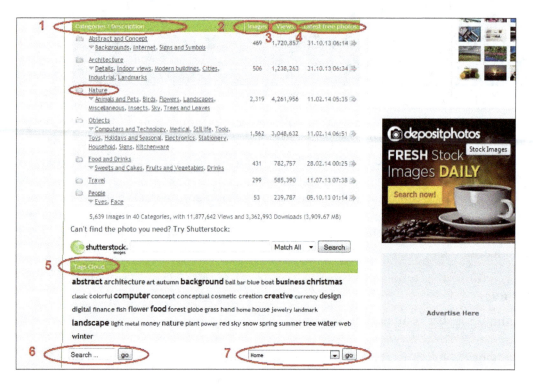

Scroll down and you will see the bottom half of the home page where you can search for and download free pictures on this site. Freepixels offers four ways of searching for photos: (1) *Categories/Descriptions*, (5) *Tags Cloud*, (6) search by word box, and (7) a dropdown menu box, all shown below:

The *Categories/Descriptions* section shows three columns right of the subjects listing: (2) *Images* – number of pictures in that category, (3) *Views* – number of views by past visitors in this category, and (4) *Latest Free Photos* – numbers signifying the times they were uploaded. Now, let's say we chose the Nature category as circled in the picture immediately above. We then have a subcategory screen as shown in the next picture:

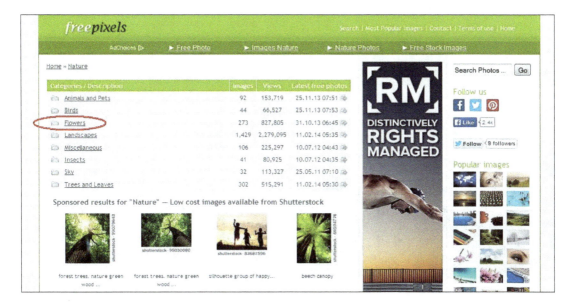

Suppose we selected the *Flowers* subcategory as circled in the image above. We would see subcategories of pictures of flowers as shown below:

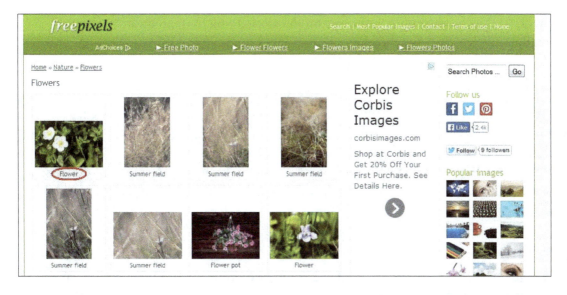

Above, is (only the top portion) of a page of pictures in the *Flowers* category. The number of pictures you'll see on this page depends on how many pictures are in that category. Simply choose one by clicking on the link below the picture or on the picture itself. You will then see the download page as shown below (say we chose the *Flower* picture as circled):

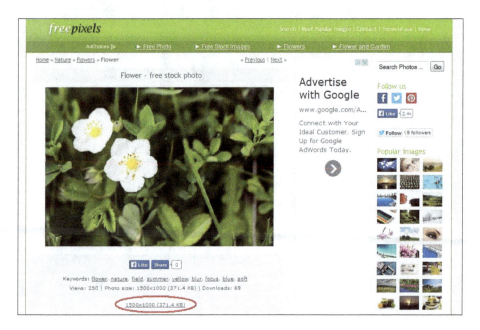

To download the picture above, just click on the circled link at the bottom. Whatever application the picture is downloaded under, it will remain in it until you, the user makes use of it.

Though freepixels has a great variety of pictures of certain subjects, don't count on finding one that will suit your project to a "T". If you really need a detailed picture, such as a "Bedlington Terrier" being groomed, you will have to choose a pay site to find it. After all, pictures on freepixels are too generalised and lack images that are great to use when teaching. Hence, detailed photos of dog tricks, training, or physical features of dog taken up close are not likely to be seen in freepixels. For those, you'll want to resort to larger, pay sites.

j) FreeRange

FreeRange www.freerangestock.com strives to provide free, quality images to commercial or non-commercial creators. There is one catch: you must download the Funmoods toolbar to enable these free downloads to take place.

This site pays each contributing photographer whenever a visitor clicks on an ad next to a photo they've submitted. FreeRange is selective when approving photos non-employed photographers have submitted, to ensure they are high quality and not too commonplace. Photos they accept must be artistically and photographically appealing or they directly identify an item or event. Also, FreeRange has its own in-house talented photographers. Pictures are shot on a 4000 dpi DSLR (Digital Single Lens Relfex) camera. Once received, these photos are cropped, sharpened, and colour corrected to the finest quality photos possible. Considering these factors, you can be sure any picture you download here will be absolutely superb.

k) ImageAfter

On *Image*After* www.imageafter.com you have almost one million photos to choose from their online collection. You are free to download and use any image or texture from their site and use it as you choose - personally or commercially.

By looking at its layout, this is not your typically designed site. Some of its boxes require you to hit [enter] to execute the choice. Also, the boxes and type are rather small so if you need a bigger display, you'll need to hit [CTRL] [+]. Below is a screenshot of their home page:

There are ten search and display functions here as circled above and numbered accordingly:

1. **Images** – If you wish to view images, just click on the arrow to the right and a dropdown menu of subject choices such as architecture, art, nature, etc will appear. You'll have to move the slider down to view all the choices.

2. **Textures** – For a display of their many textures, just select this dropdown menu and pick from its many selections.

3. **Search** – Simply type in a word and an auto-complete function will take place. Say you type in the word "bird." You will see the phrase appear as "birds", "bird's eye", "birdcage", "bird house", "bird feet", etc. Highlight the one you want and press enter.

4. **Extras** – This dropdown menu brings you to their other pages such as: *forum, latest images, by colour, random images, preferences, news, newsletter, links, terms, about, helping,* and *API.*

5. **Sort by** – This function allows you to sort your search results in ascending order "up" or descending order "down" in four ways: *name, size, date,* and *hits.*

6. **Filter by** – If you're looking for a specific colour of image or texture to coordinate with the colour of your website, you can search by colour. There are several shades of yellow, orange, red, blue, purple, and brown to choose from.

7. **Images pp** – Here you can choose how many images you want to appear on each page (anywhere from 8 to 320). If the magnifying glass has a "+" in it, you can click it to make the images larger (or "-" to make them smaller).

8. Click on this dropdown menu to go to a specific page in your search results or click the right arrow key to go to the next page or the left to go to the previous page.

9. **Clippings** – This is a button with a scissors symbol that enables you to view your "clippings" library. Before you can do that, you have to add pictures to it. Simply browse the pictures below and click the scissors symbol on the ones that you want to store for later viewing.

10. **"Are you feeling lucky punk?"** - Rather than choosing a subject, allow this site to pull up random pictures. This enables you to see other content *Image*After* offers and if you're lucky, you'll find some images or textures that you like.

To make functions (5) through (8) visible, you must search for an image or texture. *Image*After* is a site that promotes Shutterstock. Hence, if you don't find the picture (or texture) you want on *Image*After*, the search box in the following picture will enable you to find it on Shutterstock:

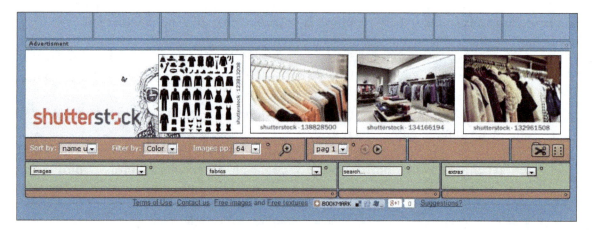

The pictures in this box act like suggestions on what you may be interested in. Each has its own photo ID number as it is assigned on Shutterstock. To order one, simply click on it. Registration on this site is free but you need to associate your account with one of your email addresses. After creating an account, respond to their follow up email message to verify that your email address is correct.

l) ImageBase

Imagebase www.imagebase.net is a collection of high-resolution photos that can be used absolutely free for personal or commercial use. They can be used for educational or non-profit purposes as well. No referencing the original photographer (David Niblack) is necessary. Also, you need not register and all pictures are readily accessible whenever you want to download them.

m) Photo Pin

When looking for photos, *Photo Pin*, also referred to as Creative Commons, www.photopin.com is a great place to start. This site helps bloggers to find pictures and insert them into their posts easily. It has millions of images supplied from Flickr but is not associated with them. Photo Pin just uses their API to find these images. In fact, their selection is so vast, you can easily spend an hour browsing here.

Simply plug in the search terms you're looking for into the search box shown in the next picture:

Again, they have a section with free stock photos. Most likely, these were pictures they once tried to sell but very few, if any of their members actually purchased them. This section is analogous to a "free box" at a garage sale. Although you can find nice quality pictures here, the selection will be rather limited. As they say, "beggars cannot be choosers."

I chose the term "Bedlington Terriers". Though this breed is not nearly as common as the others, in fact, many people have never heard of them, it acts as a great search term. I was able to pull up many pictures of these dogs. However, my search also pulled up a lot of other images that had nothing to do with them. Once you find an image that you would like to use and have selected it, you will be given a block of HTML code (enclosed in a square) that you must paste into your blog which provides a back link to their site. This provides attribution for each of their photos you use. See below:

Select the size you want, in the example it's the Large, and download it by clicking the link to the right (as circled).

n) Pixabay

One of the simplest free photo sites to navigate and use is www.pixabay.com

Two ways to find photos is by (1) the search box and (2) the *Explore* menu.

Once you search via the search box or Explore menu, additional search criteria appear as circled and numbered above:

1. **Latest images or popular images**
2. **Image type** – choose by photo, clip art, or vector
3. **Category** – browse through one of Pixabay's categories e.g. *architecture, backgrounds, beauty / fashion, business / finance, computers, education, emotions, food & drink, health / medical, holidays, industry / craft, music, nature/landscape, people, places, religion / monuments, science, sports, transportation / traffic,* or *travel / vacationing.*
4. **Orientation** – landscape or portrait display
5. **Explore** – *Editor's Choice, Latest Images, Leaderboards, Photographers, Cameras,* or *Blog.*

To the far left will be a number representing the total amount of free images available in your search. Directly under the *Explore* menu will be page selection buttons and left and right arrows to go to the previous page or next page as circled in the picture below (2).

Suppose you want to select the first picture on the left in the top row. Simply, move the mouse over the image and an enlarged image will appear. Okay, what about the *Primroses Flowers Plant White Primrose Spring* picture instead? Your first step would be to click on that image. See the figure below:

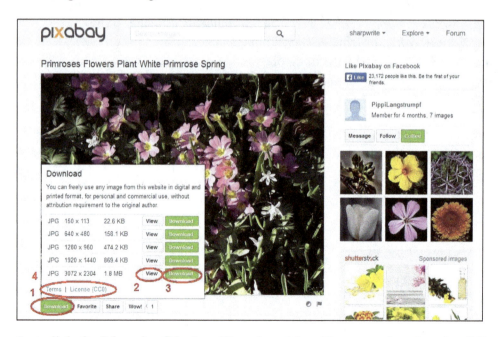

Just click the [*download*] button (1) and a table will appear showing the different sizes and file types (if applicable). You may view the size you're interested in (2) and if it looks satisfactory, you may download it (3). Before you do, you'll want to review the Terms and License (CCO) to see what the requirements are for using this image. That's all there is to it. Registration is free. Feel free to upload your own pictures onto this site under your personal profile. Upload at least ten images and you can avoid their ads. Finally, sometimes in your search results there will be a section containing Shutterstock photos. It is enclosed in a rectangular region and is posted at the top listed as such. Just avoid this section unless you want to buy one of their images.

o) Ancestry Images

www.ancestryimages.com This website provides free images for historians, genealogists and people undertaking family history, local history research or ancestry.

p) Pixel Perfect Digital

www.pixelperfectdigital.com is a great source to turn to for free background textures, stock photos, and other graphic material which may be used for personal or commercial purposes. All their pictures are supplied through a Creative Commons Attribution License and all Pixel Perfect Digital requires of its users is to credit them for the photos used. Pixel Perfect Digital's home page offers five ways to search for that ideal picture as circled and numbered:

1. **Galleries** – Search their galleries according to category.
2. **Featured** – Certain pictures have been singled out, calling special attention to them.
3. **Newest** – See which images have been recently added.
4. **Popular** – Discover which pictures are most commonly downloaded.
5. Search box with *Advanced Search* enables you to set the specific parameters to expedite the search process.

The first four require that you hunt and peck through numerous pictures that are not so well organized and this can take you as long as you have the patience to look. Therefore, we'll do a search using *Advanced Search*.

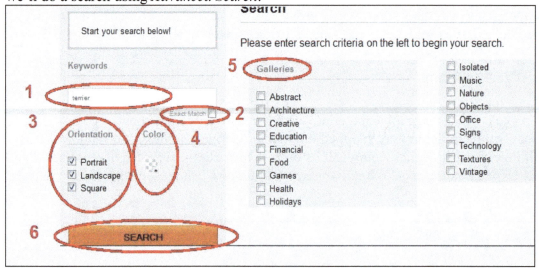

Normally the *Galleries* listing is one long column below the search parameters. Here you can find the picture you're looking for by the functions circled and numbered above:

1. **Keywords** – Enter the keyword or phrase of the picture you're looking for.
2. **Exact Match** – If you want your results to pull up an exact match, say if you're searching for something with a name or title, check this box.
3. **Orientation** – Would you like this picture to be in the form of a portrait, landscape, or square? You can check two or all three.
4. **Colour** – If your creation (such as a website) has a colour theme, you'll want pictures with coloured backgrounds that compliment it, not clash. Hence, click on the icon and move the pointer around to get the custom colour you want.
5. **Galleries** – Search for your picture from one or more of 18 galleries by checking the appropriate boxes.

6. **Search** – Once you've set all your search parameters, click this bar and the search shall begin.

Now that we know how to find the best image possible on *pixel perfect digital*, what must we do to select it? The next image shows an example. Here, we selected Newest to see what photos recently arrived. At random, I've decided to choose the fourth picture from the left to download (1). However, you may jump ahead or review pages of images if you so desire (2). As you may have noticed, www.Dreamstime.com hosts some of these pictures. Remember that Dreamstime is a pay site and if you don't want to pay for your images, avoid the paid section (as sectioned off in a white background).

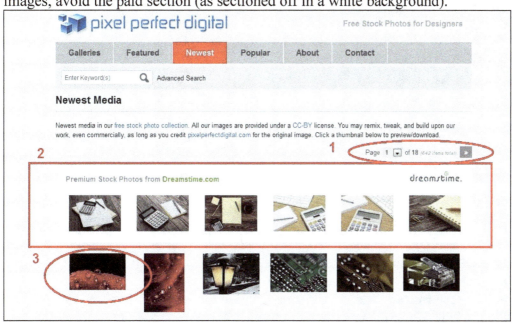

In the picture above, you can search until you find the picture that suits you (1). If you do not want to purchase a picture avoid the Dreamstime section (2). To demonstrate a download example, we'll select the image as circled (3). Below shows the download stage:

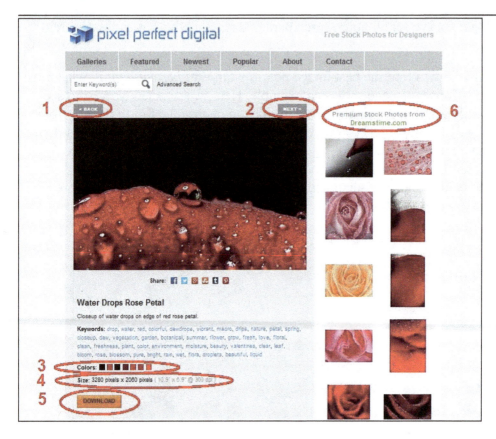

There are specific details and features to observe before downloading:

1. **The back button** – see previous pictures in the search results
2. **The forward button** – see other pictures within the search results
3. **Colours** - the colour themes this picture is available in
4. **Size** – the dimensions of the picture in pixels
5. **Download** – the button to download the image
6. **Dreamstime** – similar pictures available on Dreamstime (usually pay images)

You need not register on this site. However, before selecting a picture, make sure you don't wander off into the Dreamstime site. Again, pictures there require credits or a subscription which means registering on Dreamstime and purchasing them.

q) rgbstock

www.rgbstock.com offers a wide assortment of high-quality images, illustrations, background textures, and wallpapers for free. You are free to use these pictures for personal or commercial use. Members use them for business websites, blogs, public presentations, broadcasts, films, magazines, books, brochures, flyers, and text books. The figure below shows four ways to find a particular image subject you're looking for (as circled and numbered below:

1. By choosing *new photos, popular*, or *random* from the top menu.
2. The upper search box. (You must press [enter] to activate the search).
3. Search by category by clicking a link or choosing a category from the dropdown menu.
4. The royalty-free stock photos search box at the bottom of the page.

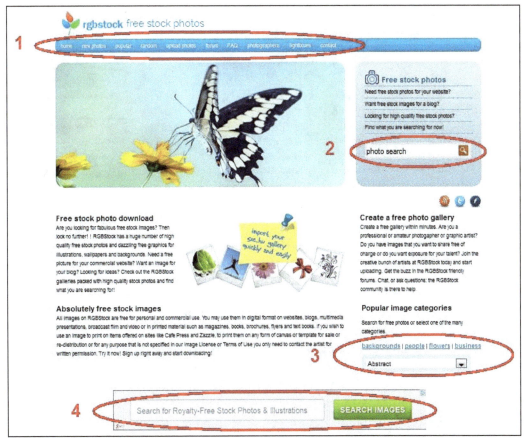

Once you find an image you would like to download, double click on it anywhere within the image itself. See the figure below:

For each image you consider, you'll want to focus on seven things as circled and numbered above:

1. The photographer's user name and avatar (if there is one).
2. The search box as it can help you find similar pictures.
3. The categories which this picture falls under. They can help you find images on the same subject.
4. RGBStock.com license – look this over before you download the picture.
5. Review the terms of use before you download the image.
6. See the actual size of the photo before you download it.
7. Finally, if everything is OK, download the image.

Registration is free and you will have your own light box to save images to while offering them to others who browse this site in the future.

r) Stock Photos for Free

Here is another self-intuitive site for downloading free photos. www.stockphotosforfree.com offers several search tools to enable its users to find the ideal image. Once you have registered and logged onto this site, you will see the following page:

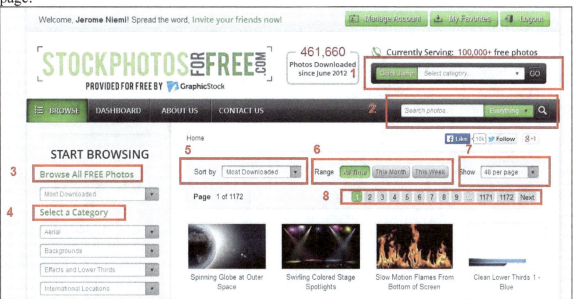

You can find your photos in eight ways as enclosed in rectangles and numbered above:

1. Category search box – enter keywords or phrases to find a photo you like
2. **Quick Jump** – brings you to one of their categories
3. **Browse All FREE Photos** – look over their entire library
4. *Select a Category* – choose one of their dropdown categories such as *Ariel, Backgrounds, Effects & Lower Thirds, International Locations, Nature & Animals, People – Talent Released, Slow Motion, Specialty & Other, Time Lapse,* and *US Cities & Locations.*
5. **Sort by** – sort A-Z or Z-A, highest rated, most favoured, or most recent
6. **Range** – see pictures that were printed *This Week, This Month,* or *Most Recent*
7. **Show** – choose how many images you want displayed on each page
8. **Page search** – search their entire library one page at a time

Once you find that ideal picture, your next step, of course, is to download it. The downloading process is very simple. Just mouse over the image, double-click, and download. To demonstrate, we'll download the *Slow Motion Falling Money* image as shown in the next image:

Never mind the watermark in the picture. That will be gone once you have saved it onto your hard drive. See below:

As highlighted above, there are four things you may want to pay attention to when considering downloading this image: the file name (1), number of downloads (2), category (3), and keywords (4). With these in mind, you can find more images like this one. If you absolutely want this picture, click [*Download*] (5) or just want to reserve it for future viewing, click [*Add to Favorite*].

Registration is totally free and requires an email confirmation.

s) FreeImages

www.freeimages.com, (used to be known as www.sxc.hu). The site offers totally free stock images, many large, high-resolution photos, for its members to download and print. Whether you need wallpaper for your desktop or just or an illustration for a presentation or blog, there are 400,000 images to choose from in the following categories: *abstract, architecture, business, computers, concepts, food, nature, objects, people, places, seasonal and events, signs, streets and cityscapes, transportation*, and the *world*.

This site welcomes contributors as well. Even though they don't earn a residual income from uploading their images to this site, they get a greater amount of exposure, as those who download and use them disclose the photographers' usernames in their creations.

On the home page you can search for your image in five different ways:

1. **The search box**
2. **Advanced Search** – shows several boxes in which you can select search parameters such as what to search for, which categories to search, search by photographer, or date range when the picture was taken or uploaded.
3. **Tabs** – choose one of the seven tabs: *Home, Blogs, Tutorials, Users, Randomizer, Light boxes,* or *Statistics*. In addition to pictures, there are blogs and tutorials on photo related subjects. Randomizer brings up random images. Statistics gives numeric data on various users, how many downloads they received, and countries and cities that use this site.
4. **View Popular / View New** – See what images are popular and which ones have been recently uploaded.
5. **Browse categories** – As mentioned above (as shown below)

Once you find an image, double-click it and you will receive a page of data like the example shown as follows:

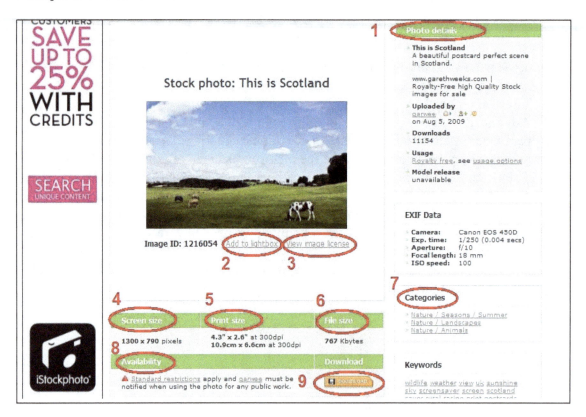

There is a great deal of information about the picture. Included are options for saving it as well. The most important factors are circled and numbered in the figure above:

1. **Photo Details** – Here you will find the title and description of the photo, the user who uploaded it, the number of people who've downloaded it, and the usage options (how the photo may be used).
2. **Save to light box** – If you want this photo, you can save it to your personal light box.
3. **View image license** – This link brings you to a page of the terms and conditions to comply with when using this image.
4. **Screen size** – This shows the picture's dimensions in pixels.
5. **Print size** – How large the picture will be when printed out.
6. **File size** – Storage requirements for the picture in kilobytes.
7. **Categories** – Which categories this picture appears under. This is helpful in finding images similar to this one.
8. **Availability** – Requirements for using this picture such as referencing the photographer.
9. **Download** – Click this button to save the image to your hard drive.

Registration is free and so is the usage of the photos. Just remember, before you download a picture, note its contributor and usage terms. Finally, give credit where credit is due. This helps the photographer gain greater exposure.

If no free pictures are available for your search term, the site will show you payable pictures.

t) FreePhotosBank

www.freephotosbank.com All photos are free to use for a book, websites, magazine, etc.. but you must credit the work.

u) Unsplash

www.unsplash.com Here you can find free high resolution images and do whatever you want with them. They have 10 new photos each day.

v) PicJumbo

www.picjumbo.com Totally free photos for personal and commercial use.

w) PickupImage

www.pickupimage.com Free download of high quality images and public domain photos.You can modify, copy and distribute, even for commercial use, without asking permission.

x) Wikimedia Commons

www.commons.wikimedia.org *Wikimedia Commons* publishes content on virtually every subject and also provides free images and art work to the general public. However, you must check the copyright on each picture you find to make sure it's OK to use. This site is free for anyone to make contributions e.g. to upload an image.

If you don't understand copyright, don't worry, they have a section describing it. The URL to their site is:
http://commons.wikimedia.org/wiki/Commons:Free_media_resources/Photography

If you've been on Wikipedia before, you know that their site is not graphically appealing, but filled with small printed sections and numerous links. Hence, I did not make a screen shot of their home page. Anyway, if you click on the above link, you will be brought to a vast number of sources, too many to list or count, of various categories of pictures and abundant sites providing free graphical material.

Sure enough, they're bound to have images to suit your purposes. You might have to do more browsing and searching than you would on most other sites as you will likely be led through several pages cluttered with links leading to pictures or sites featuring them. *Wikimedia* offers a great library of images on subjects such as *plants, animals, science, chemistry, physics, outer space, medicine, government, historical things or places, famous people, movies, music, cities, countries, airplanes*, and much, much more.

y) Public Domain Images

In the United States, images owned by the US government are generally Public domain.

- The Web page www.archives.gov/faqs/ explains the details of what is considered public domain and has links to features to search the National archives online data bases. The Library of Congress also has some its Public domain holdings online www.loc.gov/pictures

- The best space photographs in the world are free to use as well. All images taken by NASA, as a Federal Government agency, are public domain. There are a few restrictions which can be seen here www.nasa.gov/multimedia/guidelines/index.html

- The Website Public domain photos www.public-domain-photos.com has over 5,000 images to choose from.

- www.publicdomainpictures.net is another site for free images

Many universities and museum websites have images from their holdings which are public domain as well.

To search for images go to the *Flickr Advanced Search* and check the box next to "Only search within Creative Commons-licensed content" and then search as normal:

z) Other Images Sites

- NewOldStock www.nos.twnsnd.co (not.com). Here you can find vintage photography from public archives. These photos are free of known copyright restrictions.

- Superfamous www.superfamous.com These photos can be used, also for commercial use, as long as you provide credit.

- Death To The Stock Photo www.deathtothestockphoto.com Photos are sent to you every month, by email.

- Gratisography www.gratisography.com High resolution photos for commercial or personal use. Simply click on image to download.

- StockPhotos www.stockphotos.io This is a free stock photos sharing community with over 25,000 images. Commercial use is allowed as long as you credit properly.

- All-Free-Download www.all-free-downloads.com , you can download icons, vectors, brushes, photos, templates, etc..... on this site.

- Historical Stock Photos www.historicalstockphotos.com Free photos for personal websites and emails.

- PhotoGen www.photogen.com High resolution photos, free, for personal and commercial use.

6) Image Search Engine Sites

There are also images search websites. Here are a few:

a) Google Advanced Image Search

Not to be confused with Google's regular image library, *Google Advanced Image Search* online service can help you find royalty-free images which you can use at no cost and without infringing on photographers' copyrights. It is simple to use and takes less than one minute to find great photos.

Google advance image search is a great search feature and will return the greatest number of images for any keyword. However, it has a weakness in that you cannot always identify the conditions of use. In the advanced image search, you can select for ONLY royalty image to be shown in the search results

Simply follow the steps below:

1. Go to Google.com and type in the words "Google advanced image search" in the search box or go to the link www.google.com/advanced_image_search.
2. You will see the following online form:

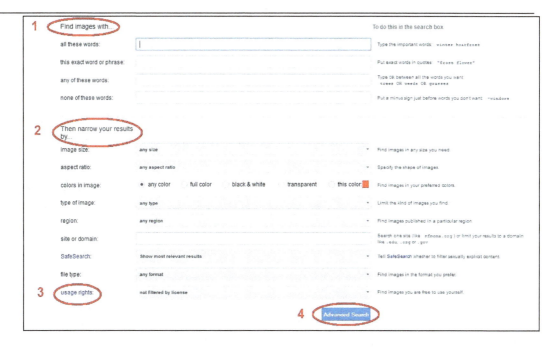

3. Fill out the sections with as much data as you like: (1) Insert as few or as many words or phrases to accurately define your search. (2) Specify the size and type of images you want. (3) Go down to usage rights and click on the arrow on the right side of the box.

4. Once you do, you will find a dropdown menu like the one below:

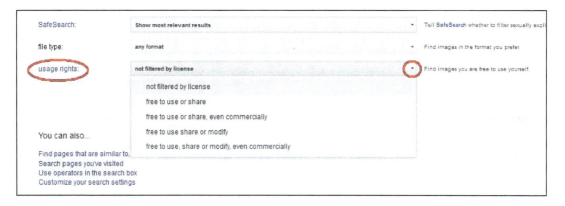

5. Choose one of the six selections: *not filtered by license, free to use or share, free to use or share, even commercially, free to share or modify*, or *free to use share or modify, even commercially.*

179

6. Right click and choose [*Save Image As*].

You may supply the form with as many parameters as you wish or accept the default values. The more settings you leave at default, the greater the number of pictures you'll find.

Or another way to use Google Images:

Go to Google and type in a keyword, in the examples below, I've typed in Labrador.

Go to Images and click on [*Search Tools*].

Once you've clicked on Search Tools, you will see the drop down menu where you can choose which images you want Google to search for. In the screenshot below, I've searched for "Labeled for reuse" and hit Search.

Google will now show you images that are suitable for reuse.

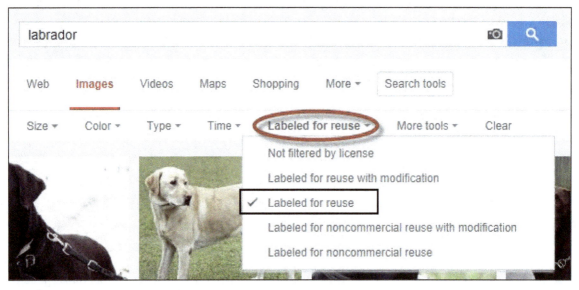

b) MorgueFile

MorgueFile www.morguefile.com is easy to use. Morguefile has a smaller database then many of the other free depositories. The images, however, are very good quality, the rights clearly spelled out and the search feature is very focused. You can download photos within minutes of confirming and creating your account.

Please see below:

Their home page has several ways for finding pictures as circled above and numbered accordingly:

1. The search box – Enter keywords or phrases to enable you to find images.
2. The site menu – As shown, MorgueFile is chosen, but if you cannot find your desired images there, you have instant access to the following sites: *iStock, Getty, Dreamstime, DepositPhotos*, or *Fotolia*. Though they are not free sites, they are additional resources to turn to.
3. **Popular** – Choose this to find the most popular downloads.
4. **Recent** – See pictures that were uploaded to *MorgueFile* recently.
5. **Last downloaded** – Find out what was downloaded by others lately.
6. **Most downloads** – View those images that get downloaded the most.

As you view the images that come up in your search, you will find them displayed like the samples in the next picture:

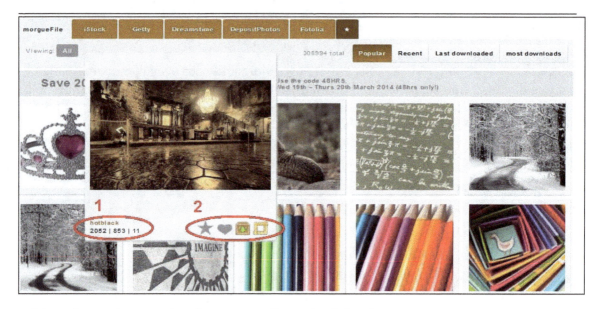

With each one that you thumb over, you'll see the following as circled above:
1. The contributor's name, # of views, and # of downloads.
2. From left to right, these symbols are 'comment', 'like', 'download image', and 'edit it'.

For more information on the picture, double-click the image itself. For example, we double-clicked the image chosen above and got more info as shown in the next picture:

The info above is as circled and numbered accordingly:
1. **The Info tab** – This must be selected to show all the info pictured above.
2. **Keywords** – Select to see what keywords are associated with this picture
3. **Comments** – Choose to make comments or view comments others have made
4. **Download** – Click to download the image to your computer.
5. Comment, share, or resize this photo.
6. Data on this picture such as the number of *Likes, Favorites, Views, Downloads,* and *Comments*.
7. Size and resolution of picture.

When the *Info* tab is selected, you'll see the author with his/her avatar (if they have one), the pic's file name, and below that, how long ago the picture was uploaded to *MorgueFile*. *MorgueFile* is a great resource that offers royalty-free and free images to its members. However, they strongly recommend that you credit the photographer as the source in your creations. Authors would also like to know how you plan to use their work. When you find a picture you would like to use, please read the contributor's comments below it and do as they ask. Likewise, provide them a link or an URL where your creation containing their picture(s) can be found. Most of all, thank them for their image(s).
Registration is free and comes with their license. With this license you may:
- Remix the image, modify or resize it to your liking
- Use it for commercial purposes
- Use it without attribution to the author

However, you cannot:
- Sell, license, sublicense, rent, transfer or distribute it in its original form.
- Claim ownership on this photo without making significant alterations to it.

c) Compfight

www.compfight.com makes it easy to find whatever type of image you're looking for super fast. Their search engine is specially created to effectively find pictures that are great for blogs, comps, inspiration, and research. Although, they're not affiliated with Flickr, they make great use of its API.

On this page there are search aids as:

1. The search box (notice how I typed in Bedlington terrier?)
2. Free Graphics
3. HD Video Clips (Hey! There are videos you can use here).
4. Freepix.com – another site with free pictures.

After doing a search, I found 976 images (as circled in the upper left section. Simply ignore the section below it as that applies to GraphicStock's website (which has nothing to do with Compfight).

Suppose you wish to select the image in the upper left corner as circled in the picture above. First of all, move the mouse over the picture you want and notice the blue rectangle with the 'x' in it. This means that image comes in more than one size. For a photo that is available in only one size, the rectangle below it will reveal its dimensions.

Once you've decided on this picture, view the license agreement (1) to find out what its author expects from you. Before you download the picture, copy and paste the HTML code (3) in the yellow box below. By copying this code into your project, you are inserting a link that will refer visitors back to the author's site. Finally, select the image size by clicking the corresponding [*Download*] button. In the picture above, the large sized picture has been selected. The picture will then be saved to your hard drive.

d) Veezzle

Rather than going to a single site to search for free images, *Veezzle* www.veezzle.com pulls up pictures from Flickr, Wikimedia Commons, rgbstock, and the Open Clipart. Their home page is composed of a simple search box:

Now, let's say I want to do a search on "Bedlington Terriers." Below is like a shrunken or "bird's eye" view of the search results (see the next picture):

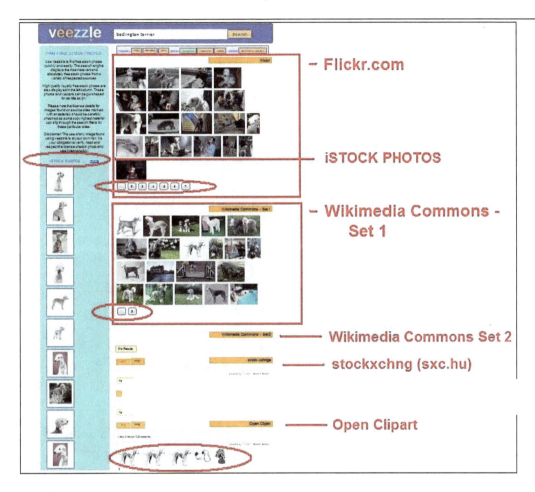

The top section is the results for Flickr. Here, you have seven pages worth of free images to choose from. Below that is the Wikimedia Commons Set 1. This site brought up two pages. Set 2, stock.xchng, and rgbstock had no results. The Open Clipart displays 5 drawings of the Bedlington terrier.

In the cyan section to the left are pictures available on istock photos and Getty Images (not shown). Hence, if you're dissatisfied with the search results on the left, you may opt to buy images from either of these sites. Some of the pictures from this site sell for as little as $1 (£0.60).

Veezzle warns its viewers that although these pictures are free, the ones with an asterisk (*) have licensing restrictions. Some copyrighted pictures may also slip through its filters, so investigate each picture you download before using it. They also state that you use their pictures at your own risk.

e) EveryStockPhoto

Instead of going to individual sites to find photos, you may visit
www.everystockphoto.com to bring up images from various websites as Flickr,
image*after, photoXpress, stock_xchng, etc. This site indexes and searches millions of
freely licensed photos.

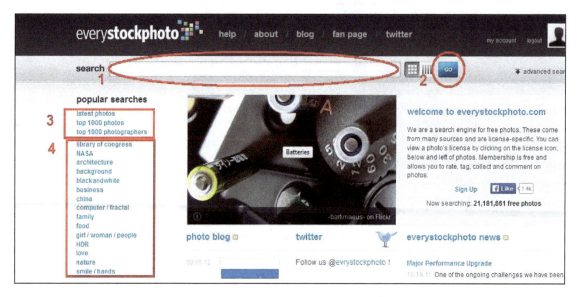

Here, you can search for your picture by entering a keyword or phrase into the search box
(1) then clicking [*GO*] (2), by latest photos or top photographers (3), or by subject (4).

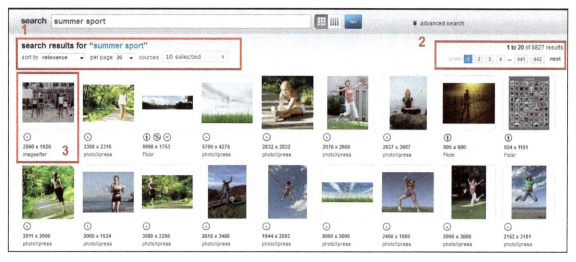

Let's say you wanted to find a picture in the *summer sport* category. First, you can start out by governing your search results (1) by setting the *sort by* box to *relevance, size, popularity*, or *date indexed.* Second, you can have 20, 50, or 100 pictures appear on each page. Third, you can choose how many of the 11 sources or websites you want EveryStockPhoto to find results from. Fourth, you can flip ahead one or more pages or to the beginning or end (2).

As shown in the image above, let's say you choose to download the first picture from the top row (3). With each picture there are CC symbols stating what can or cannot be done with these photos. If you're unsure of what they mean, review the Creative Commons section in this book. Also, you'll see the dimensions of the picture and the website it came from.
To get started, double-click on the picture itself as shown below:

Once you've chosen that ideal image, there are five things you may want to pay attention to:

1. The four tabs: *Info, License, Disclaimer*, and *Report*. As shown, the Info tab is selected giving general data about the picture. License shows whom the picture is licensed under. Disclaimer states your responsibilities when using this picture. Report is available for you to report problems you find with the picture such as poor quality, inappropriate content, etc.
2. *Resolution* or pixel dimensions of the picture.
3. *License* as to what site it is licensed by. You'll need to be familiar with the licensing requirements from each source or site you accept in your search results.

4. *Views* meaning how many people viewed this photo.
5. *Avg. Rating* is the average rating people gave to this photo.

The *Tag Cloud* section can be helpful if you choose to use this picture. It can give you ideas on what keywords to use in your project. Finally, to download, double-click on the image and select the Download photo icon on top (as circled). It will then load onto your computer's hard drive. See below:

f) Foter

www.foter.com hosts over 228 million free Creative Commons images from various online sources and the entire system is also available in a WordPress plug in. Where else can you find such a great variety of free photos? These are all free of course. Foter is among the simplest sites to use and registration is free. This site enables you to find free stock photos and add them to blogs, forums, websites, and other forms of online media. Simply find the photo you want, download or save it, and copy and paste the image into an arts application such as Microsoft Paint.

There are three easy ways to search for that ideal photo: (1) input a keyword or phrase into the search box, (2) choose a stock photo category, and (3) browse Foter's pages for the photo you want. The categories to choose from are: *Amazing, Animals, Art, Baby, Beach, Birthday, Car, Cartoon, Christmas, Family, Food, Hotel, Kids, Love, Music, Nature, People, Senior, Travel, Water*, and *Wedding*.

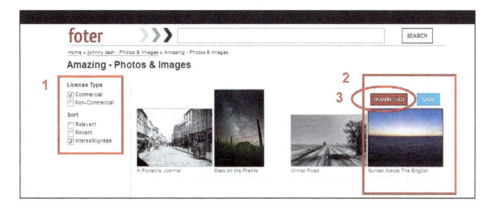

Before choosing a picture, you may want to consider the *License Type* and *Sort* sections (1). Check all the boxes that apply to your search: *Commercial, Non-Commercial, Relevant, Recent*, and *Interestingness*.

Now, suppose you wanted to download the picture *Sunset Across the English* (as highlighted above (2)). Just mouse over it until the *Download* (3) and *Save* buttons appear and click [*Download*]. Double-click the [*Download*] button and you'll see a dialog box as shown below:

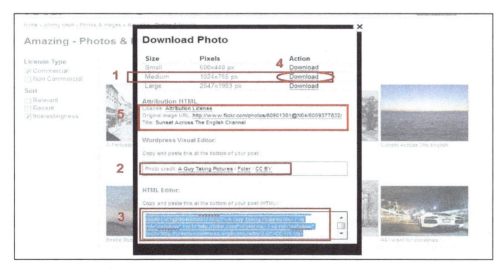

When downloading, follow these simple steps: (1) choose the size picture you want, (2) if using WordPress, insert the enclosed credit under the photo, giving credit to the photographer, (3) copy the highlighted text into your HTML editor when applicable, and before you download (4), let's not forget about (5): the Attribution HTML which inserts a link back to the author of the photo. Once you click the download link of the size picture you want, it will appear on your computer (with the link where the picture can be found above it). Copy or link the picture, whichever is appropriate in for your project. Making these insertions is quicker than entering the attributions manually.

g) FreeStockPhotos

www.freestockphotos.com Free photography for commercial and personal use.

h) Creative Common Search

http://search.creativecommons.org/

Put in your search keyword and tick the criteria for the product you want.
Then, tick the box for what you are looking for, in this example: Google images.

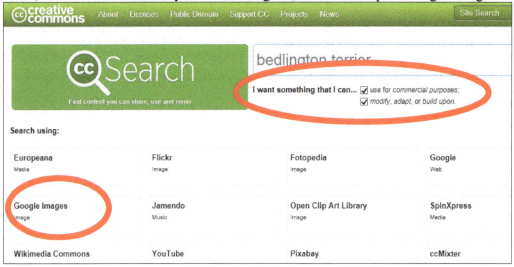

i) Wylio

www.wylio.com You can find Creative Common Pictures here and re-size and embed them. You can resize up to five images free per month.

j) Fotopedia

www.fotopedia.com A great search engine for Creative Commons pictures

7) Pay Image Sites with Free Photos

This part is dedicated to sites where photos or stock images are sold, but where selections of free images are available too. Each site mentioned has its own library of royalty-free (RF) images to choose from.
You can think of their RF bins like the clearance racks at most stores. These pictures in the RF bin are free but are often not available in many different sizes.

If finding photos for free is a high priority or a must, you'll need to take some time to browse each site's library. Likewise, if you find a site with just the right pay images you need, maybe you'll want to resort to creating an account on their site and buying some as needed. Creating your own account to browse is free on all these sites.
Before you sign up with the first pay site that impresses you, compare the pricing options of several other sites. Many of them have packages that are priced by the month while others are only priced based on a per-photo or set of photos basis. If you want a monthly plan, make sure that it fits in with your budget. Cancelling the plan later may, or may not, be easy depending on the site's policies. Read the details over carefully before committing to a plan.

Most of these payable sites have two buying structures:
- you either buy credits eg. one picture can be three credits, whilst another one can be 11 credits. Usually credits need to be used up one year after you've purchased them.
- or you buy a subscription e.g. for $211 (£130) per month and you can download 25 pictures per day.

The price per picture depends on the size and the license. Because of this, it is very difficult to say how much the price is for one picture but I'll give you some idea later. Prices vary for pictures as the person who puts the pictures on the site, to sell their pictures, determines the price.

a) Fotolia

www.fotolia.com Fotalia has over 30 million royalty free images. They offer free royalty free pictures every day. You can use these images anywhere in the world. You could visit the site every day and download all their free pictures and so build a portfolio of free pictures. Sometimes you will see the same pictures on different days though.

Fotalia strives to offer low-cost graphics to its members. It is one of the oldest stock photo websites on the web. Their material is especially suited to brochures, reports, school projects, slides, and websites.

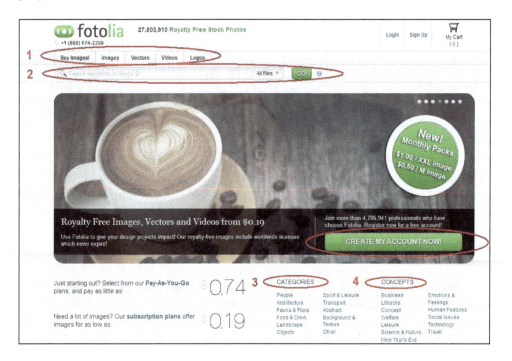

As you hop on Fotolia's site, you will find 4 ways to search for images or videos:
1. The top menu selections: *Buy Images, Images, Vectors, Videos*, or *Logos*
2. The search box where you can insert keywords or an image ID
3. Categories
4. Concepts

Their *Categories* section contains the following subcategories: *People, Architecture, Fauna & Flora, Food & Drink, Landscape, Objects, Sports & Leisure, Transport, Abstract, Background & Texture,* and *Other.*

The *Concepts* section includes subcategories as: *Business, Lifestyle, Concept, Welfare, Leisure, Science & Nature, New Year's Eve, 2014, Emotions & Feelings, Human Features, Social Issues, Technology,* and *Travel.*

To access their material either log-in or sign in at the top right corner or click the *Create My Account Now!* button in the center (as circled). Fotolia offers a Pay-As-You-Go plan or subscription plans. Although their prices are displayed as shown in the previous picture, they may not be the same when you visit this site and create an account. Registering for an account is free.

Price per picture:

$42 (£25) for 26 credits.

This means one credit is $1.62 (£1).

Assuming you want a medium size with a standard license, one picture will cost you six credits, therefore $9.72 (£6). Well, I never said buying stock photo images is cheap.

If you just want an extra small picture, it will cost you only 1 credit.

Size (?)	Pixel / Inches	Price
Standard XS	424 x 283 (0.1 MP)	1 credit
Standard S	848 x 566 (0.5 MP)	3 credits
Standard M	1687 x 1126 (1.9 MP)	6 credits
Standard L	2723 x 1818 (5.0 MP)	8 credits
Extended RF License	2723 x 1818 (5.0 MP)	100 credits

⦿ ON-DEMAND PURCHASE (CREDITS) ⓘ   ◯ MONTHLY PACK

b) Dreamstime

www.dreamstime.com Founded in 2000, today *Dreamstime* is one of the mainstream providers of online pictures. This friendly community based site offers royalty free stock photos contributed by photographers all over the world. Every day their database is renewed with thousands of fresh new images. They have obtained over 6,000,000 members, more than 157,000 photographers, and currently amassed over 21,000,000 photos, clip art images, illustrations, and vectors.

On the home page, you have a few options for finding some free photos. Click on the [*Free Image*] tab, choose a topic from the menu or input a keyword or phrase describing the photo you're looking for.

If you're strictly looking for free images on this site, you may be faced with slim pickings. If you're not finicky about the size or quality of the image, you may be in luck. The more generalised your search is, the more likely you will find images. For example, if you just want dog images but you don't care what breed, free ones are easy to find.

However, if you need a specific type, say a Cocker Spaniel puppy, your chances of finding free ones are not nearly as good. Hence, you may either resort to purchasing credits or a subscription plan from *Dreamstime*, or look elsewhere. When you hover over a picture, you will see level 1, level 2, etc... A level 5 picture will cost you more than a level 1 picture.

Price per picture (for a level 2 picture):

$35 (£21) for 30 credits.
This means one credit is £1.17 (0.70p).
Assuming you want to purchase a medium sized picture at 300dpi (minimum size needed for printing in books), that will cost you 10 credits, therefore $11.70 (£7).
The same picture in extra small at 72dpi (for web-use) will cost you 5 credits or $5.85 (£3.50).

A level 5 picture in the same size will cost you 16 credits or $18 (£11).

○ Extrasmall	480x320px	6.7" x 4.4"	@72dpi	
○ Small	800x533px	11.1" x 7.4"	@72dpi	
● **Medium**	**2121x1414px**	**7.1" x 4.7"**	**@300dp**	**0.8Mb**
○ Large	2738x1825px	9.1" x 6.1"	@300dpi	
○ Extralarge	3464x2309px	11.5" x 7.7"	@300dpi	
○ Maximum	5760x3840px	19.2" x 12.8"	@300dpi	4Mb
○ Tiff	8146x5431px	27.2" x 18.1"	@300dpi	126.5 Mb
● Royalty Free			Price: **10 credits**	
○ Extended licenses			Format: .jpg	

For $220 (£131), you can download 25 pictures per day, so a total of 750 images. In this case, each image will cost you $0.29 (£0.17).

c) 123rf

www.123rf.com has over 30 million royalty free photos. I use this site a lot for pictures to insert in my niche books. This is stock photography at affordable prices.
Price per picture:
$49 (£29) for 40 credits.

This means $1.23 (£0.73) for one credit.

Assuming you want to download a medium size picture at 300dip, that will cost you 3 credits or $3.69 (£2.19). Their subscriptions are more expensive that Dreamstime.

Standard License	Extended License	Additional Multi-seat License	
Resolution	Print Size ∨		Credits
Web Use (72dpi)			
○ s JPG 367 x 450 px	13.0 cm x 15.9 cm		1
○ M JPG 625 x 767 px	22.0 cm x 27.1 cm		2
○ ML JPG 1237 x 1518 px	10.5 cm x 12.9 cm		3
◉ L JPG 1848 x 2269 px	15.6 cm x 19.2 cm		4
○ XL JPG 2824 x 3466 px	23.9 cm x 29.3 cm		5
○ XXL JPG 3239 x 3976 px	27.4 cm x 33.7 cm		6
○ XXL TIFF 4048 x 4970 px	34.3 cm x 42.1 cm		10

d) Dollar Photo Club

www.dollarphotoclub.com Like your local dollar store, everything here is $1 (£0.60), ALWAYS! However, to become a member, you will have to pay a $10 (£6) monthly membership fee. This allows you to download 10 high resolution images per month and any additional images are also only $1. Unused downloads are transferred to the next month. You will then see their home page as shown in the following screenshot:

The Dollar Photo Club offers these features:

- 26,000,000 images and vectors to choose from, all royalty-free

- Pictures ready for business use
- Unlimited print runs and times an image can be used
- Ready to post on social media sites

I thought I would test this site out just to see how good it is by typing in the keywords "Bedlington Terrier." Like no free or other low cost site I've been to, it came up with 46 pictures in all. Hence, I personally recommend that if you're set on free images, you must become a member of Dollar Photo Club. Once you do, you can buy and download an unlimited number of photos for $1 (£0.60) each.

8) Other Good Stock Photo Websites

Some photo stock websites offer pay as you go plans and other offer subscription plans. Some offer both.
Free photo websites:
www.creativity103.com A library of free abstract designs
www.animalphotos.info Thousands of animal images under Creative Commons
www.carpictures.cc Thousands of car images under Creative Commons

Here are a few other good stock photo websites, payable:

- www.bigstockphoto.com
- www.graphicstock.com You can create a free account and download 20 images per day, for 7 days.
- www.photodune.com
- www.stockpholio.com
- www.shutterstock.com
- www.istockphoto.com
- www.depositphoto.com
- www.stockfresh.com
- www.lockerz.com
- www.smugmug.com
- www.corbis.com
- www.photo-wizard.net
- www.photobucket.com
- www.webshots.com
- www.imgur.com
- You can find a comparison of some sites here:
http://en.wikipedia.org/wiki/List_of_photo_sharing_websites

Chapter 11) Free Clip Art & Vectors

For some, rather than regular photos, they would prefer clip art images. This is especially true if the nature of your creation is to be animated. Sometimes clip art communicates better than photos since the main object tends to stand out more. When conveying messages or posting instructions, not only does clip art communicate better, it give viewers the impression that the creator of the site or other project has some imagination. Likewise, there are numerous sites that offer free *vectors*. Vectors are art-like or cartoon type pictures much like clip art, but are used in instructions and diagrams to show how things work, or for statistical information as in charts, graphs, or illustrations. They are used in research projects, presentations, especially those made in Microsoft Power Point, store signs, business cards, flyers, brochures, business logos, flags, maps and the like.

1) Excellent Free ClipArt Sites

The following are some free clipart sites. Amongst them all, you are highly likely to find something that suits your needs. All of them are easy to use and pictures can be downloaded in seconds. Best of all, they are all FREE!

a) Absolutely Free ClipArt

Whatever you're looking for, Absolutely Free ClipArt www.allfree-clipart.com is likely to have it. In fact, this site has thousands of free clipart images and their library is updated monthly. Simply go to their site, find a category you're interested in and follow it through until you find that ideal clipart.

Their categories are as follows: *Animals, Arrows, Baby, Birthday, Buildings, Business, Computers, Education, Food, Flowers, Games, Holidays, Household, Medical, Music, Occasions, People, Science, Signs, Smiley, Sports, Transportation, Weather, Wedding and Zodiac.*
Again, all images are free and no registration is required. Find an image, right click it, and select [*Save Image As*] on the pop-up menu.

b) ClipArt Etc

If you're looking for historic type images or drawings, *ClipArt Etc* http://etc.usf.edu/clipart has free images strictly for non-commercial use. These are all black and white images, mainly based on American history and the middle ages. See their home page below:

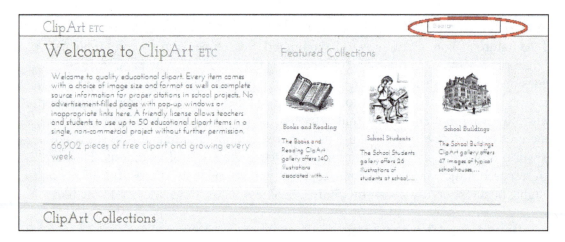

Currently, they have nearly 67,000 and their library is continuously growing. Their subcategories are as follows: *Alphabets, American History & Government, Ancient & Medieval History, Animals, Art & Architecture, Business & Industry, Community, Flags & Emblems, Home, Literature, Mathematics, Military, Music, People, Places, Plants, School, Science, Sports & Recreation*, and *Transportation*.

Most categories branch out into subcategories and though there is a search box at the top (as circled), you might have to search through several layers to find what you're looking for.

Once you find that particular image you need, left click to bring it onto the screen and right click and from the menu select [*Save Image As*] to save it onto your computer. Pictures come in different sizes and the dimensions of each are written in the lower right corner.

c) DeviantART

If you love to create and share true quality art, *DeviantART* www.deviantart.com is one excellent source of artwork. Even if you're not into fine art, this site is likely to have fabulous, colourful images and clipart like the kind you see in animated movies like the Lion King.

This is a very popular site for digital and traditional media artists to show their work. There are also lots of photos on the site. Thousands of brilliant pictures and you can download without registering! The image quality is very large for some pictures so these are suitable for any media use.

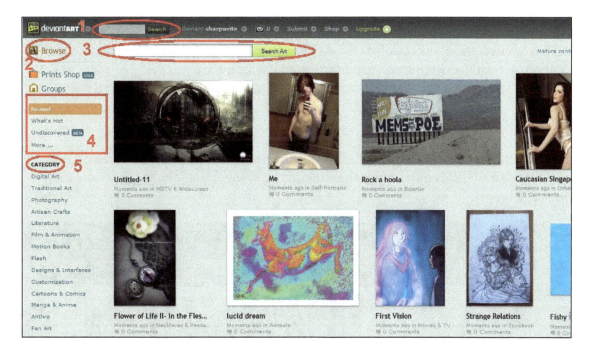

There are at least five ways to search for pictures on this site (as circled and numbered):

1. The keyword search box
2. The browse button
3. The *Search Art* search box
4. The newest and popular section
5. *Category* section

Right click on the image and from the pop-up menu select, *Save Image As* and by default, it should go into your *Downloads* folder. Make sure you read the terms and conditions or license for the image.

Membership is free. Once you are a *deviant* (their term for member), you can:

• View over 20 million distinctive art pictures.
• Show, expose, and share your works of art with other members or art aficionados.
• Sell prints and digital downloads of art pieces you've created.

- More than 32 million members support this art community, making it the largest in the world.

Signing up involves multiple steps as you will need to supply information such as your birth date and gender, along with a personal profile. DeviantART will also ask you to fill out a form with several blanks regarding things as your favourite books, writers, movies, TV shows, musicians, video games, gaming platforms and other things like that. You only need to complete the blanks you're OK with sharing. Preferably, they are looking for serious artists with education and career-oriented backgrounds.
They have a free and a payable membership.

d) From Old Books (FOBO)

If ancient art is your forte and you cherish works from the 19th century or earlier, *From Old Books Org* (FOBO) may be just the site for you www.fromoldbooks.org View their home page below:

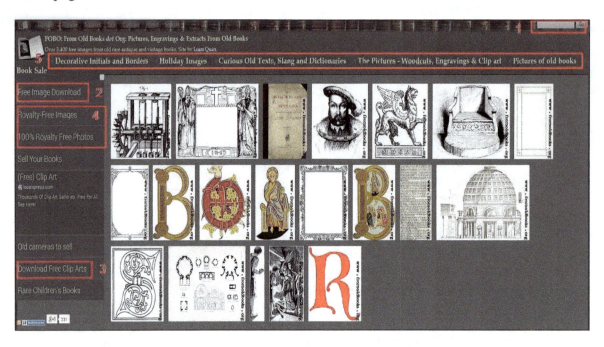

Above you can see there are several ways to find images here as pictured and numbered:
1. The search box in the upper right corner. One little glitch: it is small and not so noticeable.

2. **Free Image Download** – This brings you to the Stock Free Images site with different categories as: *Popular Free Stock Images, New Free Stock Images,* and *Pro Stock Photos From Dreamstime.*
3. **Download Free Clip Arts** – Click here to go to Soft32's site (http://open-clip-art-library.soft32.com/). Here, there are over 3,000 clip art images classified in categories such as animals, computers, signals, etc. Again, these pictures are free and can be used for any reason since the contributors of these pieces of art have waived their rights including copyright according to the *CCO Public domain Dedication.*
4. **Royalty-Free Images** – Some are 100% royalty-free and others can be downloaded instantly in any size.
5. The top menu – browse the top menu for specific categories as:
    a. Decorative Initials and Borders
    b. Holiday Images
    c. Curious Old Texts, Slangs and Dictionaries
    d. The Pictures – Woodcuts, Engravings, and Clip Art
    e. Pictures of Old Books
    Note that each of the five selections has their own submenus.

Suppose you want to download the *Celtic knotwork dragon ornament* (third picture from the left in the second row). Double-click on the image and download accordingly:

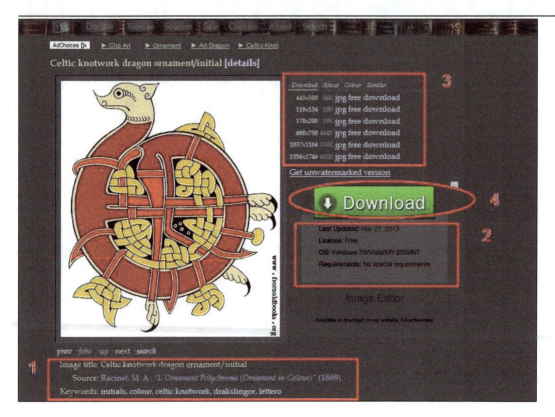

Here are the most important things to pay attention to when downloading an image like the one above (as numbered and highlighted):

1. Review the image title and the source. There is also copyright information below (not shown in the above screenshot) that you'll want to look over.
2. General requirements – review this to ensure it's OK to use this image.
3. Look at the different picture sizes available and choose the one you want.
4. Download the picture.

No registration is required. Simply find a picture you want according to the instructions above and download it.

e) HassleFreeClipArt

On the *HassleFreeClipArt.com* site www.hasslefreeclipart.com you can download clipart images in seconds - all for free.

Simply find a category you're interested in and follow it through to find that ideal image. Once you've found the image, view it then right click it and choose [*Save Image As*] from the dropdown menu. Use the search box in the upper right corner (as circled) or the categories on the left side.

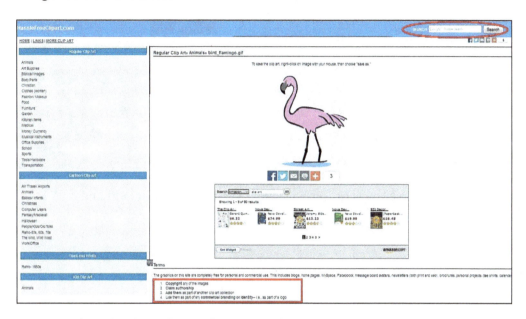

You may download any image for personal or commercial use. All *HassleFreeClipArt.com* asks is that you don't copyright the image or claim ownership of it. Also, you may not add them as another part of a clipart collection or incorporate one of them into a business logo.

f) Vector Portal

When searching for a free vector, or perhaps several of them, it is best to visit a website that specializes in them. *Vector Portal* www.vectorportal.com makes free stock vectors that creators or designers are allowed to use in commercial projects. Artists who want to present their works to Vector Portal's visitors do so as well. Vector Portal ranks within the top 10 vector sites chosen by graphic designers.

As shown above, there are five ways to find that ideal vector (as highlighted and numbered above):

1. Upper top menu
2. Lower top menu
3. The search box
4. The filter box
5. By category

Before downloading your first vector from this site, you'll want to make sure there is a file zipping program on your computer such as WinZip. Some of these pictures are so large that they come in.zip files. Once the.zip file has downloaded to your machine, you can then extract it and save it in the directory of your choice on your hard drive.

Once you find the image you're interested in, simply click the download button to the lower right of it. Suppose you wanted to download the *Funky Flower Vector Graphics* immediately below the filter search boxes (4). You would do so as shown in the picture below:

1. View the image as shown.
2. View the details to see if this is what you want.
3. Look at the tags (optional) to find others similar to this one.
4. Click the [*download*] button to download the vector.

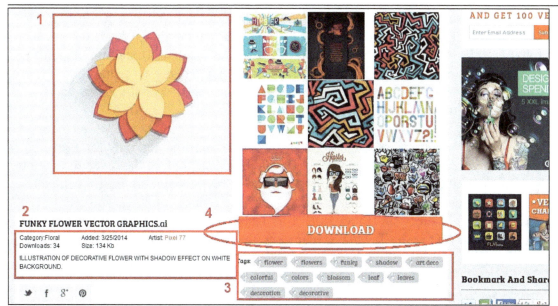

And that's all there is to it. No registration is required, but you can subscribe to receive 100 free vectors.

g) Public Domain Cliparts

www.public-domain-photos.com has over 8,000 free clipart images to choose from.

h) Animation Factory

www.animationfactory.com Over 500,000 animated clipart images, backgrounds, powerpoint templates, videos, sound effects, etc...

i) Open Clipart

www.openclipart.org A great collection of Creative Commons clipart.

2) Other Free ClipArt Sites

There are so many out there, in fact, too many to count. Many of them are straight-forward about offering free clipart images. All you need to do is get on their site and download them (some without even registering). Others ask that if you use an image, you provide a back link to their site. Some may offer free clipart images, but only from their limited, not-so-popular libraries.

Still, others require you to jump through hoops to find them. As for some, you may have to navigate through several menu choices. Others are promotional websites that lead you to pay sites like istockphoto.com, shutterstock.com, etc. Hence, you must read all content carefully when browsing these so-called "free clipart sites" and don't confuse the term *royalty free* with *free images*. Most of all, you must acknowledge their terms and conditions before registering with them. Free, quality images are not always easy to find and may require time and patience on your part.

Yet there is one other common catch. Some of these sites are free, but only for a seven day trial period. If you wish to try them out, just be sure to cancel before the seven days are up or else you automatically become a member. Just don't be too quick to leave a bank account or credit card number on any of these sites - not unless you are absolutely impressed with their selection. If they offer astonishingly superb images that no other site does, the choice is up to you. Try out as many sites as you can before you buy a membership.

Following is a list of some other clipart sites:

ClipArt Castle – www.clipartcastle.com

Diehard Images – www.diehardimages.com

Free-Graphics.com – www.free-graphics.com – right click and save.

FreeGraphics.org – www.freegraphics.org

Incredible Art Department - www.incredibleart.org also public domain images

Microsoft Free Clipart Downloads – www.free-clipart-pictures.net

MyCuteGraphics – www.mycutegraphics.com – right click and save.

ProDraw Graphics – www.prodraw.net – right click and save

Clipart - www.clipart.com 10,000.000 downloadable images. Payable: download up to 250 clipart images per week.

Chapter 12) Free Background Textures and Wallpaper Designs

Note: expect a lot of unwanted email in your inbox and advertising on your site if you use any of the following tools.

Sometimes people get tired of the same old wallpaper on their desktops or would rather post their content on something other than a plain white background. Before going out and buying a background design or wallpaper, it pays to look around at free sources. This chapter lists many sites that offer either or both.

Just like people love to decorate their homes, they love to personalise their computers or mobile devices. It's like giving their PCs, tablets, or phones a personality of their own. Others just get tired of seeing the same old background on their desktops or want to try something new. Therefore, background textures and wallpapers have become increasingly popular.

Likewise, website creators and owners like to acquire the most suitable backgrounds for their sites. Themes they choose usually complement the nature of their business or the theme of their blog. A great background convinces visitors and readers that a site owner is genuine and has made a great effort to attract people; likewise, their products, services, or blogs are of fine quality. Having a unique, well designed background implies that the site owner has a great imagination and really loves what he or she does. After all, it beats looking at icons or reading black print on a plain white background.

Background textures and wallpaper designs are offered for free on most sites that offer free images. However, their selection might be quite limited. If you're looking for something really distinctive, it is best to find the design (or picture) you plan to use from a site that specializes in wallpapers or textures. Hence, this chapter is devoted to sites where you can find them.

1) American Greetings

Although *American Greetings* www.americangreetings.com/downloads/wallpapers.pd mainly specialises in printable greeting cards, they offer a great variety of free wallpapers. If this is what you're looking for, it's quickest to go directly to the URL above instead of

their home page www.americangreetings.com.
Whether you use a Mac or PC, these designs can be installed on either platform. *American Greetings* offers many sizes in wallpapers including widescreen designs.

Their wallpapers work well, regardless of the resolution your monitor is set at (640x480, 800x600, 1024x768, 1280x1024 and 1600x1200). Before you can download a wallpaper picture, you must register with the site.

Registration is free, unless you want to become a member of their ecard program. This will enable you to print ecards throughout the year for any occasion and will also remind you of peoples' birthdays and anniversaries coming up so you won't miss a single one.

2) Desktop Nexus

Desktop Nexus www.desktopnexus.com is a community that incorporates technology enabling its members to interact and share real time feedback with photographers and artists. Visitors to this site can subscribe to RSS feeds and thus receive updates each time a new wallpaper image within their favorite categories has been added.

Every wallpaper design uploaded to this site is automatically cropped, resized, re-mastered, and stretched to fit the size of the downloaded customer's screen. This enables creators from around the globe to share their wallpapers via Desktop Nexus.

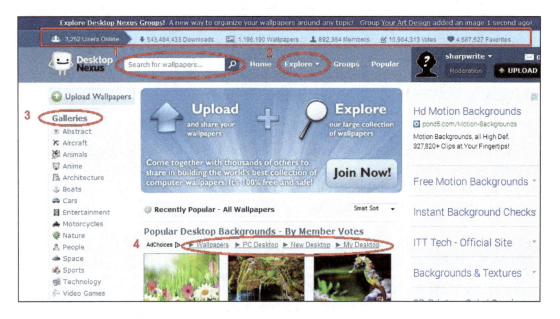

If you were to log onto this site, you can see how popular it is by the stats in the top row. Currently, Desktop Nexus has over 1.2 million wallpapers to choose from. Best of all, they are all free. To find that ideal desktop background for your computer, you can do one of four things:

1. Enter a keyword or phrase into the search box
2. Click *Explore* and choose a category
3. Select a category under the *Galleries* section
4. Browse through *Popular Desktop Backgrounds – By Member Votes* by selecting one of the four links: *Wallpapers, PC Desktop, New Desktop,* or *My Desktop.*

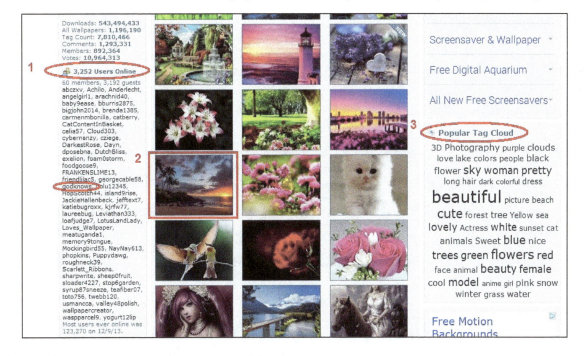

Still, there are three more ways to search for a great wallpaper scenes (as circled in the screenshots above):

1. By viewing the profiles of members currently online. Not only can you download a wallpaper design and take it away with you, but you can associate with members that are currently online, look over their profiles, and see what works they have contributed to date.
2. By scrolling up and down the page and looking at the middle section with pictures. All you need to do is double-click one you like to get a full sized image. If you're sure this is the one you want, choose a resolution size then right click it and select

[*Set As Desktop Background*]. For instance, you can view the member "godknows" by moving your mouse over his (her) listing and clicking it like you would a link.

3. If you're at a loss for words or the suggestions above don't seem to help, you can click a word in the [*Popular Tag Cloud*] box.

The sections directly above and below the Popular Tag Cloud box are simply referrals to other wallpaper, backgrounds, or screensavers online sites. Finally, the very bottom of this page has a [*Show More*] box to see more pictures and groupings of links to obtain site information, holiday wallpapers, recently active groups, and partner sites.

3) MyFreeWallpapers

If you are seeking a free wallpaper or background image but your interests are geared more towards movies, games, or music, www.myfreewallpapers.net is a great place to look.

The next two pictures show search options available on this site's home page:

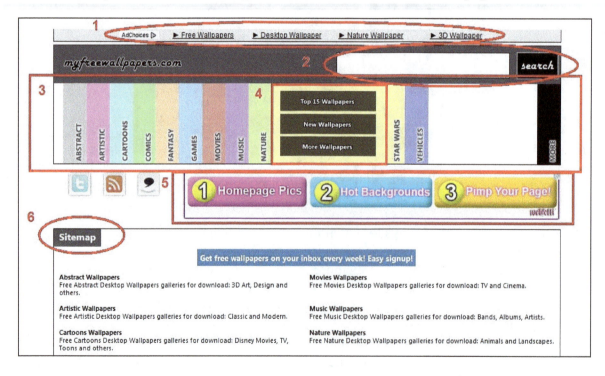

Here, you can search for that perfect wallpaper in the following ways (as circled and numbered in the two pictures immediately above):

1. In the *Ad Choices* menu: *Free Wallpapers, Desktop Wallpaper, Nature Wallpaper,* and *3D Wallpaper*.
2. Enter a keyword or phrase in the search box.
3. Choose a category in the colour menu above.
4. By choosing one of the buttons: *Top 15 Wallpapers, New Wallpapers,* or *More Wallpapers*.
5. From one of the three coloured buttons: *Homepage Pics, Hot Backgrounds,* or *Pimp Your Page*.
6. From one of the categories in the *Sitemap* section above.
7. From one of the categories in the myfreewallpapers.com (beige) box
8. From a link in the bottom menu (video game format wallpaper selections).

Once you find the picture that you'd love to have as a wallpaper, click on it to view the full image as shown below:

You will see three icons on the top right:
1. Share – the heart symbol picture
2. Email – email this picture to someone or even to yourself
3. Info – info about this wallpaper such as the link to share it, website and blogs reference link, and forum and boards URL.

That's all. Now you have a new wallpaper background, one you can't find anywhere else.

4) Wallpapers

If you love great outdoor scenes or like to change your wallpaper frequently to reflect the time of the year, visiting *Wallpapers.com* www.wallpapers.com is a must. They have some stunning wallpapers.

Below shows some nifty features about Wallpapers.com:

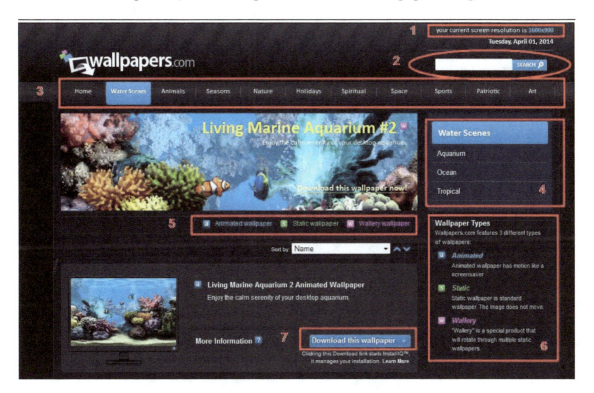

As you're looking for the ideal wallpaper to install on your system, there are seven features on this page you will want to pay close attention to:

1. **Your resolution size** – In the upper right corner, this site tells you the resolution size of your screen. This makes finding and downloading the correct wallpaper easy.
2. **Search box** – Enter a keyword or phrase that you want your design to be based on.
3. **Top menu** – Choose from their several categories: *Water Scenes, Animals, Seasons, Nature, Holidays, Spiritual, Space, Sports, Periodic,* and *Art.*
4. **Subcategories** – These are simply categories within the main category.
5. **Wallpaper types** – Choose from *animated, static,* or *wallery* types.
6. Same as (5) but explains types of wallpapers: A*nimated* wallpaper has continuous motion like a screensaver, a *static* wallpaper is a still picture, and a *wallery* wallpaper is like a slideshow of different static pictures.
7. **Download this wallpaper** – By clicking this button, the installation is started and managed accordingly. Also, several types of free software are offered during installation as Norton Security, Gameio, Free Ride Games, Yahoo Toolbar, WeatherBug, Smart PC Cleaner, and more. Watch your screen carefully and decline all the programs you don't want.

Although their selection may not seem so large, these pictures are unique and of high quality. If you become tired of the wallpaper you previously downloaded, you can change it. If you decide you don't want any of them, you can use their Uninstall feature at the bottom right of the screen (not shown).

5) WallpaperStock

www.wallpaperstock.net/downloads.html is yet another site with a great variety of wallpapers you can use for your desktop, tablet, or cell phone. Although they don't say how many they have, they certainly have lots of them. Using their site is quite self-intuitive.

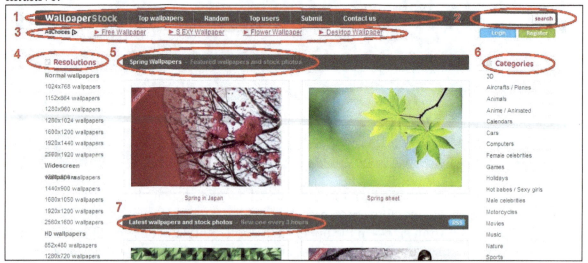

Finding a great wallpaper here is easy, especially with their many ways to search (as circled and numbered in the figure above):

1. WallpaperStock's top menu - *Top wallpapers* and *Random.* (Top Users, Submit, and Contact Us).
2. Search box – enter a keyword or phrase
3. *Ad Choices - Free Wallpaper, S EXY Wallpaper, Flower Wallpaper*, and *Desktop Wallpaper.*
4. Resolution – choose a specific size in *Normal wallpapers, Widescreen, HD wallpaper, Tablet*, or *Mobile.*
5. The top pictures section – usually reflects the time of the year.
6. Categories – as listed below
7. Latest wallpapers and stock photos

The categories of wallpapers are as follows: *3D, Aircrafts/Planes, Anime/Animated,*

Calendars, Cars, Computers, Female celebrities, Games, Holidays, Hot babes/Sexy girls, Male celebrities, Motorcycles, Movies, Music, Nature, Sports, TV shows, World, Other, Top votes, and *Top downloads*.

Once you have decided on a great image you want on your desktop, double-click on it and download it according to the instructions on the screen:

1. Save the file in the Downloads folder on your computer
2. Select that file and install it like you would any other application.

Within seconds, this new image will be your desktop background.

There is so much to see on this site, so take your time and browse. Checking out their other wallpapers will add to the personal experience of finding that perfect wallpaper.

6) WebShots

www.webshots.com You can download free High Definition wallpaper on this site. New photos are added every day.

7) In Summary

No longer do you need to look at the same wallpaper design throughout the usage life of your computer (unless you want to). You can change your desktop background as often as you wish, even if it's every day.

When it comes to free wallpapers, screen savers, and backgrounds, there are many sites out there that offer them. Likewise, nearly all of the sites listed throughout this book offer them as well. Simply type in a phrase like "free wallpapers" into your favorite search engine and numerous listings will appear. If you are looking for a wallpaper design for a portable device as a tablet or mobile phone, you will want to insert that type of device into your keyword phrase.

Many of these free wallpaper sites have ads on their pages for other services. Just be careful not to click on a link or use a search box that is designated for a pay service. Good luck and have fun!

Chapter 13) Audio and Video

Please remember that audio and video can take up a lot of space on your computer so if you don't have a lot of free space, make sure you purchase an external drive so you won't receive messages like: "sorry, hard drive full."

The use of audio and video files on your website can be a big help as videos are an extremely important aspect of online marketing these days. The copyright restrictions on these items are the same as with images and also as with images, currently the search engines do not penalise for duplicate video content. If you do use these items on your website do it carefully. Many users do not like music blaring out at them especially if they are browsing whilst at work. If you are using these items consider carefully if they will be on auto-play, and make sure that a mute button is easy to find in the top portion of your website.

If you will be creating your own products to sell, you might consider making and selling videos. Well, you don't need a penny to do so.

Making videos these days is super easy: most smart phones have video recording possibilities and very often, these videos are good enough quality to use on the web.

- You can upload your video free to www.youtube.com or to www.vimeo.com, two of the biggest video websites.

- On www.viralvideochart.com you can see a chart of the most popular viral videos. If your video is in the Top 10, you know you've done well!

Let's have a look at how you can produce your videos totally free.

1) Software For Audio and Video

While professional quality video software editing tools can cost a fortune, there are some very good ones that are free. In fact for most uses, you most likely already have a very good video editor that was pre-installed on your computer when you purchased it.

- Imovie (video editing software) comes pre-installed on Apple machines www.apple.com/mac/imovie

- Windows Movie Maker is also video editing software that is available on PC's.

www.windows.microsoft.com/en-us/windows/get-movie-maker-download

- Avidemux www.avidemux.sourceforge.net/ is an open source program that is designed for quick modifications. It gives a few additional features to the already installed programs.

- Ezvid www.ezvid.com is a very nice video package. Among its features is screen capture. You can create a video of what is happening on your screen and even do a voice over, either at the time of recording or later in the editing process.

- If you are a perfectionist and want everything perfect, then Lightworks www.lwks.com is your answer. A little more difficult to learn but it is Professional quality with a capital "P". The editors of movies such as "Notting Hill" with Julia Roberts, "Bruce Almighty" and "Evan Almighty", "Braveheart", "Pulp Fiction" and many more used this software to edit those movies.

- Audio editors are also widely available. Nero, which was one of the first companies to develop PC based audio equipment, has the Nero Wave Editor www.alternativeto.net/software/nero-waveeditor/about This free software can handle a wide range of tasks.

- Wavosaur www.wavosaur.com is a full feature audio program, that many users enjoy because of the ease of use.

- Powtoon www.powtoon.com An easy way of creating animated videos. Free and payable version available.

- A special mention here goes to Skype. Skype www.skype.com is a free computer-to-computer communication package. It allows a user to send text messages, audio calls and video conferencing. Most smart phones are also able to use Skype for free if they have a Internet connection. For a small charge, phone calls can be made to landlines and cell phones not capable of making the free calls.

Skype does not record audio or video calls, however, there are a number of third party apps that will record your calls.

- DVD video soft has a highly rated free program, www.dvdvideosoft.com/products/dvd/Free-Video-Call-Recorder-for-Skype.htm however be careful during the installation as it will want to add other programs.

- Supertintin www.supertintin.com is considered the best in the Skype forums. However its free version limits recording time to five minutes. The paid version does not have that limitation and it currently sells for $30 (£18)

- With Callgraph, which you can download from www.scribie.com/free-skype-recorder, you can record Skype conversations. Ideal if you want to record an interview and sell that as a product. This is only available for PC. I am not a Mac user so I cannot recommend a product for Mac. Just Google the subject.

- Audacity Audio software is an open source full audio package www.audacity.sourceforge.net. Suppose you have recorded an interview you've done with Skype, you can then edit the recording with Audacity e.g. cut bits out, add some royalty free music, add a slide with your website on, etc.. Audacity runs on a Mac and a PC.

- www.audio-tool.net is another free audio recorder

- Techradar www.techradar.com

- VirtualDub www.virtualdub.org

- Wistia www.wistia.com Global video delivery on any device, anywhere in the world. Free version available and payable version with lots more features.

a) Great payable video editing software and tools

- AudiAcrobat www.audioacrobat.com is a payable online tool to create audio and video.

I have used all these video editing software programs (all payable):

- Corel VideoStudio Pro

- Cyberlink PowerDirector

- Pinnacle Studio

- Magix Movie Edit pro

- Sony Movie Studio Platinum

- Sony Vegas Movie Studio

b) Autocue or teleprompter software

If you are going to record yourself e.g. with your mobile phone, and you are a little bit nervous that you are going to say the wrong thing, you can use auto cue software and let that run whilst you are speaking. This will prevent you from saying the wrong things. Simple let the script run on your computer (at your eye-level) and read it whilst you are speaking. You will have to practise a little bit first to make sure that you don't look as if you are reading it from a screen, that will look unnatural for the person watching your video. Newsreaders all use a teleprompter and so do a lot of speakers and presenters. Free auto cue software:

EasyPrompter: www.easyprompter.com
CuePrompter www.cueprompter.com

c) Converting videos

Once you've done your video, you will, very often, need to convert it to different formats.

- Handbrake www.handbrake.fr Handbrake is perfect and is free. You can download it and convert almost any video format to almost any other video format.

- YouConvertit www.youconvertit.com is a free online tool where you can convert almost any media type to different formats e.g. documents, images, audio, video, etc...

- Zamzar www.zamzar.com is another free online tool to convert from one file type to another e.g. images, documents, videos, etc...

d) Burning CD and DVDs

- CDburner from www.cdburnerxp.se
CDBurnerXP is a **free** application to burn CDs and DVDs, including Blu-Ray and HD-DVDs. It also includes the feature to burn and create ISOs, as well as a multi language interface. Everyone can use it for free. It does not include adware or similar malicious components. Only for Windows.

- CDburner from www.discoapp.com is also free and is for Mac users.

e) Webinars

In case you want to hold a webinar but don't have the funds to pay for the expensive well known www.GoToWebinar.com, you can use AnyMeeting. Find it on www.anymeeting.com. They have free options, of course, with limitations such as a maximum of 200 attendees.

f) Voices

You don't like your own voice? Get some else to do a voice over at www.voices.com or www.voice123.com (payable).

2) Free Resources

There are two basic ways to consider audio and video content for your website. It is either hosted on your site or embedded. Embedded video is the manner that sites like You tube www.youtube.com uses. The video file stays on their server and you have no means to edit it.

Embedding is also the way news organisations such as

- Market news Video www.marketnewsvideo.com/embed

- Reuters www.reuters.com/tools/rss

- ABC news http://embed.ly/embed/features/provider/abcnews

use to present updated news on their website. In addition to the items just mentioned and the sources listed for free content, there are other places to look.

- Hulu www.hulu.com is a great source for movie trailers and television programs. Only available for people in the USA. You need to be careful when you select your clips that it is available in the region your target audience is located.

- Archive www.archive.org is a huge source of video and audio files: over 125,000 concerts as an example. While not all the content is free to use, the audio section has over 150,000 files in its Creative Commons and public domain archives. Generally you will have to download these files and host them on your site.

- MusicBakery www.musicbakery.com Great place to download royalty free music. They have free clips and payable ones.

3) Screen Capture Software

As an Internet Marketer, you might want to record what you are doing on your computer, in other words: record your screen. Screen Capture Software is what you need.

- AwesomeScreenshots www.awesomescreenshots.com lets you capture your page or part of it and annotate it with arrows, text, etc.... You can use this screenshot to insert in a video.

- Jing is screen capture software and you can download it free from www.techsmith.com/jing.html. You can make short videos of 5 minutes or less. If you need longer videos, you can just record 3 videos of 5 minutes and then put them together with Audacity, to make a 15 minute video.

- www.camstudio.org Not to be confused with Camtasia Studio, CamStudio is an open source video screen capture software application. Camstudio is able to record all screen and audio activity on your computer and create industry-standard AVI video files and, using its built-in SWF Producer, can turn those AVIs into lean, mean, bandwidth-friendly

Streaming Flash videos (SWFs)

- ScreenCastOMatic is downloadable free from www.screencast-o-matic.com. It is screen capture software. You can record and save the file as MP4, avi or other video formats. Your video can be up to 15 minutes long but you can't edit the files. For only $15 - £9 per YEAR, you can get the Pro version. That is as good as free!

- www.smallvideosoft.com/screen-video-capture is easy-to-use software for PC or Mac.

- A brilliant payable version to record your screen is Camtasia, which you can download from www.techsmith.com/camtasia.htm l. All my videos in www.WorldwideSelfPublishing.com are recorded with Camtasia.

- You can also use www.jingproject.com which lets you record five minutes maximum for a video. If you need 20 minutes of video you can record four videos of five minutes. This is free of charge.

TOP TIPS (but payable options):

-To avoid people stealing or copying videos from your site, you can use www.viddler.com to store your videos. People can then only see the video on the domain name that you tell them. The visitor will not be able to download the video from that domain name.

-Other interesting sites that you can use for storage services for your videos are:
www.EZS3.com
www.aws.amazon.com/s3/

- With www.EasyVideoPlayer.com you can upload and store your videos without having to deal with the complicated Amazon S3 storage. All you need is an account with Amazon S3 and EasyVideoPlayer will upload the video automatically to your Amazon S3 account. Amazon S3 is not free but it is as good as free as you pay about $10 (£6) per month to get thousands of people watching your videos.

Once you have finished a video, you can upload it to video sites in order to get traffic. ALWAYS use your keywords in the title and description when submitting a video.

The best video sites to upload your videos to are (some are payable):

- AOL – www.on.aol.com
- Google Video – www.video.google.com
- Viddler - www.viddler.com
- Ustream - www.ustream.tv
- YouTube - www.youtube.com
- Brightcove – www.brightcove.com
- Buzznet – www.buzznet.com
- Daily Motion - www.dailymotion.com
- Dropshots – www.dropshots.com
- Fark – www.fark.com/video
- Flixya – www.flixya.com
- Screenjunkies – www.screenjunkies.com
- Jibjab - www.jibjab.com
- Liveleak – www.liveleak.com
- Metacafe – www.metacafe.com
- Vimeo – www.vimeo.com

TOP TIP: When you submit videos to video websites, make sure to give them keywords. If you upload the same video to several sites (with the same video description), the search engines will look at this as duplicate content. What you can do to avoid this and to make every video unique is the following:

- Give the video a different title. So if you are uploading to three videos sites, give each video a different title.

- Make each video you are uploading a few seconds shorter or longer by inserting some extra slides or extra music. One of the criteria that Google looks at to decide if the video is duplicate content is the duration of the video. If one video is 10 min 20 seconds and the other video is 10 min 30 seconds, Google will think it is a different video, certainly when it also has a different title.

This is extra work, but well worth it.

- Tube Mogul - www.tubemogul.com Sign up here to have all your videos automatically uploaded to up to 20 video hosting sites all at once.

- A word of warning about the payable video submission Senuke:

www.senuke.com "It is Complete & Utter Search Engine Domination. Period. It is the Most Powerful SEO Automation Software Ever." These are their words, not mine. But it is indeed powerful stuff for getting traffic. The downside is that it costs $147 (£88) per month. There is a $67 (£40) per month version (SEnuke X Lite) that only does Niche Research and Social Network Submission, which in my opinion is not worth getting at all. If you have the money; pay for the full version and see if you like it. You have 14 days to try it free.

A big advantage of SEnuke is that you do not need a website, you can just promote an affiliate link hoping that it will be picked up by people. You can also generate your affiliate link from within SEnuke.

They submit videos to video sites, social networking sites, social bookmarking sites, RSS feed sites and more.

How does it work? You fill in your name, nickname and email and Senuke submits your article, video, and so on to all the sites. You do not even have to create an account with all the different sites as Senuke does this for you.

SEnuke is great and the software does work but as usual there are a few things to know:

- Although they submit to article sites, this is not their strength. All articles will be exactly the same, so considered duplicate content.
- If you do not learn how to use SEnuke properly, you will spam the sites to death and nobody will take any notice, including Google. You will have to become a SEnuke expert and get to grips with all the functions otherwise more harm than good can be done.
- The biggest problem with SEnuke is:
  - o All the accounts will be created on the same day.
  - o The time of the creation of the accounts will all be approximately the same.
  - o The dates of the submission will all be within a day or a few days.

These three problems will immediately raise three red flags for Google and your work will have zero results in the search engines.

The solution for this is to pick some accounts for submission today and pick a few other accounts tomorrow. You could also set up new accounts every week and spin the name and title but then is there any point paying $147 (£88) per month if you have to do it all the non-automated way, while you pay for automation?

In case of video submission: you can try to fool Google by giving each video that you submit a different title, so Google thinks each video is different. However, the automation aspect has no value in this case as you'll have to give a new title, submit to one video site, give a second video a different title and submit it to another video site, give the third video, you will have to do this for 30 sites. You might as well set up an account with all 30 sites and submit the video yourself.

Whatever you do with SEnuke, you have to remember that the automated publishing will never contain unique content, as the same stuff will be published to all sites and you know by now that Google likes unique content. **If you are in a niche with very low competition, SEnuke can work.**

Conclusion: SEnuke is excellent if you want to get traffic to your sites or affiliate links, hoping that people will find them all over the web. But if you want to rank in Google, it's not the best.

A few more tools:

- Myliveactor www.myliveactor.com An actor will create your video

For video making sites:
- www.audacity.sourceforge.net free audio editing
- www.videomaker.com/youtube/

4) Make a Video Totally for Free

- Splasheo www.splasheo.com Creates videos, fast and easy. Free download.

TOP TIP: Try this out – making a video has never been easier. You can use this method for any videos you want to make. EVERYTHING is free including all the software you will use to make the video.

Here is a step-by-step guide on how to make your own video completely free by using free pictures, free articles and free video making software.

First step: Go to www.freeimages.com and save some royalty-free pictures regarding your niche on your hard drive. For example, if your niche is about controlling your panic attack, you can save pictures about somebody who is angry and somebody who is calm.

Second step: Go to www.gimp.org and download it free. Import the picture(s) and right-click on the picture to save it as a 700 width picture, which is a good size. Tick auto scale. **Third step:** Get a PLR article regarding your niche or write a short article yourself. The latter is the better option.

Fourth step: Download Audacity: www.audacity.sourceforge.net. With Audacity you will read the article and record your voice whilst you read it.

Fifth step: Open Windows Movie Maker which you should have on your PC if you are using Windows. If not, download it. In Windows Movie Maker you can import pictures, put your voice that you have recorded over the pictures and leave your website domain name at the bottom of the video. Save the video when ready.

Sixth step: Submit your video to the sites listed under "free traffic from video marketing" ALWAYS use your keywords in the title and description when submitting a video.

5) Free and Low Cost Videos for Re-use

If you're looking for videos that you can use at little or no cost, this section lists sources on where to find them. Considering how hard it is to make video footage for your website, especially if you lack the skills and a quality video camera or camcorder, you may want to resort reusing others' videos. Just like images, there are numerous videographers who like to share their works, providing you agree to publish a link in your creation that leads viewers back to their site.

a) Archive.Org

www.archive.org. I have already mentioned this site but not for videos. Based in San Francisco, the Archive was founded in 1996 and has grown thanks to donations from the Alexa Internet and other agencies. *Archive.Org* is a non-profit, large Internet library offering texts, videos, audio clips, moving images, and software for free download. With this permanent access service, historians, researchers, teachers, students, individuals with disabilities, and the general public have access to historical collections that have been reserved in digital format.

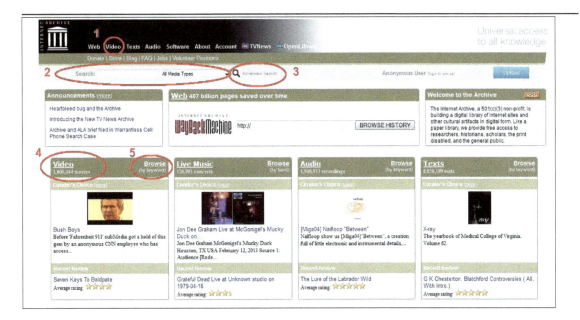

When searching for a video, there are key factors to pay attention to:
1. The *Video* selection in the top menu which brings up video listings only
2. The search box and categories dropdown menu
3. The *Advanced Search* function where you can find videos based on search parameters
4. The *Video* section which brings up video categories (same as 1)
5. The *Browse* link which brings up icons and listings of numerous companies and subjects that lead to videos

Click the *All Media Types* dropdown menu button to find the following categories: *Animation & Cartoons, Arts & Music, Community Video, Computers & Technology, Cultural & Academic Films, Ephemeral Films, Movies, News & Public Affairs, Prelinger Archives, Spirituality & Religion, Sports Videos, Television, Videogame Videos, Vlogs*, and *Youth Media*. These categories can be viewed in more detail by the Video heading (1 or 4) in the above picture.

In the *Advanced Search* screen (3), there are several criteria which you can input to find only the videos you want. You can use one or more of the following: *Title, Creator, Description, Collection, Media Type, Date*, and *Date Range*. There are also three custom fields where you can choose additional criterion. See the section below:

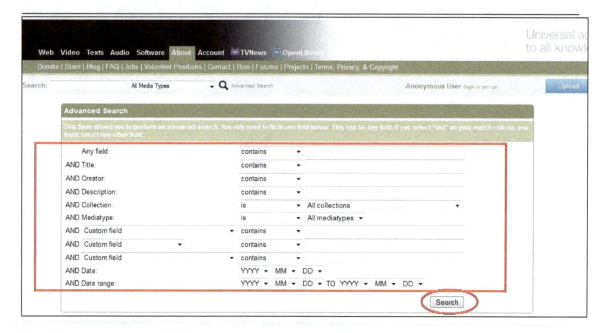

Fill in one or a combination of fields to find only the videos you want. More sections appear on this page, each is pretty much self-explanatory.

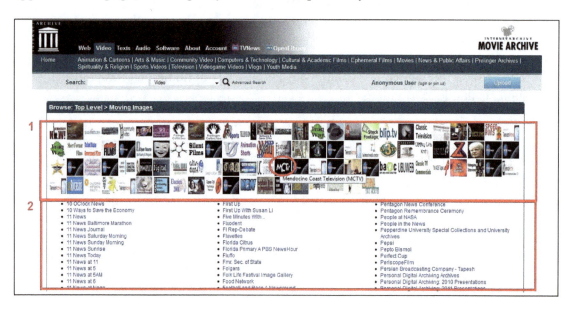

The top section (1) of the above page is icons for various news broadcasters or TV channels. Slowly move the mouse over them and a tool tip will appear indicating what each one is. Hence, the 14th picture in the third row is MCTV or Mendocino Coast Television (MCTV). Section 2 is specific listings where videos can be found. Scroll down and you'll see hundreds of listings on this page.

Once you know the ropes (which are quite simple) of navigating Archive.Org, your next steps are to find a video and download it. The following screenshot shows a bird's eye view of the downloading page:

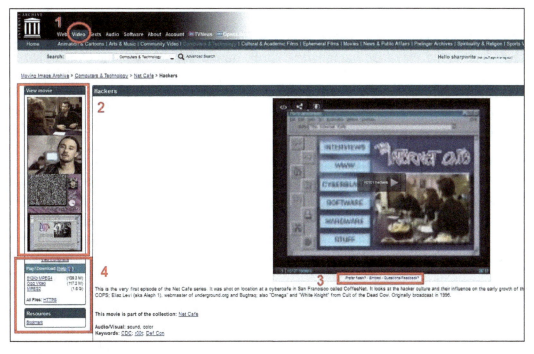

Just pay attention to these details before downloading:
1. Make sure you're in the VIDEO section to ensure what you're about to download is a video.
2. View the thumbnails in the video, which are still frames taken from it. Below it is a link that says *view thumbnails*.
3. Look at the links directly below the video: *Prefer flash? / Embed / Questions/Feedback?* The Prefer flash link is simply a toggle between flash and HTML5. If you want to use Flash, click on it and it will say Prefer HTML5 or vice-versa. This link works just like an Enable / Disable button on your browser.
4. On the left, you'll find the *Play / Download (help?)* box. Personally, I think they could have made this larger and/or easier to find. Since it's so small and too far off to the side, you may want to view the magnified picture below:

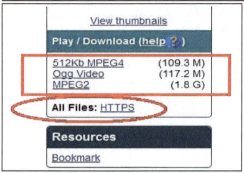

Instead of downloading a single or default file type, you can choose from whatever formats are listed in the Play / Download box. In the above example you have three choices:

512kb MPEG4	(109.3 M)
Ogg Video	(117.2 M)
MPEG2	(1.8 G)

This, of course allows you three file format choices (for the video entitled "Hackers"). It specifies the three file types and the storage requirements or space they'll take up on your hard drive (*M* means megabytes and *G* means gigabytes). Apparently, the one that takes the most space has the highest quality, but what you choose to download is a matter of personal preference. For some, quality is extremely important and they have lots of hard drive space, while for others, they just want the video and hope they have the room store it on their portable device. File types and sizes available may vary among different videos, especially considering each one's time length.

Finally, the *All Files*: HTTPS link simply provides a list of all files which compose the video in their format. Choosing this option is only necessary for computer geeks or those who only want to use only some of its file, say for picture, but not sound.

Registration is free and their selection is large.

b) BottledVideo

www.BottledVideo.Com: *Free Footage for the Masses* is a promotional site created by an individual who has prospered selling video footage in the past. This site is merely a 100% free stock footage source to offer students and amateur videographers material for their projects.

Below is a "bird eye's view" of their home page:

Finding the ideal video on this site may take some time and patience as their video organisation system is something to be desired. However, they have a few tools as highlighted above:

1. The Video, Categories, and Site Info menu along the top
2. The search box directly below (1)
3. The row of buttons in the middle of the page which are: *Most downloaded, Featured, Most popular, Random*, and *Random*

In reality, there are no categories. It's just that the videos are arranged in alphabetical order according to title. Also, all videos are watermarked until downloaded.

Once you find the video you want, double-click on it. If you want the free version, make sure to click on the appropriate radio selection, then click [*Add to Cart*]. However, be sure this is the one you want since you cannot verify the title of it at this point. All you see is their crypic digital code for the picture (HD197-119 as in the above example).

Note, their free stock footage is not HD quality or 16*9 format. All their free videos are simply 640*480 crop versions of their HD masters. All 16*9 midrange are $15 (£9) each and full HD clips are sold at $25 (£15) a clip.

Still, this is a great resource for videos if you don't mind hunting and pecking. Registration is free, but they will ask for your full name, complete address, and website you're using. After all, their mission is to help promote you, as you help promote them.

c) Market News Video

One way to help bring visitors to your website is through using free videos from *Market News Video* www.marketnewsvideo.com. This site strives to create and distribute quality videos pertaining to the stock markets and publicly traded companies. Although their videos are free, there are advertisements linked to them which cannot be removed. Hence, their revenue is generated through sales of their advertisements and licensing fees.

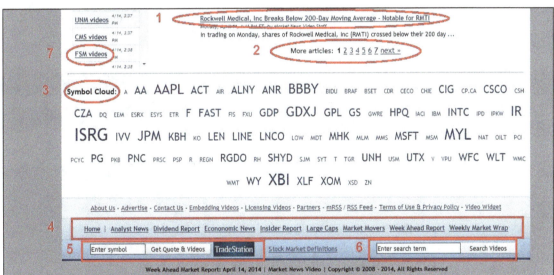

As circled in the illustration above, there are seven ways to locate the video(s) you wish to embed on your site:

1. Choose a video by clicking on its title.
2. Browse the pages of videos this site has to offer.
3. Select a [*Symbol Cloud*] tag.
4. Pick a category from the highlighted menu.

5. Search for a video by symbol.
6. Enter search terms in their search box
7. Choose a category link from the left scrollable section.

Options 4 – 6 are also available at the top of Market News Video's home page. Assuming you already have your own website, you can embed their videos into it by visiting their embedding link at www.marketnewsvideo.com/embed. This can be done by utilizing their RSS feeds or their video widget. Likewise, you can copy and paste a simple snippet of HTML code as found on the page of the above link.
For licensing details, see their page: www.marketnewsvideo.com/licensing

d) Stock Footage for Free

As for finding a large library of free video footage from producers around the globe, nothing says it more than its name www.stockfootageforfree.com. These works are royalty-free and can also be used for commercial purposes. And there are never any fees, EVER! No fees, no catch, unlimited downloads, as advertised on their site.

To view additional videos, either choose *FREE STOCK FOOTAGE* from the menu above or insert a keyword word or phrase in the search box on the right (both are circled).

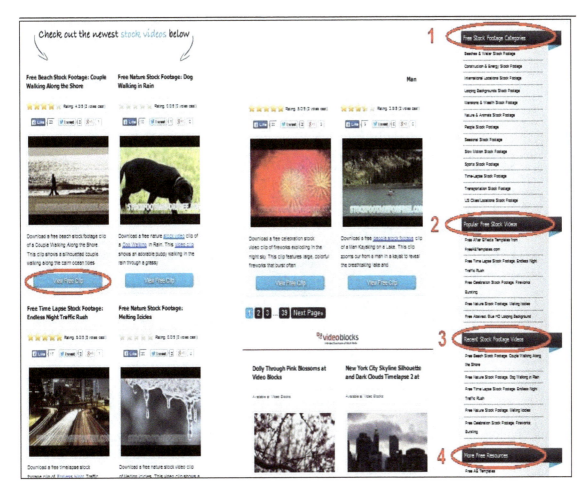

Scroll down and you can find lots of videos including their latest arrivals. However, if none on this page interest you, you may want to browse the menus and categories on the right. The menus are as follows: (1) *Free Stock Footage Categories*, (2) *Popular Free Stock Videos,* (3) *Recent Stock Footage Videos*, and (4) *More Free Resources.*

Once you find a video you're interested in, click on the button *View Free Clip* (see the example circled on the left in the above picture). Suppose we selected the *Free Beach Stock Footage: Couple Walking Along the Shore* picture as shown below:

Before downloading it, you may want to watch it. Click either circled arrow to play it. If you're happy, click the [*DOWNLOAD*] button below and it will be saved onto your computer.

e) Videezy

Professional and novice videographers can meet and share videos in the *Videezy* community www.videezy.com. They have video clips, background loops, music tracks and sound effects. Currently they offer over four million video clips to use. If you happen to be a videographer yourself, you may share your b-roll, backgrounds and miscellaneous video creations with the world. By doing this, you can promote yourself as well. Some videos are available for free downloading, but for some, licensing requirements apply before you can use them on your website or creation. You have seven days of free downloads.

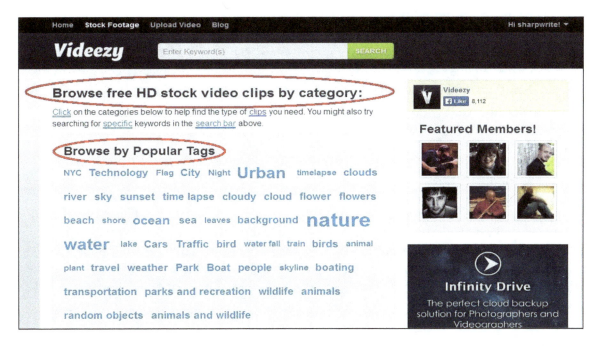

There are five ways to find **free** videos on Videezy:
1. Do a keyword search in the search box at the top of any Videezy page.
2. Scroll through the top section: *Feature Free HD Stock Video Footage* section (top of home page).
3. Scroll down the *Newest Videos Uploaded* section towards the middle of their home page
4. On the *Stock Footage* page, choose a tag in the *Browse by Popular Tags* section (shown in the third from the top picture).
5. On the *Stock Footage* page, scroll through the Browse by *Vendor Category* section.

The categories in the last section are as follow: *Abstract, Animals and Wildlife, Archive Footage, Arts and Culture, Backgrounds, Clouds, Elements and Effects, Fire and Smoke, Food and Drink, Industry, Music Related, Nature, People, Random Objects, Sports, Technology, Time Lapse, Transportation, Travel, Urban,* and *Water*.
Finally, once you've located the video you want, double-click on it and follow the simple downloading instructions.

f) Videvo

With its "no strings attached" policy, videvo www.videvo.net has become one of the most prominent resources for free video footage and motion graphics. As of this writing, they have 1300 HD clips and are adding new ones on a weekly basis. Since its creation in 2012, this Oxford, UK based site has grown quite rapidly to a point where it is one of the largest HD free stock sites on the web today. Their footage can be used for commercial purposes too.

Searching for that ideal video can be done in the following ways:

1. By choosing *BROWSE, FOOTAGE*, or *MOTION GRAPHICS* in the top menu
2. By inserting a keyword or phrase in the search box to the right
3. By choosing a category from the menu immediately below (1). Its categories are as follows: *Animals, Food and Drink, Industry, Medical, Music, Nature, People, Production, Space, Sport,* or *VFX.*

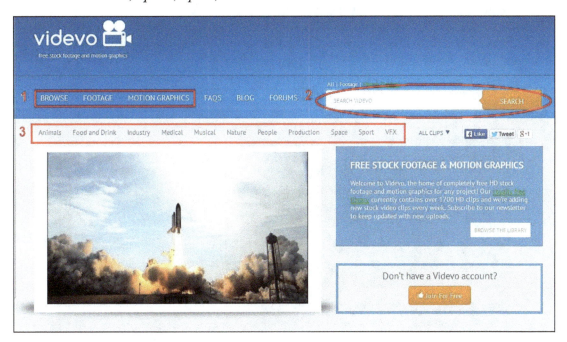

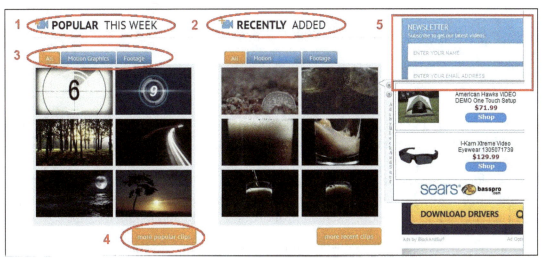

Likewise, you can search for your video in other ways:
1. Under the *POPULAR THIS WEEK* section
2. Under the *RECENTLY ADDED* section
3. By choosing *ALL, Motion Graphics*, or *Footage* to filter your search
4. By viewing *more popular clips* under either section

Also, on the right (5) you can subscribe to get updates on new videos as they're uploaded onto this site.

Once you have found the video you would like to use, download it according to your video downloader's instructions. See the picture below:

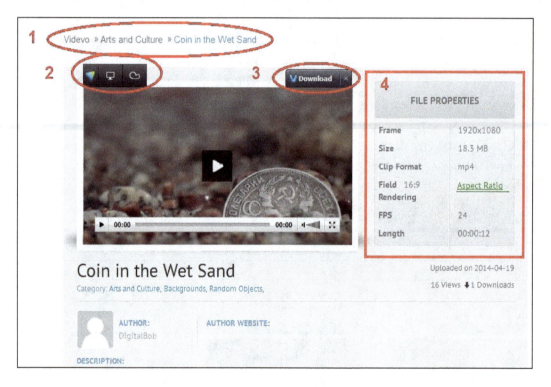

Before you download a video, observe the following:
1. Its title and category and subcategories (which also appears below the video)
2. Options such as playing, sharing, etc.
3. The video downloader's *Download* button
4. But most of all, the file properties such as the frame size, storage size, clip format (file type), *Field Rendering* (screen proportions), FPS, and length of clip.

Finally, joining is free and they require the minimal amount of information, such as your name, email address, username, and password.

g) Jamendo

www.jamendo.com is the world's largest free music library or at least that's what they say. You can listen, download and share music.

h) CCMixter

www.ccmixter.org Files to download under Creative Commons license.

i) SoundCloud

www.soundcloud.com With over 40,000,000 registered users, this is a great site that allows its users to upload, share, promote and download music files.

j) Videoblocks

On www.videoblocks.com you can find a large selection of royalty free videos.

k) Hulu

On www.hulu.com you can also find free videos to embed into your site. Make sure to check out the rules.

l) FreeSound

www.freesound.org Thousands of sounds, all under Creative Commons License.

m) Free-Loops

www.free-loops.com 7000 free sounds, drum loops, instruments and more.

n) Search Engine for Media files

You can search for CC licensed media e.g. audio, videos, books, etc..

www.freebase.com

o) Payable stock videos

 A lot of the payable stock photo sites also have videos. Simply type in your keyword and select videos. Most of the videos are fairly expensive though. Here are a few payable video sites:

www.alamy.com

www.pond5.com

www.istockphoto.com

www.videohive.net Over 95,000 royalty free videos to download

www.graphicriver.net

www.fotalia.com

www.dreamstime.com

www.photospin.com

www.revostock.com

www.gettyimages.co.uk

www.shutterstock.com

www.123rf.com

www.fotosearch.com

www.canstockphoto.com

www.depositphotos.com

www.stockvault.com

Of course you can always embed videos from www.youtube.com on your blog or website.

Chapter 14) Marketing Support Tools and Varia Tools

There are a number of tools that can be built into your website that will help your marketing effort.

1) Auto Responder and Bulk Mailers

The money is in the list! You've heard it before. You can indeed earn money by building a list but with auto responders like

- www.aweber.com

- www.icontact.com

- www.getresponse.com

and others, there is a monthly fee. You want to avoid that in the beginning of your Internet Marketing venture.

There are few free auto responders as far as I know and even fewer free ones that are worth the risk of using. Here are a few good free ones:

- Livewire at www.livewire.com is one program that should meet all of your needs.

- MailChimp at www.mailchimp.com is another outstanding program. You can send 12,000 emails to 2,000 subscribers free. No contract, no credit card required. You can expand your email list with their payable options. One slight negative: each email that you send to your subscribers will contain a small advertisement from MailChimp at the bottom.

- Imminica Mail www.imnicamail.com is free up to 1000 subscribers and a maximum of 6000 emails per month.

- Listwire www.listwire.com There are no fees with Listwire, however many subscribers you have. They also insert a small ad at the bottom of each email that you send to your subscribers.

- BananaTag www.bananatag.com lets you find out what happens to your emails after you've sent them e.g. when was the email opened? who opened it? was it opened from a mobile phone or a desktop PC? etc... Works perfect with Outlook and Gmail. They have a free version and a payable one.

2) File Storage, Back Ups and Transfers

Things are changing rapidly in the file transfer arena. A few years ago there were many companies offer these services either free or for a fee. Today that number is dropping mostly because of cloud storage.

- One site that is left that does the file transfer service is We Transfer www.wetransfer.com. This service allows you to transfer files up to 2gb for free. You can upload them and have them available for a limited time e.g. for others to download. There is no limit on how many files you can upload.

Some say it is always a good idea to back up your files to the cloud, just in case your computer crashes or totally packs up. I am not personally a big fan of this as I rather store MY files on MY computer, not somewhere in the clouds.

Often called cloud storage, you are able to access all the files you upload from any Internet connection. They also have the ability to share folders if you wish. While there are many providers, some of the leading providers are:

- Google drive www.google.com/intl/en/drive

- Dropbox www.dropbox.com

Google Drive and DropBox are free and you can share folders. Using a share folder you can make files available at any time. In Dropbox each time you add a share folder for someone who is not already a Dropbox user you will get extra storage when they register. Both of these services also work well on mobile devices. You can back up photographs you take on your cell phone if you wish.

- Box www.box.com

All these have a limited of free storage but you can store unlimited amount of items if you use their payable services.

3) Chat Software for Customer Support

Live customer service by online chat is a double edged sword, something you should think about carefully before doing. Depending on the focus of your business, customers will expect a certain number of hours of availability each week. Anything less than 12 hours a day, 6 days a week and you will be looked upon as unreliable. Not be online when your site says you will be and people will think you are a scam artist. A number of companies offer excellent customer support chat software for free for a limited number of users.

Many times this is the same program that large companies pay thousands of dollars for. You will come across the terms "seat" and "user". They are different ways to count customer service use. A seat is someone logged in: you could have a limit of 3 seats but have 10 users. Only 3 could be logged in at a time. Others go by users, if you have three users then if you are covering 24 hours you only have one at a time.

More and more people prefer to chat live rather than waiting for a response to their email.

- Purechat www.purechat.com is a completely free program with a unlimited number of users.

- Livezilla is a chat system and a ticket tracker, www.livezilla.net, it allows one free operator.

- EtalkUp www.crunchbase.com/organisation/etalkup Restricted users allowed for the free version. The free version doesn't have the full visitor tracking feature.

4) Trouble Ticket Management

You should have a system to keep track of incoming customer support issues.

- Freecrm www.freecrm.com provides five users

- Freshdesk www.freshdesk.com allows three users for ticket management and email support.

- Osticket www.osticket.com offers free software to host on your server with unlimited use.

5) Raffle Management

Running a raffle or giveaway contest can be very time consuming. The easiest free software to use to help manage raffles is Rafflecopter www.rafflecopter.com

6) Competitive Analysis Tools

Checking on how your competition is doing things can help keep you on track. There are many excellent tools out there but most are very expensive.

- A few have free versions that will provide you with some basic data. Majestic SEO is a good program, with a limited free version that gives a good deal of data. Check their website at www.majesticseo.com

- LXR Marketplace has a few free tools that can be used www.lxrmarketplace.com/seo-competitor-analysis-tool.html

- Ahrefs has two tools that are some of the best available, they have a free version www.ahrefs.com and they also have a plug in for Firefox browsers.

- Open Site Explorer from SEOMoz, allows you to compare the SEO of different sites. www.moz.com/researchtools/ose

7) Other Free Varia Tools

- www.7-zip.org a free alternative to WinZip to zip your files

- View and print PDF files: www.get.adobe.com/reader

- Allow your PC to run faster by cleaning up: www.piriform.com/ccleaner

- Free Open Source FTP program www.filezilla-project.org

- www.shortkeys.com Set up replacement text for any user defined keystrokes

- Free Mindmapping software: www.freemind.sourceforge.net

- Evernote www.evernote.com Brilliant tool for taking notes

- Toggl www.toggl.com is a free time tracking tool. They have a free and a payable version at $5 (£3) per month.

- UptimeRobot www.uptimerobot.com You can be notified when your site goes down. This is a free service.

- Which Test Won www.whichtestwon.com ideal to test your marketing knowledge. See if you know which versions performed best.

I have already mentioned these two next tools under the video chapter but as these tools can be used for all different types of files, I am mentioning them here again.

- YouConvertit www.youconvertit.com is a free online tool where you can convert almost any media type to different formats e.g. documents, images, audio, video, etc...

- Zamzar www.zamzar.com is another free online tool to convert from one file type to another e.g. images, documents, videos, etc...

- Remember The Milk www.rememberthemilk.com This site will send you email reminders. Also available as an app.

- GetPocket www.getpocket.com Put anything in Pocket if you want to view it later. You can view it on your tablet, computer or phone. Over 11 million users. Get it, it's free!

URL-shortening services or link-cloaking software
Sometimes an affiliate link is so long and looks so unattractive that you might want to shorten it before sending it to potential customers. That's what URL-shortening means.

You can get from this URL:

www.amazon.co.uk/Head-Ti-S6-Titanium-Tennis-Racket/dp/B001DMKZSQ/ref=sr_1_2?s=sports&ie=UTF8&qid=1294687755&sr

To this URL:
www.tennis-racket/Tintanium When people click on this they will be re-directed to the Amazon website as shown above with your affiliate link.

Here are two URL-shortening websites:
www.bitly.com
www.tinyurl.com
www.tiny.cc
www.snurl.com
www.bit.do
www.tinypic.com You can upload images and create a shortening url for those images.

Make sure that you read the terms and conditions as some of these websites will automatically delete your URL if it's not used or clicked on for a certain number of days.

Chapter 15) Setting Up an Online Store and Taking Payments

More and more shops appear online daily. Virtually anything can be bought online. In case you want to build an online shop, rather than a website, I am covering an online store briefly.

Using third party services is the easiest way. Third party companies handle all the billing for you. You can also get your own merchant account. The problem with the latter is this will create monthly expenses so I won't talk about them in this book as this book is about free resources.

I explain eCommerce in more detail in my book "Drop Shipping and eCommerce" so I am only very briefly going to touch this subject in this book. If you are interested in running an online store, get yourself a copy. I admit in the book that it is not easy and it is time consuming, but if done correctly, you can earn a lot of money with it.

Building an online store can be simplified in these few steps:

- Find a niche

- Find products to sell either as an affiliate, as a drop shipper or stock the products

- Get a domain name

- Get hosting

- Decide on payment options for your customers: third party or your own merchant account

- Design your store

- Send traffic

Here are some free options:

- Use Paypal as your payment processor. Paypal doesn't charge a monthly fee but charges you a percentage on each transaction amount plus a small fee per transaction. So in a way, this is free as you are only charged if you have sold something, that means your charges will be deducted from your profit. Paypal is ideal to start with but also has many disadvantages. My Drop Shipping book explains all this very well in some detail. It simply is too much to explain here.

- www.easydigitaldownloads.com is a free Wordpress Plugin that lets you sell digital downloads via your Wordpress site. You can sell your own downloads without spending any money.

- Create an eBay store.

- Create an Amazon store. Amazon will take care of charging your customer.

- www.2checkout.com is a great company to deal with. They do charge a very small set-up fee but no monthly charge.

- A great payable option for a store is www.ekmpowershop.com or www.ekmpowershop.co.uk. They do charge a very low monthly fee and you will need your own merchant account.

- A totally free way to create a store is to put products on your store, all with affiliate links. That way, all you need is a domain name and hosting and all the rest is done for you. All you need to do is find affiliate products to sell.

- For UK readers: on www.boutiquelocal.co.uk you can set up a free store. The only cost here is that you pay 10% commission on each sale. Boutique Local has teamed up with Paypal. This is proof that they must be reliable, otherwise Paypal wouldn't team up with them. You do need a Paypal account.

Unfortunately I do not know of any completely free way to set up a professional store. Hence the reason why I don't write in detail about it in this book. Most companies that will create a free store for you, will ask you to sign up for their hosting so you will create monthly expenses that way.

Here are some sites that claim that you can build a free store. I have not used any of these and I suspect that there will be some expenses or big limitations if you use their free versions e.g. you can only have five products or they will charge you a percentage or a fee per sale. Check it out as free might not always be free because of hidden expenses once you have signed up.

www.moonfruit.com

www.freewebstore.com

www.miiduu.com

www.tictail.com

www.zpecommerce.co.uk

www.create.net

www.prestashop.com

www.yokaboo.com

www.cafepress.com ideal for selling stuff with your own personalised design.

www.etsy.com ideal for selling products you make yourself.

Other platforms for selling digital products/payment processing (payable):

www.clickbank.com

www.digiresults.com

www.gumroad.com

www.plimus.com

www.rapbank.com

www.paydotcom.com

www.dealguardian.com

www.payzeno.com

www.jvzoo.com

www.clicksure.com

www.1shoppingcart.com

www.nanacast.com

www.stripe.com

www.payspree.com

Chapter 16) Things To Do Before Sending Traffic

Once your website has been designed, there are four vital things you must do or must know before sending any traffic to your site.

1) You Must Publish Your Website.

Your website needs to be published so that people can find it. With a lot of software these days, you don't have to worry about publishing your site, as the software should do this automatically for you. Publishing your site is free, all the time. I know some people don't know this as people have asked me this in the past.

Publishing your site is done by a protocol called *FTP: File Transfer Protocol*. It is a way of sending files securely from one computer to another. We are all involved in FTP without realising we are doing it. If you buy a song or an eBook from the web and download it to your computer, you are using FTP, because you are transferring the files from the host computer to your computer.

There are three ways to publish a site:

- When using WordPress, publishing is done automatically, so you do not need to do it. Press "F5" and the latest version will be visible online or click the "Update" button.

- When using a web design program like Webplus or Microsoft Expression Web, there is a "publish to" button. You need to fill in some technical information that your hosting company will be able to give you. The information that you will need will be available from your account with your hosting company. Most of the time, all you need is your username, password and IP address.

- If using Filezilla, you drag the files from your computer to the Filezilla server. Filezilla is FTP software and it is free. There's a huge amount of help available on the site, where you can also download it: www.filezilla-project.org.
Filezilla looks a bit scary to start with but, believe me, it is easy after you have used it a few times.

Unfortunately it is impossible to explain in detail how each web design program publishes your site. Simply Google how to do it and there will be videos on YouTube to show you. Note: The homepage of your website *must* always be called index.html when using Webplus.

I suggest that you submit your site for publishing to these search engines:

- Submit your site to Google here: www.google.co.uk/submit_content.html (or just Google "add url"). You must submit every website, even if you have designed it with WordPress. From experience I know that Google will see your site much quicker if you submit it.

- Submit your site to DMOZ (PR8) here: www.dmoz.org/add.html. DMOZ is a huge database of human-added websites. A back link from them to your site is a great thing to have and will greatly increase the amount of traffic you receive. If you do not get listed here at your first attempt, make some changes to your site and apply again to be listed. It will be worth the effort.

- Submit your website to Bing: www.bing.com/toolbox/submit-site-url

- Submit your site to Yahoo: http://search.yahoo.com/info/submit.html

Once you have submitted your site, you can check if Google has found it by typing in Google: "site: www.yourwebsitehere.com" and Google will show your site and the pages it has indexed. If Google displays a message "Your site did not match any documents", it means that Google has not indexed your site yet.

You can also just type your URL in the search box at www.google.com. If your site appears in the results, Google has indexed it. If three weeks after submission, your site is still not indexed, I suggest you submit it again. The best way to speed up getting indexed is by submitting to social bookmark sites and by getting back links to your site.

You can focus your submission efforts based on your target market, with this interesting information according to www.hitwise.com:
- Yahoo! searchers are younger and affluent
- Google searchers are often older, male and have a larger income
- Bing searchers are often female, within the best 'converting to buyers' ratio

Although 88% of all searches are through these top three search engines, below is a list of some other search engines that you can submit your site to.

www.dogpile.com
www.entireweb.com
www.exactseek.com
www.excite.com
www.gigablast.com

You could also use www.addme.com for manual submission to 14 search engines.

You can find a list of the smaller search engines here: www.thesearchenginelist.com.

Be prepared to receive a lot of follow-up emails or SPAM from several search engines after you have submitted your site. Do NOT submit your site until your site is up and running and ready to take orders from customers.
My book "Finding Niches Made Easy" contains a lot more search engines, including advanced search techniques.

2) You MUST TEST All the Links on Your Website

All the steps you take to make your online shop a success are useless if no one can find your website.

No traffic = No visitors = No profit

Before sending traffic to your site you need to TEST, TEST, TEST everything on your site.

TEST – TEST – TEST – TEST – TEST – TEST

This is crucial; I cannot stress this enough. Have you ever come across websites with "error 404" or other errors? Or pictures that are only half shown? Or text that runs over a picture? Of course you have. Very often this is because the webmaster does not check the website regularly. You have no chance to earn money with links that do not work. You need to check your links on a regular basis—your page links as well as your affiliate links. When you re-organise files on your computer, check your site. Depending on which company or host you use and how you have published your site, this can affect the website. When pictures have changed folders on your computer, those pictures might not show up on your website. The pictures will show as a blank frame with an "x"—very unprofessional.

This is what you have to check regularly:

1. Check that all your internal page links are working.
2. Click and test [Add to Cart] buttons on your pages. All good shopping carts have a feature called "Test run" where you can make a test purchase to see if all runs smoothly. After you have done that, you go back and click the [Go Live] button.
This is how it looks in 1shoppingcart: L3011 means the system is Live. If you want to do some testing, simply change it to T3011 (T for Test) and that means you are in test mode and you can test the order buttons on your website. Don't forget to change it back to L3011 when you're done testing, otherwise customers will receive error messages saying their payment cannot be processed.

3. Check that all your pages display as intended.
4. Check that your email auto responder is working properly. Opt-in with your own email address for testing purposes.
5. Check that all hyperlinks to internal pages are linked to the correct page.
6. Check that customers can see in a few seconds what the site is all about.
7. Can the customer see the contact information easily?
8. Check that all your videos are playing correctly and load quickly.
9. Check if your website looks good opened with the different Internet browsers: Internet Explorer, Firefox, Google Chrome, Opera, Safari (for Apple computers) and so on.
10. Ask three friends to look at your website and give you their comments and criticism. Looking at a website from other people's point of view can teach you a lot. Other people will see things that you don't.

3) You Must Make Sure That You Can Check How Your Website is Doing

Now that your website is tested and published, you must make sure that you can see how it is doing. When you have made it to the first page of Google, you need to stay there. Once you are on the first page does not mean that you will stay there forever.

If you just want to know how many visitors have looked at your site, you can place a visitor counter on your page. Just search for "visitor counter" and you will find plenty. The visitor counter websites will give you a code that you put on your site.

A free alternative to analyse how your site is doing is by using Google Analytics, which is totally free www.google.com/analytics. I have already mentioned this.

www.google.com/webmasters/tool is also free and gives you extra tools for your website

Visit www.google.com/alerts and put your three main competitors on alert. Google will let you know when your competitors are active on the web.

4) You Must Avoid Being Banned by Google.

Your site can be banned by Google for several reasons. One reason is by applying Black Hat SEO to your site. Also, NEVER use link farms or automated back linking.
Whilst talking about being banned: if possible, when you first start out, open 3 or 4 different PayPal accounts if you have different bank accounts. That way, when one of your accounts is banned, you can learn from it and use one of the other accounts.
It is VERY difficult to set up a new account if your account has been banned once as PayPal can check your IP address and know it is you again, opening a new account.

Chapter 17) Getting Free Traffic

Now that you know how to build a site and how to test it, you need to generate traffic, because remember:

No traffic = No visitors = No profit = No Success

I believe in the following rule: if you drive traffic in a way that is humanly possible, it is acceptable. If all of a sudden you have 1000 links to your site, and it was only submitted to Google two days ago, Google knows this is impossible for you to have done, and concludes you must have used some sort of automated software to create the links. Google does not like anything automated: automated websites, automated links, automated submissions, automated social marketing, and so on.

If you have a non-competitive niche you might well get and stay on the first page simply with good SEO applied to your site. If that is all you want to achieve, there is no need for you to apply any of the traffic methods in this book. However, don't forget that a lot of people do not use Google, therefore you will not reach all potential customers with just Google.

There is no such thing as "one best way" to drive traffic. You need to drive traffic to your site in different ways. Choose a few methods that you think you will enjoy.

TOP TIP: Never count on one way of driving traffic. You must try to build multiple streams of traffic.

There are over 100 traffic methods in my book *"From Newbie To Millionaire"*. It is simply too much information to cover in this book. 77 of the traffic methods listed in my book are totally free. Here are just a few methods.

1) Free Traffic from Article Marketing

Good article marketing = more visitors to your site = increased sales

Article marketing still works. I know several people who are making money with it. A well written article will rank in Google for the keyword you've optimised it for, as well as offering valuable backlinks to your domain. Most article sites will only allow you a maximum of two links per article, and these generally have to be contained within the author box at the end.

There is one other bonus to creating good articles for article sites: if your article is good then other people will post it as content on their own sites. This means each time your article is used, you get more backlinks from the links in your author box!
Article marketing rocks when done well! Article marketing is free traffic at its best.
- It works quickly as your article is mostly published in the next three days after submission.
- Google loves article directories, and this will help with your rankings for your keyword.
- It is long-term traffic, as once your article is in the directory, it will stay there. If you have chosen an untapped niche your article will constantly show up in Google. Of course if you haven't, there will be new articles and you will have to write and publish new articles as well to stay ahead.
- There are automatic submission packages available that submit your article to lots of different article directories in one click. I do not recommend using these simply because if the same article is submitted to 20 different directories, they will not be unique articles. Google does not like duplicate content or duplicate articles, so will probably only list one of your articles.

TOP TIP: Write 20 unique articles and manually submit them to 20 different article directories. This is a lot more work BUT you have the chance to be seen by Google on 20 article websites, not just on one. Each of your articles would be seen as unique content by Google, and so will have a better chance of showing in the search engines.

A well optimised article can rank in Google all on its own, as well as allowing you to have two backlinks to your site.

5 Things each article MUST have:

- Keyword in the beginning of the title: Your title must have your keyword in it but it's equally significant that it's in the beginning of the title to maximise your chances of ranking. Here's an example where somebody is searching for panic attacks:
"5 Top Tips to manage your panic attacks" is a good title BUT " Panic Attacks Gone Forever – 5 Top Tips" is better because the keywords are first.
- Keywords and keyword phrases. Use the keywords from your niche research and write an article on several keywords.
- GOOD Article Content. Articles must read easily and provide useful information. Please do not use PLR as content, unless you re-write it and don't copy somebody else's article. Google will look at it as duplicate content and your article will simply not show. Readers love figures, statistics, facts and tips.
- Keyword density. Spread your keywords over the article. About 3% to 4 % keyword density will give you a chance to rank in Google with your article.
- YOUR links: Don't forget to put a link to your website at the bottom of the article. Some article submission websites also allow you to put a link in the middle of the article. A brief description of your site and a resource box should always be placed at the end of your article. This link can be an affiliate link or a link to your website.

10 steps for successful article marketing:

1. Find good long tail keywords to target with your keyword research tool.
2. Find a catchy title and search in Google to make sure it is unique. eg. If your title is "10 things you did not know about preventing headaches" you must copy that text, (including inverted commas to get the exact match) and paste it into Google. As you can see from the screen shot below, no results are found for exactly the same sentence, so that means your title is unique.

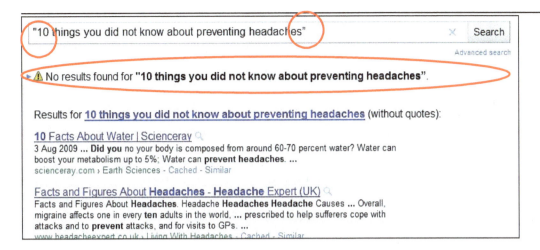

3. Join message boards and blogs and see what the hot topics around your niche are. Yahoo Answers is also a good place to see what sort of questions people are asking www.answers.yahoo.com You could write an article on one of these questions. Usually if people ask a question in Yahoo, they will also search elsewhere for the answer.

4. Write an article between 400 and 600 words or hire a ghost writer to write it. Make sure you check it for errors.

5. Find an affiliate product to link to at the end of your article or sell your own products.

6. Write an author's bio box.

7. Write your resource box, both a plain version and an HTML version. *

8. Put a keyword list together.

9. Start submitting your article and make sure you keep a record of the ones you have done.

10. Repeat with a different and unique article.

* If possible, it is best to use anchor text in your resource box. Some article directories don't allow you to use HTML code, so you can use a direct link like this one: http://www.lifewithoutstress.com. According to studies, anchor text works better but using your website address as a link has the advantage that Google might see your website address. The only reason why you would use anchor text rather than your URL is to get backlinks to your site.

If HTML is allowed and for maximum exposure, you can use a combination of both, something like this: "If you are looking for a life without stress (=anchor text), then check out Stress Free Tips (=anchor text) at http://www.lifewithoutstress.com (=URL)"

Don't forget to check how many links you are allowed. For most directories you are allowed at least two or three links in your resource box.

> **TOP TIP:** In order to build up credibility and get a lot of search engine traffic, you need to regularly submit articles, not just once. I suggest for maximum results and maximum exposure you submit new articles every two to four weeks. Each article must be unique.

> **TOP TIP:** Don't try to sell too hard in your article but focus on giving very good information. Save the sales pitch for when they get to your site. The only aim for article marketing is to get people to your site. If an article gives valuable information the reader is likely to click on your link at the end of the article.

Popular article directories

www.vretoolbar.com/articles/directories.php Here you can see a list of the top 50 article directories by Traffic and Pagerank.
With this many listings, you're highly likely to find enough articles sites to publish your articles.
One of my favourite ones is www.ezinearticles.com
Another one I like: www.articlecity.com

2) Free traffic from Directories and Trade Associations

A directory is a great way to source links for your site. A directory is a website that has a list of links to other sites and usually categorises in a certain order.
This is fairly simple and quick to do. Search for
- "keyword"+"directory"
- "keyword"+"directories"
- "keyword"+"trade associations"
- "keyword"+"meta-indexes" for sites with master lists of directories

Then look at all the websites that might be of interest to your niche. Sign up if need be and submit your website to the directories. Most of the time these submissions are free, but even if it costs you a few dollars or pounds a year to get extra traffic, directories are a very good resource for generating backlinks to your site.

3) Free Traffic from Press Releases

Press releases are syndicated content, which means that when you post one, a lot of other sites will automatically take it and post it onto their WebPages too.

Most Internet marketers and/or webmasters don't realise the importance of press releases and therefore under use them but they are a fantastic way to get extra visitors to your site or to your affiliate link site.

You can use these to promote products, the launch of your site or a new section or just to raise awareness of what you're offering. Plus, optimising the press release for the keywords you're targeting will also allow it to rank in Google almost overnight!

Google loves press releases, but only if they follow a certain set of rules:
- The information you're giving must be newsworthy and specific - promoting a product, a service, a site launch, a new eBook or book and so on.
- It should not be written like a sales letter - write it as if it was going to appear in a broadsheet newspaper. It needs to be factual and well worded.
- Craft the best possible headline and then use that headline in the first sentence. You have to make your headline sound like a newsworthy topic. "Announces" or "review" or "interesting result" are good words to use. The headline should ideally not be longer than ten words.

In the first paragraph you should make it clear who you are and what you're offering. The body copy should be between 250 and 300 words.
- Explain why the reader should care - Why/how/when/where are you promoting this?
- Avoid using sensationalist adjectives like "insane", "crazy" - again, this is NOT a sales letter.
- Include ALL your contact details.
- Include city and date of the release.
- You MUST spell check and proofread.

4) Free Traffic from Video Marketing

You can submit your videos, mostly with a link to your website to several video websites. If you cannot put a link with your video, make sure your URL is shown on the video itself. You might have to become a member first before you are able to submit a video. Most of these video submission websites are free but for some you will need a paid account. Always use your keywords in the title and description when submitting a video.

Refer back to the Audio and Video chapter to find video websites to submit your video to.

5) Free Traffic from Social Networks

TOP TIP: I wouldn't use software that automatically gets you thousands of followers/friends on Twitter, Facebook or any other social networking site. Normally the followers will be bogus in some way - either fake accounts or people who have been spammed to death. The only way you will ever get any real, potential buyers is by doing it the good old-fashioned way - yourself!

Social networks are places where people can interact and meet new people. Users can share things they like, upload photos, chat and do almost everything they can do in real life. Social networks aren't just for kids: everyone's using them.

Explaining all the different social networks would take an entire book, so I will explain them only briefly and, as already mentioned, I am not a big social media fan for business purposes but I do read a lot about social networks just to make sure I am "up to date." According to research Facebook now gets more page impressions than Google BUT there is a huge difference from an IM marketing point of view: Facebook users are mostly on Facebook for fun and social purposes, not to buy. If somebody searches in Google for "knee pain remedy" they are clearly looking for a specific solution and so these searches will convert a lot better.

The best social networks to be a part of are:
- www.twitter.com
- www.Facebook.com
- www.linkedin.com
- www.pinterest.com
- www.instagram.com
- www.tumblr.com
- www.plus.google.com Google Plus
- www.flickr.com
- www.foursquare.com
- www.vine.com
- www.tagged.com
- www.vk.com Europe's largest social network

6) Free Traffic from Yahoo Answers

Visit www.answers.yahoo.com and answer some questions in your niche with your link at the bottom. A wide range of topics is discussed. Google likes Yahoo answers.

7) Free Traffic from Wiki-Answers

Visit www.wiki-answers.com and answer some questions in your niche with your link at the bottom. A wide range of topics is discussed. Google likes Wiki-answers.

8) Free Traffic from All Experts

Visit www.allexperts.com which allows visitors to ask questions to experts. You can apply to become a volunteer expert and answer questions. Your response to the questions is archived on the site and can generate links for a long time.

9) Free Traffic from Wikipedia.

Wikipedia www.wikipedia.org is a lot stricter and it's more difficult to list your definition or topic. However it's 100% worth your time if you think that there is an untapped niche with insufficient information available on Wikipedia.
Simply Google "adding your own Wikipedia article" and the first site shown will probably be this one: http://en.wikipedia.org/wiki/Wikipedia:Starting_an_article. This page explains what you need to do to make your own page in Wikipedia.
Google loves Wikipedia.

10) Free Traffic from Your Own Army of Affiliates

This is an easy way to make money. If you have developed your own eBook/book or you are selling your own products you MUST find affiliates to sell for you. List your products on www.clickbank.com and lots of other affiliate networks and let other people sell your products. On Clickbank, you will have to pay a one-time small fee to list your product. You will earn less as you will give away between 20% and 70% of your earnings in commission but on the other hand *you don't have to do anything at all.* Yes that's right: *once you have an army of affiliates doing the work for you, you do not have to do anything at all.*
Very simple principle: find a potential niche, develop an eBook in that niche, put it on

Clickbank and the commission will start coming in. If you have done your research right you know that people are looking for your keywords, so it is likely that a bunch of affiliates are looking for products to sell in your niche as well.

Other platforms for selling digital products/payment processing (payable):

www.clickbank.com

www.digiresults.com

www.gumroad.com

www.plimus.com

www.rapbank.com

www.paydotcom.com

www.dealguardian.com

www.jvzoo.com

www.clicksure.com

www.1shoppingcart.com

www.nanacast.com

www.stripe.com

Below is a Clickbank screenshot showing that affiliates are selling for me. Do I know these guys? No. Have I ever spoken to these guys? No. Thank you realdeals5, you are doing a good job and thank you to all the other affiliates. The sales without a name under the "Affiliate" column are sales that are directly from my website, so I don't have to pay an affiliate. You can see that the affiliates are selling a lot more than I am but I am earning a lot more from them than from my own sales, even if my income is only $9.35 (£5.50)per sale. You can also see my low number of refunds (only two out of 34 sales).

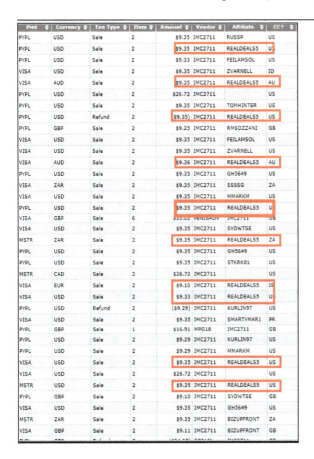

Pmt	Currency	Txn Type	Item	Amount	Vendor	Affiliate	CC#
PYPL	USD	Sale	2	$9.35	IMC2711	RUSSP	US
PYPL	USD	Sale	2	$9.35	IMC2711	REALDEALS5	U
PYPL	USD	Sale	2	$9.33	IMC2711	FEILAMSOL	US
VISA	USD	Sale	2	$9.35	IMC2711	ZVARNELL	ID
VISA	AUD	Sale	2	$9.35	IMC2711	REALDEALS5	AU
PYPL	USD	Sale	2	$26.72	IMC2711		US
PYPL	USD	Sale	2	$9.35	IMC2711	TOMHINTER	US
PYPL	USD	Refund	2	($9.35)	IMC2711	REALDEALS5	US
PYPL	GBP	Sale	2	$9.25	IMC2711	RMSOZZANI	GB
VISA	USD	Sale	2	$9.35	IMC2711	FEILAMSOL	US
VISA	USD	Sale	2	$9.35	IMC2711	ZVARNELL	US
VISA	AUD	Sale	2	$9.36	IMC2711	REALDEALS5	AU
PYPL	USD	Sale	2	$9.35	IMC2711	GH5649	US
VISA	ZAR	Sale	2	$9.35	IMC2711	SSSSG	ZA
VISA	USD	Sale	2	$9.35	IMC2711	MMARKM	US
PYPL	USD	Sale	2	$9.35	IMC2711	REALDEALS5	U
VISA	GBP	Sale	6	$33.02	PENISADV	IMC2711	GB
VISA	USD	Sale	2	$9.35	IMC2711	SYDWTSE	US
MSTR	ZAR	Sale	2	$9.35	IMC2711	REALDEALS5	ZA
PYPL	USD	Sale	2	$9.35	IMC2711	GH5649	US
PYPL	USD	Sale	2	$9.35	IMC2711	STKRK01	US
MSTR	CAD	Sale	2	$26.72	IMC2711		US
VISA	EUR	Sale	2	$9.10	IMC2711	REALDEALS5	IE
VISA	USD	Sale	2	$9.33	IMC2711	REALDEALS5	U
PYPL	USD	Refund	2	($9.29)	IMC2711	KURLIN97	US
VISA	USD	Sale	2	$9.35	IMC2711	SMARTYMAR1	PR
PYPL	GBP	Sale	1	$16.91	MPG18	IMC2711	GB
PYPL	USD	Sale	2	$9.29	IMC2711	KURLIN97	US
PYPL	USD	Sale	2	$9.29	IMC2711	MMARKM	US
VISA	USD	Sale	2	$9.35	IMC2711	REALDEALS5	US
VISA	USD	Sale	2	$26.72	IMC2711		US
MSTR	USD	Sale	2	$9.35	IMC2711	REALDEALS5	US
PYPL	GBP	Sale	2	$9.10	IMC2711	SYDWTSE	US
VISA	USD	Sale	2	$9.35	IMC2711	GH5649	US
MSTR	ZAR	Sale	2	$9.35	IMC2711	BIZUPFRONT	ZA
VISA	GBP	Sale	2	$9.11	IMC2711	BIZUPFRONT	GB

11) Free Traffic with 'Share' Icon on Your Site

You must have seen these sorts of buttons before:

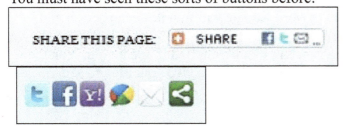

I suggest you put a "share it with" icon on your site, even at the beginning when you will not have many Facebook fans or Twitter followers (everyone has to start somewhere). More people will talk about your website. More people will see your website on all the share-it sites. These 'share it with' buttons are free and you can download them from

www.sharethis.com
www.addthis.com
www.buttonland.com Lots of free buttons to download here.
Also, put a "Tell a Friend" icon on your site. This tool is included in most software packages.

12) Free Traffic from Naming Images on Your Site

A lot of people will look under 'Images' in Google. By including a lot of images on your site and giving these images a name, you will increase traffic to your site. You must give the images a name that is relevant to the page they are on. Always make sure you include Alt and Title in your image tags.

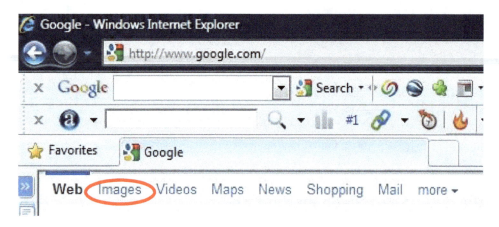

Google or any other search engines cannot recognise pictures on your website (not yet anyway) but if you give each picture a keyword Google will find it. Each page should have at least one image on it.
Google's pictures search won't find your picture of a Ferrari 458 if you are put it on the web with a reference "DCMB999002". It might show if you give your picture a name like "My Ferrari 658".

13) Free Traffic from Quizzes

There are a lot of people who love quizzes. You can visit www.proprofs.com to create a quiz. They have free and payable options. People who do the quiz are likely to send it to their friends.

14) Free Traffic from RSS Feed

If you publish an RSS feed, your site visitors that subscribe to your RSS will automatically receive new content each time you put it on your site. The people that receive your new content will visit your site, creating more traffic.

15) Free Traffic from Google Alerts

Sign up to www.Google.com/alerts and get emailed at regular intervals, whenever anyone blogs or talks about your niche. You can join the forums and blogs that are active in your niche and get free traffic to your site. You can contact the webmasters of the websites that are active in Google Alert and ask them to put your Clickbank product on their site. Use your imagination and business mind.

16) Join Forums

This is also to promote yourself as an expert. Be discreet with links to your site. Always stay on topic.

17) Guest Blogs

Early in the book I mentioned getting people to guest blog on your site. Try to get blogs on other people's sites as well, with links to yours. The blogs should be on sites that are in the same field as yours.

18) Free Traffic from Friends and Family

Tell all your friends, colleagues and family about your website. They will tell their friends and their friends will tell others, etc.... and before you know it, hundreds of people will look at your site.

Chapter 18) Safety

As already mentioned, a lot of things you download free from the web contain viruses and spyware. It is crucially important that you install antivirus and/or antispyware software on your computer.

You can educate yourself about security by visiting this site: www.w3.org/security

The most important thing to remember is that the free resources will protect your PC but are usually not as efficient as the payable versions. Let's say that often the free ones have a 97% detection against spyware and viruses. But of course, 100% protection is what you need, ideally.

Here are a few sites that give you free protection, they also have a payable option.

www.avira.com

www.mrg-effitas.com

www.comodo.com

www.zonealarm.com

www.avg.com

www.malwarebytes.org

www.forticlient.com

www.superantispyware.com I once had a virus on my computer and each time I typed in a website url, it was directed to another url. I tried to get rid of the virus with six different programs but this one - the payable version - got rid of it.

Some popular payable options:

- www.bullguard.com

- www.norton.com

- www.mcafee.com

- www.kaspersky.com

- www.bitdefender.com

Worpress security:

- www.acunetix.com is a free plugin that monitors your security weaknesses.

- www.ithemes.com is a security plugin which adds security to your blog (payable).

- www.wordfence.com is a security plugin which has been downloaded over two million times. There is a free and a payable option.

- www.wordpress.org/plugins/exploit-scanner searches your Wordpress site for signs that may indicate that malicious hackers have been at work or tried to get to your site. This is a free plugin.

- www.wordpress.org/plugins/antivirus Plugin that will scan your theme templates for malware.

- www.wordpress.org/plugins/bulletproof-security Another free security plugin, used by over 1 million users.

- www.wordpress.org/plugins/all-in-one-wp-security-and-firewall Wordpress security and firewall pugin.

I you want to find out more about Malware, Spyware and how to keep your Windows PC Secure, here is a book about it, available on Amazon, published by myself but written by a ghost writer. Title: "Oh No! My Computer's Acting Weird". It is not free though-).

Conclusion

You now have all you need to know to get started making your own website with free tools. As you can see there are tools that replace the expensive tools web developers use and there is a great deal of free content to make your website your own.

Once you get started, you might get to a point where you are unsure of how to continue. If it is a tool you are confused about, go back to where you downloaded the tool. A great thing about open source content, those items made with Common Creative tools, is that many of the developers are very willing to help with questions.

WordPress has forums where users share their experiences and ask questions. A great thing about these forums is that it is likely your question has already been asked, so just search the forum for your question. If that does not work, paste your question in Google and see what results come up or visit Youtube or Udemy for instructional videos.

The most important things to remember are:

- NEVER steal a picture, video, article, etc...

- NEVER accept a picture from someone else without being 100% sure that the person has the copyright for the picture

- ALWAYS read the terms and condition before you use a picture, video, article, etc.

- Install virus and/or or spyware detection

- Free hosting usually means slow hosting therefore visitors will leave your site very quickly

- Use long tail keyword to focus on for SEO

- Content is King

- Test all the links on your website before sending traffic

TOP TIP: GET STARTED! Use the crayons in the box to paint your picture. You can still colour in a nice picture with a few crayons missing. Start TODAY with the tools and knowledge that you have. You will never know it ALL! You will gain more knowledge as you go along and you will learn from the mistakes that you make. That's what I did.

Once you are making some money, the secret to going from earning a little bit to earning a lot is duplication. Duplication is how a small business can grow to an enormous enterprise. McDonalds© started with one restaurant and they now have almost 34,500!
Exactly the same principle can be applied to websites: you start with one and then add another, add another, and another, etc.....

**The only place where your dreams become impossible is in your own thinking!
Duplicate what works to make your dreams come true!**

This quote, of course, only applies if you want to become a professional Internet Marketer, not if you only want to build a personal website or one company website.

Whatever website you are planning to build, good luck!

Kind regards

Christine Clayfield

Christine Clayfield

Internet Marketer, Author, Entrepreneur, Infopreneur, Book Publisher, Public Speaker

www.FindingNichesMadeEasy.com
www.FromNewbieToMillionaire.com
www.DropshippingAndEcommerce.com
www.FromNewbieToMillionaireTestimonials.com
www.WorldwideSelfPublishing.com

www.ChristineClayfield.com

All Resources and Tools in One Place.

For your convenience, here are all the websites again, all together.

Chapter 1) What Skills Do You need To Succeed?

No websites listed

Chapter 2) What Is Your Niche?

Do some research and find a niche market which you think will be profitable and then start building a website which will earn you money from this niche. The tools listed will help you research market trends and find those all important right long tail keywords

Adwords www.adwords.google.com / www.adwords.google.co.uk
Wordstream Keyword Niche Tool www.wordstream.com/keyword-niche-finder
Google Trends www.google.com/trends/
BoardReader www.boardreader.com
Google Keyword Planner www.adwords.google.com/ko/KeywordPlanner/Home
Topsy www.topsy.com

Chapter 3) Free Writing Tools

The most important thing you'll need on your site is content, and this chapter and the websites listed will help you find the right software for all your writing needs.

Open Office www.openoffice.org
Libre Office www.libreoffice.org
NeoOffice www.neooffice.org
Google Docs www.docs.google.com
Think Free www.thinkfree.com
Notepad www.notepad-plus-plus.org

- Textwrangler www.barebones.com/products/textwrangler/

Pdf converters
FreePdfconvert www.freepdfconvert.com
Pdf converter www.doc2pdf.net
Cute pdf www.cutepdf.com
Pdf 995 www.pdf995.com
Pdf Forge www.pdfforge.org
Tiny Pdf www.tinypdf.com

Chapter 4) Your Website

Wordpress is one great way to create your first website but this chapter lists and reviews other free options and explains how user friendly each one is. There's great advice on the "dos" and "donts" of design, including user-friendly site navigation and using graphics and music.

Wordpress Tools

www.wordpress.com / www.wordpress.org / www.wordpress.org/themes
www.wordpressthemesbase.com

Website building
Freewpthemes www.freewpthemes.net
Google Sites www.sites.google.com
Akismet www.akismet.com
Inbound Now www.inboundnow.com
NVU www.nvu.com
MojoPortal www.mojoportal.com
Joomla www.joomla.org
Cushy CMS www.cushycms.com
Pligg www.pligg.com
Drupal www.drupal.org
Webs www.webs.com
SilverStripe www.silverstripe.org

Wix www.wix.com
FileZilla www.filezilla-project.org
PageBreeze www.pagebreeze.com
CoffeeCup www.coffeecup.com
KompoZer www.kompozer.net
Seamonkey www.seamonkey-project.org
Validator http://validator.w3.org

Free CSS Templates

Templated www.freecsstemplates.org
Free Web Templates www.freewebtemplates.com
Templates Box www.templatesbox.com
e-web Templates www.e-webtemplates.com
Template World www.templateworld.com
Free Templates Online www.freetemplatesonline.com
Minisite Graphics www.minisitegraphics.com
DIY Website Graphics www.diywebsitegraphics.com

Cookie Law

Cookie Law www.cookielaw.org

Designs

Web Pages That Suck www.webpagesthatsuck.com
Colorcombos www.colorcombos.com
Colourlovers www.colourlovers.com
Colourblind: http://colorfilter.wickline.org
Yahoo http://developer.yahoo.com/yslow (not available for Windows Explorer)
Elance www.elance.com
Fiverr www.fiverr.com
20 Dollar Banner www.20dollarbanners.com
99designs www.99designs.co.uk
Agents of Value www.agentsofvalue.com
Freelancer www.freelancer.com
Guru www.guru.com

Ifreelance www.ifreelance.com
Microworkers www.microworkers.com
Amazon Mechanical Turk www.mturk.com
oDesk www.odeskresources.com
People per Hour www.peopleperhour.com
Browser Shots www.browsershots.org
Handbrake www.handbrake.fr
Zamzar www.zamzar.com
Sitepal www.sitepal.com
Cartoon Your World www.cartoonyourworld.com
Web My Face www.mywebface.com

Chapter 5) Domains, Hosting and Email

Here you'll find all the information you need to give your website a domain name and how to choose a hosting company that gives your business a professional edge. Also lots of info on useful sites to visit to get a free email account.

Free Access Internet
Free Dialup www.freedialup.org
Free Internet Name www.free-Internet.name
All Free ISP www.all-free-isp.com

Wifi Freespot www.wififreespot.com

12 Free www.12free.co.uk

My Free ISP www.myfreeisp.co.uk

Domain and Host companies
GoDaddy www.godaddy.com
HostGator www.hostgator.com
Weebly www.weebly.com
Codotvu.com www.codotvu.com
Freenom www.freenom.com
Uk.to www.uk.to

1and1 www.1and1.com

Free hosting
Freehosting www.freehosting.com
Byethost www.byethost.com
Weebly www.weebly.com
50webs www.50webs.com
Batcave www.batcave.net
Bravenet www.bravenet.com
GoDaddy www.godaddy.com
1and1 www.1and1.com
Hostgator www.hostgator.com
WordPress www.wordpress.com / www.wordpress.org

Free email accounts
Google https://mail.google.com/
Yahoo www.yahoo.com
1and1 www.1and1.com

Chapter 6) SEO
Good SEO is vital for your website. This chapter lists lots of free online training you can access for free, as well SEO, keyword search, web optimisation and analytical tools so that your website gets the attention it deserves.

Training
Udemy www.udemy.com/whiteboard-seo / www.udemy.com/seo-for-content-creators/
MOZ www.moz.com/beginners-guide-to-seo
Seo-hacker www.seo-hacker.org
Hobo Internet Marketing www.hobo-web.co.uk/seo-eBook
Amazon website www.amazon.com / www.amazon.co.uk
Google Webmaster www.google.com/webmasters/docs/search-engine-optimization-starter-guide.pdf.
Yoast www.yoast.com

Duplicate Copy
Plagiarism Org www.plagiarism.org
Copyscape www.copyscape.com / www.copyscape.com/banners.php?o=f
www.copyscape.com/premium.php
Grammarly www.grammarly.com
Small SEO toolbox www.smallseotools.com

Keywords
Google Keyword Planner www.adwords.google.com/ko/KeywordPlanner/Home
Soovle www.soovle.com
Wordstream Keyword Niche Tool www.wordstream.com/keyword-niche-finder
Keyword Discovery www.keyworddiscovery.com/search.html
Bing Search Tool www.bing.com/toolbox/keywords
Word Pot www.wordpot.com

SEO Tools and Webmaster Tools
Google Analytics www.google.com/analytics
Google Webmaster Tools www.google.com/webmasters/tools
Bing www.bing.com/toolbox/webmaster
Wordpress www.wordpress.org/plugins/google-analytics-for-wordpresss/
Footprintlive www.footprintlive.com
Accesswatch www.accesswatch.com
ExtremeTracking www.extremetracking.com
Statcounter www.statcounter.com
Web Trends www.webtrends.com (paying)

Chapter 7) Legal Content

You should be very aware of the serious potential penalties if you use duplicate or plagiarised copy on your site, or infringe someone else's copyright. The current legislation is explained here along with practical tips on how you can make sure you don't breach the rules. The terms of the various licenses offered by Creative Commons are also explained, as is the phrase "Public Domain" with links to websites where you can find such work. Copyright law and Personal Rights are also covered together with limits on their use. Finally, you'll find a list of the "must have" elements for your website pages in relation to these topics.

Copyright laws
explanation about DMCA:
http://en.wikipedia.org/wiki/Online_Copyright_Infringement_Liability_Limitation_Act
explanation about OCILLA:
http://en.wikipedia.org/wiki/Digital_Millennium_Copyright_Act
Cornell College website www.copyright.cornell.edu/resources/publicdomain.cfm
 UK Government Intellectual Property Office www.ipo.gov.uk/types/copy.htm
U.S. National Archives www.archives.gov/research/ansel-adams

Use of materials
Creative Commons www.creativecommons.org / www.creativecommons.org/licenses/

Public Domain Work
Public Domain Review www.publicdomainreview.org
Digital Library www.digital.library.upenn.edu/books/cce
Web Law www.web.law.duke.edu/cspd

Books
Google Books www.books.Google.com
Gutenberg www.gutenberg.org
Authorama www.authorama.com
Bartleby www.bartleby.com
Bibliomania www.bibliomania.com
Literature www.literature.org

Archives
Archive www.archive.org

Model and Property releases
American Society of Media Photographers www.asmp.org/tutorials/property-and-model-releases.html

Legal Policy (free and paid legal policies for your website)
SEQ Legal www.seqlegal.com
Legal Zoom www.legalzoom.com and www.legalzoom.co.uk

Contact Form
Wordpress http://wordpress.org/extend/plugins/contact-form-7.
Site Map
Wordpress http://wordpress.org/extend/plugins/xml-sitemap-feed

Audio Testimonials
Audio Generator www.audiogenerator.com
Article Video Robot www.articlevideorobot.com

Cookies
Cookie Law www.cookielaw.org

Signature
My Live Signature www.mylivesignature.com

Chapter 8) Content is King

This chapter contains a wealth of ideas on places to go online where you can get great free content for your website. These include blogging, article websites, news feeds, PLR material, maps, images and video. You'll also find sources for free "add-ons" you can put on your site such as chat rooms, surveys, quotations, even greetings cards.

Tool bar
Virtual Real Estate www.vretoolbar.com

Creating Content
Free Conference Call www.freeconferencecall.com

Guest Blogging
Kissmetrics www.blog.kissmetrics.com/guide-to-guest-blogging/

Myblogguest www.myblogguest.com
Blog Synergy www.blogsynergy.com
BloggerLinkUp www.bloggerlinkup.com

Article sites
DMOZ,
www.dmoz.org/Business/Publishing_and_Printing/Publishing/Services/Free_Content/
The Virtual Real Estate www.vretoolbar.com/articles/directories.php
Article city www.articlecity.com/rss.shtml
Amazines www.amazines.com
Articlebase www.articlesbase.com
Ehow www.ehow.com
Scoop.it www.scoop.it
ContentGems www.contentgems.com

News Feeds
Bloglines www.bloglines.com
Feed Validator www.feedvalidator.org
RSS feeds www.rssfeeds.com www.rssreader.com
Rocket News www.rocketnews.com/feed
Fresh Content www.freshcontent.net
Feedzilla www.feedzilla.com

Gadgets and Widgets
Free Sticky www.freesticky.com
Google Gadgets www.google.com/ig/directory?synd=open

Private Label Rights
Specialreportclub www.specialreportclub.com
Cloneforsuccess www.cloneforsuccess.com
Contentgoldmine www.contentgoldmine.com
Gutenberg www.gutenberg.org
Allprivatelabelcontent www.allprivatelabelcontent.com

Plrpro www.plrpro.com
Resellrightspack www.resellrightspack.com
Site Content Ideas www.sitecontentideas.com
Easyplr www.easyplr.com
Super-resell www.super-resell.com
Theplrstore www.theplrstore.com

Souces of Free Content and Ideas for Content
I Need A Great Story www.INeedAGreatStory.com
Curation Soft www.curationsoft.com
Alltop www.alltop.com
Quora www.quora.com
Googlemaps www.maps.google.com www.maps.google.co.uk

Audio and Music Clips
Sourceforge www.sourceforge.net
Applian www.applian.com
PublicDomain4U www.publicdomain4u.com
RoyaltyFreeMusic www.royaltyfreemusic.com
Shockwave-sound www.shockwave-sound.com
Slicktracks www.slicktracks.com

Visitor Counters and Trackers
Stats4all www.stats4all.com
Extreme tracking www.extremetracking.com
Bravenet www.bravenet.com

Weather Forecast
Weather www.weather.com
Qwikcast www.qwikcast.com
Accuweather www.accuweather.com
Weatherzone www.weatherzone.com
Myweather2 www.myweather2.com

Worldweather www.worldweatheronline.com

Free Chat Room
Bravenet www.bravenet.com
Polls and Surveys:
Bravenet www.bravenet.com
Surveymonkey www.surveymonkey.com

Horoscopes
Eastrolog www.eastrolog.com
Adze www.adze.com
Astrology.com www.astrology.com

Jokes
Comicexchangewww.comicexchange.com
Jokesgalore www.jokesgalore.com

Games
Flashgamesforyourwebsite www.flashgamesforyourwebsite.com
Gamesforwebsites www.gamesforwebsites.com
Miniclip www.miniclip.com

Quotations
Greatquoteslibrary www.greatquoteslibrary.com
Brainyquote www.brainyquote.com
Quotationspage www.quotationspage.com
ReciteThis www.recitethis.com
QuotesCover www.quotescover.com
Quozio www.quozio.com
Pinwords www.pinwords.com

Greetings Cards
Regards www.regards.com

Bravenet www.bravenet.com

Financial Tools
Investing.com www.investing.com
Moneychimp www.moneychimp.com
Mortgageloan www.mortgageloan.com
Thefinancials www.thefinancials.com

Other Tools
Wisdom Commons www.wisdomcommons.org
Intratext www.intratext.com
Newspaper creator http://newspaper.jaguarpaw.co.uk
Word Cloud creator www.wordle.net
Video Recorder www.recordit.co
Audio to t4ext converter www.evernote.com
Slideshare www.slideshare.net
Pinstamatic to create Pinterest boards www.pinstamatic.com

Headline/title generators
Tweakyourbiz www.tweakyourbiz.com
Portent www.portent.com
Title-builder www.title-builder.com
Contentrow www.contentrow.com
Instantsalesletters www.instantsalesletters.com

Chapter 9) Graphic Design Tools
Various design tools to help you with your graphics.

Photoshop Alternatives
GIMP www.gimp.org / www.gimpshop.com
Paint.net www.getpaint.net
BeFunky www.befunky.com
Pixlr www.pixlr.com

Splash www.splashup.com

Design Tools
Canva www.canva.com
Timeline Slicer www.timelineslicer.com
Sumopaint www.sumoware.com
Photovisi www.photovisi.com
HTML Colour Finder www.html-color-codes.info
TinyPNG www.tinypng.com

Free Photoshop Tools
Brusheezy www.brusheezy.com/patterns www.brusheezy.com/textures
Get Brushes www.getbrushes.com
Free Photoshop www.freephotoshop.org/styles

Make A Thumbnail
www.makeathumbnail.com

Banner Creation
Banner Fans www.bannerfans.com
Fotor Banner Maker http://banner.fotor.com
3D Text Maker www.3dtextmaker.com
BannerBreak www.bannerbreak.com
Html5 maker www.html5maker.com

Logo Creation
Logo Maker www.logomaker.com
The Logo Creator www.thelogocreator.com

Favicon Creators
Favicon org www.favicongenerator.com
Favicon www.favicon.cc

Book Cover Creation
My eCover Maker www.myecovermaker.com
DIY Book Covers www.diybookcovers.com
Book Cover Pro www.bookcoverpro.com
PicMonkey www.PicMonkey.com
Slide Creation
Prezi www.prezi.com

Image Sources
Google Search www.images.google.com/advanced_search?hl=en&fg=1
TinEye www.tineye.com

Infographics
http://ui-cloud.com/free-vector-infographic-design-elements
http://all-free-download.com/free-vector/free-infographics.html
Pickto Chart www.piktochart.com
www.freepik.com/free-photos-vectors/infographic
Easelly www.easel.ly
Infogr.am www.infogr.am

Chapter 10) Images

An important warning about the dangers of stealing online photos is followed by detailed advice on finding the images you'll need from a variety of online sources and how to check that you're entitled to use them. "Royalty Free" and "Creative Commons licensing" are explained. There's a draft agreement if you're using a ghost writer and a form of words to use when approaching someone to ask for permission to use an image. Finally you'll find lots of sources of free (and some paid) sites where you'll find images, icons etc. with detailed information on how to download the images and check that you're using them legally.

Wordpress Plugin www.photodropper.com/wordpress-plugin
Tin Eye www.tineye.com
Google Inside Search www.google.com/insidesearch/features/images/searchbyimage.html
Creative Commons www.search.creativecommons.org

Google advance search www.google.com/advanced_image_search
Flickr www.flickr.com
Free Mediagoo www.freemediagoo.com
4FreePhotos www.4freephotos.com
Gratisography www.gratisography.com
Bigfoto www.bigfoto.com
Cepolina www.cepolina.com
Getty Images www.gettyimages.co.uk www.gettyimages.co.uk/embed
Free Pixels www.freepixels.com
ImageAfter www.imageafter.com
Image Base www.imagebase.net
Photo Pin www.photopin.com
Pixabay www.pixabay.com
AncestryImages www.ancestryimages.com
Pixel Perfect Picture www.pixelperfectdigital.com
Rgbstock www.rgbstock.com
FreeImages www.freeimages.com
FreePhotosBank www.freephotosbank.com
Unsplash www.unsplash.com
PicJumbo www.picjumbo.com
PickupImage www.pickupimage.com
Wikipedia Commons www.commons.wikimedia.org
Morgue file www.morguefile.com
Compfight www.compfight.com
Veezzle www.veezzle.com
Free Digital Photos website www.freedigitalphotos.net
Stock Photos for Free website www.stockphotosforfree.com
EveryStockPhoto www.everystockphoto.com
Foter www.foter.com
Free Range Stock www.freerangestock.com
US National Archives. www.archives.gov/faqs
The Library of Congress www.loc.gov/pictures
NASA www.nasa.gov/multimedia/guidelines/index.html

Public domain photos www.public-domain-photos.com www.publicdomainpictures.net
New Old Stock www.nos.twnsnd.co
Superfamous www.superfamous.com
Death To The Stock Photo www.deathtothestockphoto.com
Gratisography www.gratisography.com
StockPhotos www.stockphotos.io
FreeStockPhotos www.freestockphotos.com
Wylio www.wylio.com
Fotopedia www.fotopedia.com
All-Free-Download www.all-free-downloads.com
Historical Stock Photos www.historicalstockphotos.com
PhotoGen www.photogen.com
AnimalPhotos www.animalphotos.info
CarPictures www.carpictures.com
Creativity103 www.creativity103.com

Pay Image Sites With Free Photos
Fotolia www.fotolia.com
Dreamstime www.dreamstime.com
123rf www.123rf.com
Dollar Photo Club www.dollarphotoclub.com
Big Stock Photo www.bigstockphoto.com
Graphic Stock www.graphicstock.com
Photo Dune www.photodune.com
Stock Pholio www.stockpholio.com
Shutterstock www.shutterstock.com
Istock Photo www.istockphoto.com
Deposit Photo www.depositphoto.com
Stock Fresh www.stockfresh.com
Lockerz www.lockerz.com
Smug Mug www.smugmug.com
Corbis www.corbis.com
Photo wizard www.photo-wizard.net

Photo Bucket www.photobucket.com
Webshots www.webshots.com
Imgur www.imgur.com
Icons and buttons
Icon Finder www.iconfinder.com
Find Icons www.findicons.com
Buttonland www.buttonland.com

Chapter 11) Free Clip Arts & Vectors

This chapter lists lots of sites you can visit for free Clipart images together with download instructions.

All Free Clip Art www.allfree-clipart.com
Clip Art Etc http://etc.usf.edu/clipart
DeviantART www.deviantart.com
From Old Books www.fromoldbooks.org
HassleFreeClipArt www.hasslefreeclipart.com
Vector Portal www.vectorportal.com
Public Domain Clipart www.public-domain-photos.com
Animation Factory www.animationfactory.com
Open Clipart www.openclipart.org
ClipArt Castle www.clipartcastle.com
Diehard Images www.diehardimages.com
Free-Graphics www.free-graphics.com
FreeGraphics.org www.freegraphics.org
Incredible Art Department www.incredibleart.org
Microsoft Free Clipart Downloads www.free-clipart-pictures.net
MyCuteGraphics www.mycutegraphics.com
ProDraw Graphics www.prodraw.net
Clipart - www.clipart.com

Chapter 12) Free Background textures & Wallpaper Designs

Here you'll find details of where you can download free background textures and wallpapers for your website. Beware though, you may find you get lots of spam.

American Greetings www.americangreetings.com/downloads/wallpapers.pd

Desktop Nexus www.desktopnexus.com

My Free Wallpapers www.myfreewallpapers.net

Wallpapers www.wallpapers.com

WallpaperStock www.wallpaperstock.net/downloads.html

WebShots www.webshots.com

Chapter 13) Audio and Video

This chapter is full of advice on adding audio and video to your website including free software and tools to help you make and edit your own productions, burn CDs, hold Webinars and details of where you can upload your videos to. Sources of screen capture software and free (and some paid) video clips are also listed.

- You can upload your video free to

- www.youtube.com

- www.vimeo.com,

- www.viralvideochart.com

Software For Audio and Video

- Imovie www.apple.com/mac/imovie

- Windows Movie Maker www.windows.microsoft.com/en-us/windows/get-movie-maker-download

- Avidemux www.avidemux.sourceforge.net/

- Ezvid www.ezvid.com

-LWKS www.lwks.com

- Nero Wave Editor www.alternativeto.net/software/nero-waveeditor/about

- Wavosaur www.wavosaur.com

- Powtoon www.powtoon.com

- Skype www.skype.com

- www.dvdvideosoft.com/products/dvd/Free-Video-Call-Recorder-for-Skype.htm

- Supertintin www.supertintin.com

- Callgraph www.scribie.com/free-skype-recorder

- Audacity Audio www.audacity.sourceforge.net.

- Audio Tool www.audio-tool.net is another free audio recorder
- Techradar www.techradar.com
- VirtualDub www.virtualdub.org
- Wistia www.wistia.com

Great payable video editing software and tools
- AudiAcrobat www.audioacrobat.com is a payable online tool to create audio and video

Autocue or teleprompter software
EasyPrompter: www.easyprompter.com
CuePrompter www.cueprompter.com

Converting videos
- Handbrake www.handbrake.fr
- YouConvertit www.youconvertit.com
- Zamzar www.zamzar.com

Burning CD and DVDs
- CDburner from www.cdburnerxp.se
- CDburner from www.discoapp.com

Webinars
Anymeeting www.anymeeting.com
Gotowebinar www.gotowebinar.com
Voices
- Voices www.voices.com
- Voices123 www.voice123.com

Other Resources
- Market news Video www.marketnewsvideo.com/embed
- Reuters www.reuters.com/tools/rss
- ABC news http://embed.ly/embed/features/provider/abcnews
- Hulu www.hulu.com

- Archive www.archive.org
- MusicBakery www.musicbakery.com
- Splasheo www.splasheo.com Creates videos, fast and easy. Free download.

Screen Capture Software
- AwesomeScreenshots www.awesomescreenshots.com lets you capture your page or part of it and annotate it with arrows, text, etc.... You can use this screenshot to insert in a video.
- Jing www.techsmith.com/jing.html
- Camstudio www.camstudio.org
- ScreenCastOMatic www.screencast-o-matic.com.
- Small Video Soft www.smallvideosoft.com/screen-video-capture
- Techsmith www.techsmith.com/camtasia.html
- Jing www.jingproject.com
- Viddler www.viddler.com
- EZS£ www.EZS3.com
- Amazon AWS www.aws.amazon.com/s3/
- Easy Video Player www.EasyVideoPlayer.com

The best video sites to upload your videos to are (some are payable)
- AOL – www.on.aol.com
- Google Video – www.video.google.com
- Viddler - www.viddler.com
- Ustream - www.ustream.tv
- YouTube - www.youtube.com
- Brightcove – www.brightcove.com
- Buzznet – www.buzznet.com
- Daily Motion - www.dailymotion.com
- Dropshots – www.dropshots.com
- Fark – www.fark.com/video
- Flixya – www.flixya.com
- Screenjunkies – www.screenjunkies.com
- Jibjab - www.jibjab.com

- Liveleak – www.liveleak.com
- Metacafe – www.metacafe.com
- Vimeo – www.vimeo.com
- Tube Mogul www.tubemogul.com
- Senuke www.senuke.com

Various
- Myliveactor – www.myliveactor.com
- Audacity www.audacity.sourceforge.net free audio editing
- Video maker www.videomaker.com/youtube/

Free and Low Cost Videos for Re-use
Archive.Org www.archive.org
BottledVideo www.BottledVideo.Com
Market News Video www.marketnewsvideo.com
Stock Footage for Free www.stockfootageforfree.com
Videezy www.videezy.com
Videvo www.videvo.net
Jamendo www.jamendo.com
CCMixter www.ccmixter.org
SoundCloud www.soundcloud.com
Videoblocks www.videoblocks.com
Hulu www.hulu.com
FreeSound www.freesound.org
FreeLoops www.free-loops.com
Freebase www.freebase.com

Payable stock videos
www.alamy.com
www.pond5.com
www.istockphoto.com
www.videohive.net
www.graphicriver.net

www.fotalia.com
www.dreamstime.com
www.photospin.com
www.revostock.com
www.gettyimages.co.uk
www.shutterstock.com
www.123rf.com
www.fotosearch.com
www.canstockphoto.com
www.depositphotos.com
www.stockvault.com

Chapter 14) Marketing Support Tools & Varia Tools

Here you'll find details of free tools you can add to your website in order to build a subscriber list together with file transfer and file storage options. Also links to free download customer service and competitor analytics software.

Livewire www.livewire.com
MailChimp www.mailchimp.com
Imminica Mail www.imnicamail.com
Listwire www.listwire.com
BananaTag www.bananatag.com
We Transfer www.wetransfer.com
Purechat www.purechat.com
Livezilla www.livezilla.ne allows one free operator
EtalkUp www.crunchbase.com/organization/etalkup
Freecrm www.freecrm.com
Freshdesk www.freshdesk.com
Osticket www.osticket.com
Rafflecopter www.rafflecopter.com
Majesticseo www.majesticseo.com
 LXR Marketplace www.lxrmarketplace.com/seo-competitor-analysis-tool.html
Ahrefs www.ahrefs.com

Open Site Explorer www.moz.com/researchtools/ose

Other Free Tools
7-Zip www.7-zip.org
Adobe Reader www.get.adobe.com/reader
Piriform.com www.piriform.com/ccleaner
Filezilla www.filezilla-project.org
Net2ftp www.net2ftp.com

OneButton www.onebutton.org
Shortkeys.com www.shortkeys.com
Free Mind www.freemind.sourceforge.net
Evernote www.evernote.com
Toggl www.toggl.com
UptimeRobot www.uptimerobot.com
Which Test Won www.whichtestwon.com
YouConvertit www.youconvertit.com
Zamzar www.zamzar.com
Remember The Milk www.rememberthemilk.com
GetPocket www.getpocket.com

URL Shortening websites
www.bitly.com
www.tinyurl.com
www.tiny.cc
www.snurl.com
www.bit.do
www.tinypic.com

Cloud Storage
Google drive www.google.com/intl/en/drive
Dropbox www.dropbox.com
Box www.box.com

Chapter 15) Setting Up An Online Store And Take Payments

A brief introduction to setting up an online store with links to lots of useful free tools.

Easy Digital Downloads www.easydigitaldownloads.com
2checkout www.2checkout.com
Boutique Local www.boutiquelocal.co.uk
Ekmpowershop www.ekmpowershop.com / www.ekmpowershop.co.uk.
Moonfruit www.moonfruit.com
Freewebstore www.freewebstore.com
Miiduu www.miiduu.com
Tictail www.tictail.com
Zpecommmerce www.zpecommerce.co.uk
Create.net www.create.net
Prestashop www.prestashop.com
Yokaboo www.yokaboo.com
Cafepress www.cafepress.com
Etsycom www.etsy.com
Clickbank www.clickbank.com
Digiresults www.digiresults.com
Gumroad www.gumroad.com
Plimus www.plimus.com
Rapbank www.rapbank.com
Paydotcom www.paydotcom.com
Jvzoo www.jvzoo.com
Clicksure www.clicksure.com
1shoppingcart www.1shoppingcart.com
Nanacast www.nanacast.com
Stripe www.stripe.com
Payspree www.payspree.com
Payzeno www.payzeno.com
Deal Guardian www.dealguardian.com

Chapter 16) Things To Do before Sending Traffic

A useful summary of things you must do and test before you publish your new website and how to submit your site to the search engines. Also some advice on how to make sure Google never bans your site!

Filezilla www.filezilla-project.org

Google submission www.google.co.uk/submit_content.html

DMOZ (PR8) www.dmoz.org/add.html

Bing www.bing.com/toolbox/submit-site-url

Yahoo (PR8) http://search.yahoo.com/info/submit.html

Hitwise.com www.hitwise.com

Dogpile.com www.dogpile.com

Entireweb.com www.entireweb.com

Exactseek.com www.exactseek.com

Excite.com www.excite.com

Gigablast.com www.gigablast.com

Addme.com www.addme.com

Search Engine List www.thesearchenginelist.com.

Google Analyticals www.google.com/analytics

Google Webmasters Tool www.google.com/webmasters/tool

Google Alerts www.google.com/alerts

Chapter 17) Getting Traffic

All you need to know about generating traffic to your site using article marketing, answering questions, social media, forums, blogs and affiliates. Also some free resources you can use to keep your site secure.

Yahoo Answers www.answers.yahoo.com

Wiki-answers www.wiki-answers.com

All Experts www.allexperts.com

Wikepedia www.wikipedia.org

ClickBank www.clickbank.com

Digi Results www.digiresults.com

Gumroad www.gumroad.com
Plimus www.plimus.com
Rapbank www.rapbank.com
Paydotcom www.paydotcom.com
Deal Guardian www.dealguardian.com
Jvzoo www.jvzoo.com
Clicksure www.clicksure.com
1shoppingcart www.1shoppingcart.com
Nanacast www.nanacast.com
Stripe www.stripe.com
Sharethis www.sharethis.com
AddThis www.addthis.com
Buttonland www.buttonland.com
Proprofs www.proprofs.com
Google Alerts www.google.com/alerts

Article Directories
www.vretoolbar.com/articles/directories.php
www.ezinearticles.com
www.articlecity.com

Social Networks
Twitter www.twitter.com
Facebook www.Facebook.com
Linkedin www.linkedin.com
Pinterest www.pinterest.com
Instagram www.instagram.com
Tumblr www.tumblr.com
Google Plus www.plus.google.com
Flickr www.flickr.com
Four Square www.foursquare.com
Vine www.vine.co
Tagged www.tagged.com

VK www.vk.com

Chapter 18) Safety

Free Online PC Protection
www.w3.org/security/
www.avira.com
www.mrg-effitas.com
www.comodo.com
www.zonealarm.com
www.avg.com
www.malwarebytes.org
www.forticlient.com
www.superantispyware.com

Payable options
www.bullguard.com
www.norton.com
www.mcafee.com
www.kaspersky.com
www.bitdefender.com

Wordpress security
www.acunetix.com
www.ithemes.com
www.wordfence.com
www.wordpress.org/plugins/exploit-scanner
www.wordpress.org/plugins/antivirus
www.wordpress.org/plugins/bulletproof-security
www.wordpress.org/plugins/all-in-one-wp-security-and-firewall

Make Money With My Products

Please visit www.christineclayfield.com/affiliates/ for more information on how to earn money with my products.

Published by IMB Publishing 2014